PLENTY MORE

PLENTY MORE

VIBRANT VEGETABLE COOKING FROM LONDON'S OTTOLENGHI

YOTAM OTTOLENGHI

TEN SPEED PRESS
California | New York

CONTENTS

INTRODUCTION	vi
TOSSED	1
STEAMED	37
BLANCHED	53
SIMMERED	73
BRAISED	115
GRILLED	137
ROASTED	157
FRIED	183
MASHED	217
CRACKED	237
BAKED	257
SWEETENED	285
INDEX	334
ACKNOWLEDGMENTS	339

INTRODUCTION

VEGI-RENAISSANCE

Chunky green olives in olive oil; a heady marinade of soy sauce and chile; crushed chickpeas with green peas; smoky paprika in a potent dip; quinoa, bulgur, and buckwheat wedded in a citrus dressing; tahini and halvah ice cream; savory puddings; fennel braised in verjuice; Vietnamese salads and Lebanese dips; thick yogurt over smoky eggplant pulp—I could go on and on with a list that is intricate, endless, and exciting. But I wasn't always aware of this infinite bounty; it took me quite a while to discover it. Let me explain.

As you grow older, I now realize, you stop being scared of some things that used to absolutely terrify you. When I was a little, for example, I couldn't stand being left on my own. I found the idea—not the experience, as I was never really left alone—petrifying. I fiercely resented the notion of spending an evening unaccompanied well into my twenties; I always had a "plan." When I finally forced myself to face this demon, I discovered, of course, that not only was my worry unfounded, I could actually feast on my time alone.

Eight years ago, facing the prospect of writing a weekly vegetarian recipe in the *Guardian*, I found myself gripped by two such paralyzing fears.

First, I didn't want to be pigeonholed as someone who cooks only vegetables. At the time, and in some senses still today, vegetables and legumes were not precisely the top choice for most cooks. Meat and fish were the undisputed heroes in lots of homes and restaurant kitchens. They got the "star treatment" in terms of attention and affection; vegetables got the supporting roles, if any.

Still, I jumped into the water and, fortunately, just as I was growing up and overcoming my fear, the world of food was also growing up. We have moved forward a fair bit since 2006. Overall, more and more confirmed carnivores, chefs included, are happy to celebrate vegetables, grains, and legumes. They do so for a variety of reasons related to reducing their meat consumption: animal welfare is often quoted, as well as the environment, general sustainability, and health. However, I am convinced there is an even bigger incentive, which relates to my second big fear when I took on the *Guardian* column: running out of ideas.

It was in only the second week of being the newspaper's vegetarian columnist that I felt the chill up my spine. I suddenly realized that I had only about four ideas up my sleeve—enough for a month—and after that, nothing! My inexperience as a recipe writer led me to think that there was a finite number of vegetarian ideas and that it wouldn't be long before I'd exhausted them.

Not at all! As soon as I opened my eyes, I began discovering a world of ingredients and techniques, dishes and skills that ceaselessly informed me and fed me. And I was not the only one. Many people, initially weary of the limiting nature of the subject matter (we are, after all, never asked in a restaurant how we'd like our cauliflower cooked: medium or medium-well), had started to discover a whole range of cuisines, dishes, and ingredients that make vegetables shine like any bright star.

Just like me, other cooks are finding reassurance in the abundance around them that turns the cooking of vegetables into the real deal. They are becoming more familiar with different varieties of chiles, ways of straining yogurt, new kinds of citrus (like pomelo or yuzu), whole grains and pearled grains, Japanese condiments and North African spice mixes, a vast number of dried pasta shapes, and making their own fresh pasta. They are happy to explore markets and specialty shops or go online to find an unusual dried herb or a particular brand of curry powder. They read cookbooks and watch television programs exploring recent cooking trends or complex baking techniques. The world is their oyster, only a vegetarian one, and it is varied and exciting.

TURNING IDEAS INTO RECIPES

I get my recipe inspiration in a variety of ways. When traveling, I am constantly on the lookout for new ideas. A trip to Tunisia is a waste of time unless I come back with the ultimate method for making *harissa*; Christmas on the beach in Thailand will be cut short (much to my partner Karl's dismay) in favor of a search through swarming Bangkok alleys for the elusive best-ever oyster omelet.

My collection of cookbooks and magazines takes me on journeys into the creative minds of other cooks, or their heritage, or both. It might start off from an image or an idea that I find in a book—combining sorrel with mustard seeds, for example, or roasting carrots with orange halves—which sparks a chain reaction leading to a brand-new dish. Over the past few years I have been on a long journey to Iran—alas, a virtual one—through the pages of some of my favorite books (may I mention Najmieh Batmanglij's marvelous *Food of Life*?); I have been on similar tours to Lebanon and Japan (Michael Booth's *Sushi and Beyond* is exemplary); and I was made privy to the ins and outs of various unusual grains (through Liana Krissoff's *Whole Grains for a New Generation*) and vegetables (by Deborah Madison's *Vegetable Literacy*).

My colleague chefs at Ottolenghi and NOPI—Sami, Scully, Helen, and many others—also constantly stimulate me with their ideas, which turn into dishes and products that we serve in our shops and restaurants.

Pivotal to this book's content is the way in which initial, nascent ideas are turned into actual recipes. Since *Plenty* and my early *Guardian* columns, I have expanded my range of ingredients and techniques, but I have also vastly changed the way I work, and *Plenty More* is the result and expression of this change.

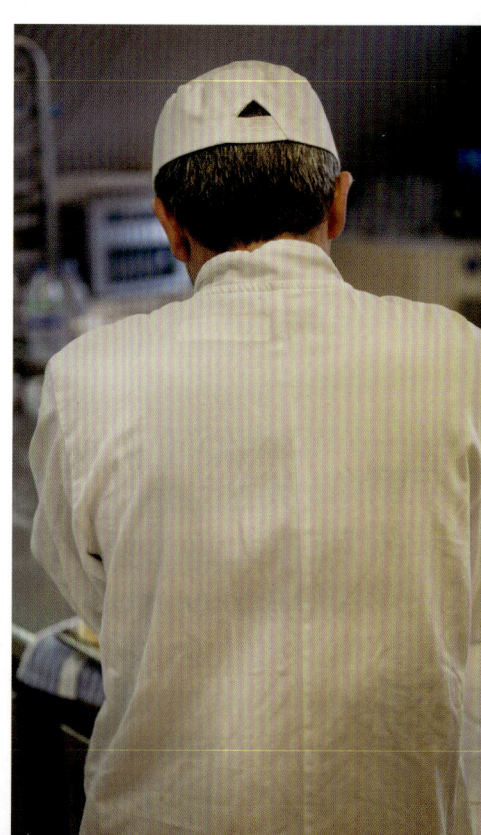

In the early days it was all pretty simple (as things often are). On a recipe-testing day, I would get up early in the morning and go out shopping for ingredients in a local market or supermarket. I'd then return home, unpack, draw out my notes and my key dry staples, and start cooking and scribbling. In the early afternoon, I'd clean up and go to the computer to note down the recipes. By the evening, there were two recipes ready to go, three if I'd been efficient and lucky.

As my shopping, prepping, and writing workload increased, I needed some help, and this was when Tara came on board.

Eventually, however, all this activity outgrew my domestic kitchen: poor Karl had his home turned into a big food lab, with bowls of half-made concoctions here or a plate of some semi-eaten thing there. There weren't many "proper" meals.

Two years ago, we took on a railway arch in Camden, central London, next door to the Ottolenghi bakery, and turned it into the official test kitchen. The story of the last two years, as well as of *Plenty More*, is in many ways the story of Arch 21, where the recipes presented to you in this book were conceived, tested, tasted, evaluated, and now finally released to the world. It is also the story of growth: from *Plenty* as a sole venture to *Plenty More* as a project shared by a group.

THE SET AND THE MAIN CHARACTERS

The Ottolenghi "hub" now occupies three railway arches. The first, taken on in 2007, we call the "bakery," yet it is so much more. It is the powerhouse behind Ottolenghi and NOPI.

If you happened to walk into Arch 20, you would most likely come across Artur, headphones on as a permanent fixture, grating lemons and squeezing juice: liter upon liter of the cloudy yellow liquid on which our little empire runs. Next you'd find Aga, hairnet on (new health and safety imperative every day), rolling *grissini* sticks. Upstairs, Mariusz and Irek dispense terrifying quantities of Lescure butter into brioche dough, puff pastry, or croissant dough. At night, Carlos lines large square pans with almond cream and rhubarb, while Robert lines bread baskets with a bubbly sourdough. Twenty-four hours a day something—flour related, jam related, curd related, chocolate related—is happening in Arch 20.

To our left is the youngest member of the family, Arch 22, where Maria works on world domination through the Internet: a recently opened Ottolenghi online shop dispensing all those exotic ingredients you either love or loathe us for having brought into your life. Upstairs, there's a little office and Ottolenghi accounts with Angelita at the helm, as close as we get to a corporate headquarters.

Arch 21 is the creative hub from which dishes, recipes, and many of our products sprout. Every day kohlrabies are diced, chickpeas soaked, yogurt blitzed with a bunch of herbs, or a leg of lamb goes in the oven with seasonal root vegetables and a bottle of wine. By midday, there are usually a couple of dishes ready to put together.

All the office dwellers then huddle together for a taster and give their two pennies' worth. Lucy, who's in charge of Ottolenghi's purchasing and my life in general, isn't hard to please but *can* be highly observant; Sarah is often harsher—a love-it-or-leave-it kind of girl—but always happy to be surprised by a "goner"; Tara tends to deliver short verdicts with effective proposals for improvement; Esme, a perfectionist in the kitchen, is mostly positive and willing to go up to take 5, 6, or 7 to make the recipe work.

Once the robust discussion is over, we go back to the ingredients list with a bunch of adjustments. Through the testing process a dish could completely transform itself from one thing to another: rice stuffing may end up as risotto, an eggplant sauce as beef-rib marinade. As painstaking as this sounds, it is highly enjoyable. Hitting on the missing piece that "solves" a dish like a puzzle is a moment of revelation. Everything falls into place when deep-fried onions add the richness so lacking in an otherwise delicious barley dish with lentils and mushrooms, or when a finishing touch of browned butter with Urfa chile flakes is spooned over zucchini with yogurt. Often this last effort properly punctuates the dish and brings all the other elements into the correct light.

In *Plenty More* I have aimed to capture some of the techniques involved in constructing a dish, in putting together components and arranging them in layers of flavor, texture, and color. If *Plenty*, through its structure and recipe selection, tried to shed light on groups of ingredients—my favorite ingredients—this book takes these favorites, adds a few new members to the happy family (*kashk*, *dakos*, and black garlic, to name just a few), and then focuses on cooking techniques and methods that best utilize their potential. Roasting lemon, for example, or braising lettuce was novel to me a few years ago. Now I am eager to share these ideas.

Exposing parts of the process that lead to the creation of a dish, telling about the culinary journeys I have recently been on, and focusing on some simple cooking techniques that elevate an ingredient and properly reveal it will, I hope, offer an additional perspective on an ever-expanding world of vegetables, grains, and legumes, a world with plenty of fantastic ingredients and dishes and plenty more to discover.

YOTAM OTTOLENGHI

A SHORT NOTE ABOUT INGREDIENTS

Ingredient measurements in parenthesis that appear after the ingredient has been peeled, chopped, sliced, etc. are always net. Unless otherwise specified, all salt is table salt, pepper is freshly ground, eggs are large, parsley is flat-leaf, olive oil is extra virgin, peppers are seeded, citrus pith is to be avoided when the rind is shaved, and onions, garlic, and shallots are peeled.

TOSSED

TOMATO AND POMEGRANATE SALAD

SERVES FOUR

I rarely rave about my own recipes, but this is one I can just go on and on about. It is the definition of freshness with its sweet-and-sour late-summer flavors, and it is also an utter delight to look at. But the most incredible thing about it is that it uses a few ingredients that I have been lovingly cooking with for many years, and believed I knew everything there was to know about, yet had never thought of mixing them in such a way. That is, until I traveled to Istanbul and came across a similar combination of fresh tomatoes and pomegranate seeds in a famous local kebab restaurant called Hamdi, right by the Spice Bazaar. It was a proper light-bulb moment when I realized how the two types of sweetness—the sharp, almost bitter sweetness of pomegranate and the savory, sunny sweetness of tomato—can complement each other so gloriously.

I use four types of tomato here to make the salad more interesting visually and in flavor. You can easily use fewer, just as long as they are ripe and sweet.

Mix together all the tomatoes, the red pepper, and the onion in a large bowl and set aside.

In a small bowl, whisk together the garlic, allspice, vinegar, pomegranate molasses, olive oil, and a scant ½ teaspoon salt until well combined. Pour this over the tomato mixture and gently mix.

Arrange the tomato mixture and its juices on a large, flat plate. Sprinkle the pomegranate seeds and oregano over the top. Finish with a drizzle of olive oil and serve.

1⅓ cups/200 g red cherry tomatoes, cut into ¼-inch/5-mm dice
1⅓ cups/200 g yellow cherry tomatoes, cut into ¼-inch/5-mm dice
1⅓ cups/200 g tiger or plum tomatoes, cut into ¼-inch/5-mm dice
about 1 lb/500 g medium slicing tomatoes (about 5), cut into ¼-inch/5-mm dice
1 red pepper, cut into ¼-inch/5-mm dice (1 cup/120 g)
1 small red onion, finely diced (rounded ¾ cup/120 g)
2 cloves garlic, crushed
½ tsp ground allspice
2 tsp white wine vinegar
1½ tbsp pomegranate molasses
¼ cup/60 ml olive oil, plus extra to finish
1 large pomegranate, seeds removed (1 cup/170 g seeds)
1 tbsp small oregano leaves
salt

SORT-OF-WALDORF

SERVES SIX TO EIGHT

My first foray into the weird and wonderful world of presenting on national television was when I took part in the BBC's Great British Food Revival *and was given the somewhat trying task of selling British nuts to the great British public. The combination of my inexperience in front of the camera and my lackluster attitude to the subject matter resulted in a performance you could fairly describe as not my finest hour ("Have you not watched the program?" was my reaction when asked about it the following year).*

Still, I did manage to develop a taste for an English eccentricity called pickled walnuts and for cobnuts, which have a fresher flavor than any other nut I know. They go brilliantly well with autumnal fruit and young varieties of cheese. Here, I roast them very slowly to make them totally crunchy and enhance their flavor. Regular hazelnuts, lightly toasted and gently crushed with the flat side of a large knife, are a good substitute.

Preheat the oven to 325°F/160°C.

Scatter the nuts in an ovenproof dish and roast in the oven for 30 minutes, until they take on some color and turn perfectly dry and crisp. Let them cool down and then crush roughly.

To make the mayonnaise, place the shallot, egg yolk, mustard, maple syrup, vinegar, and ½ teaspoon salt in the bowl of a small food processor. Whisk together, then, with the machine still running, slowly add the oils in a steady stream until you get a smooth and thick mayonnaise. Set aside.

Place the cabbage, celery, apples, and onion in a large bowl. Add the sour cream, dill, mayonnaise, sour cherries, ½ teaspoon salt, and some black pepper. Use your hands to thoroughly mix everything together—don't worry if you break the apple slices; it's all part of the look—transfer to individual plates, scatter the nuts on top, and serve.

See pictures on the following pages

⅓ cup/50 g shelled cobnuts or hazelnuts
¼ head red cabbage, finely shredded (4¼ cups/300 g)
6 celery stalks, cut into ¼-inch/5-mm slices (3½ cups/350 g)
2 Granny Smith apples, cored and thinly sliced (2¾ cups/300 g)
½ medium red onion, thinly sliced (½ cup/60 g)
⅔ cup/140 g sour cream
1 cup/50 g finely chopped dill
rounded ¾ cup/100 g dried sour cherries or cranberries (optional)
salt and black pepper

Mayonnaise
1 small shallot, finely chopped (2 tbsp/20 g)
1 egg yolk
1 tsp Dijon mustard
1 tsp maple syrup
1 tbsp cider vinegar
⅓ cup/80 ml sunflower oil
⅓ cup/80 ml canola oil
salt

SERVES SIX

FANCY COLESLAW

2 medium carrots, peeled and cut into thin matchsticks (scant 1¼ cups/140 g)
1 small fennel bulb, shredded ⅛-inch/3-mm thick (1⅓ cups/120 g)
4 tbsp/60 ml lemon juice
¼ small head savoy cabbage, shredded ⅛-inch/3-mm thick (1¾ cups/120 g)
1 large head radicchio, shredded ⅛-inch/3-mm thick (scant 3 cups/200 g)
1 medium red pepper, seeded and thinly sliced (⅔ cup/100 g)
1 red chile, thinly sliced
½ cup/100 g Greek yogurt
scant 3 tbsp/40 g mayonnaise
1½ tsp Dijon mustard
1½ tsp honey
1 tbsp olive oil
1 cup/30 g flat-leaf parsley leaves, chopped
1⅓ cups/20 g dill leaves, chopped
⅓ cup/10 g tarragon leaves, chopped
salt and white pepper

Spiced cashews
¾ cup/120 g cashew nuts, coarsely chopped
¾ tsp ground turmeric
¾ tsp ground cumin
1½ tsp paprika
¾ tsp superfine sugar
salt

After a bit of shredding and chopping, you'll have a refreshing bowlful of fresh vegetables. To save time, use a food processor to slice the vegetables: the end result won't be quite as beautiful, but it will be just as delicious. Likewise, to save time, any toasted nuts can be used to replace the spiced cashews. But if you do make them, double or triple the amount stipulated: they make a great nibble to serve with drinks.

Preheat the oven to 350°F/180°C.

Place the carrots, fennel, and 2 tablespoons of the lemon juice in a large bowl and mix well. Set aside for 20 minutes and then drain.

To make the nuts, in a small bowl, combine the nuts, turmeric, cumin, paprika, sugar, and a pinch of salt. Stir 1 tablespoon water through the mixture so the spices cling to the nuts. Spread out on a parchment-lined baking sheet and roast for about 12 minutes, until golden and crunchy. Remove and leave aside to cool.

Return the carrots and fennel to the large bowl, add the cabbage, radicchio, red pepper, and chile, and stir well.

To make the dressing, whisk together the yogurt, mayonnaise, mustard, honey, olive oil, the remaining 2 tablespoons lemon juice, ¼ teaspoon salt, and a pinch of white pepper. Pour this over the vegetables and mix well. Add the herbs and spiced nuts, stir to combine, and serve.

See picture on previous page

RAW BEET AND HERB SALAD

SERVES FOUR

This crunchy and fresh salad, with tons of sharp, peppery, "healthy" flavors, is a good way to start a meal or end it, or simply to have with lots of other summery vegetable-based dishes. It is also very effective served with grilled lamb or oily fish from the grill. Prepare all your ingredients in advance, keeping the delicate herb leaves refrigerated in a sealed container with a moist cloth at the bottom, and toss together when you are ready.

¼ cup/30 g sliced almonds
2 tbsp/15 g sesame seeds
⅓ cup/45 g pumpkin seeds
3 medium beets, peeled and cut into thin strips (2¼ cups/300 g)
1⅓ cups/40 g basil leaves, torn
⅔ cup/20 g flat-leaf parsley leaves
2 cups/30 g dill leaves
1¼ cups/20 g cilantro leaves
⅓ cup/10 g tarragon leaves
1 tsp chile flakes
2 tsp grated lemon zest
3 tbsp lemon juice
5 tbsp/75 ml olive oil
salt and black pepper

Preheat the oven to 400°F/200°C.

Mix together the almonds and sesame and pumpkin seeds and spread out on a baking sheet. Place in the oven and roast for 6 minutes. Remove from the oven and set aside to cool.

Place the beets, herbs, chile flakes, and lemon zest in a large bowl. Add the seeds and nuts, lemon juice, olive oil, ¼ teaspoon salt, and a grind of black pepper. Toss together and serve at once.

CELERY SALAD WITH FETA AND SOFT-BOILED EGG

SERVES FOUR

Feta, a bit like lemon juice or cilantro, is one of the oldest tricks in my book when trying to "fix" a recipe. "We can do the obvious and add some feta," we always say in the test kitchen when faced with a dish that seemed wow-ish on paper but didn't quite live up to the promise, "but that would just be too easy." It is, indeed, easy and it does work, but I do try to limit the number of times I resort to feta, just so that it remains special (I am less successful with lemon and cilantro, I am happy to concede).

In this recipe, though, the feta is instrumental in bridging the gap between the sharp, crunchy, and healthy-tasting salad and the warm, creamy, rich egg. The result is the most comforting of dishes.

Place the celery, green peppers, and onion in a bowl, sprinkle with the sugar and ½ teaspoon salt, and mix well. Set aside for 30 minutes to allow the vegetables to soften and to draw out some of the juices, which will make up part of the dressing.

Using a small, sharp knife, slice off the top and tail of each lemon. Cut down the side of each lemon, following its natural line, to remove the skin and white pith. Over a small bowl, cut between the membranes to remove the individual segments.

Add the lemon segments, celery leaves, parsley, cilantro, capers, chiles, olive oil, and some black pepper to the softened vegetables. Mix gently to combine.

Just before you are about to serve, carefully spoon the eggs into a pan of boiling water and simmer gently for 6 minutes. Run under cold water until the eggs are just cool enough to handle but still warm inside, then peel them gently; the yolk should still be runny.

Arrange the salad on individual plates, dot each with the feta, and place a soft-boiled egg on top, broken in the middle. Finish with a few drops of olive oil and some freshly ground black pepper and serve at once.

- 8 celery stalks, thinly sliced on the diagonal (4 cups/400 g)
- 2 green peppers, halved, seeded, and cut lengthwise into strips ¼-inch-/5-mm wide
- 1 medium onion, thinly sliced (1⅓ cups/150 g)
- 1 tsp superfine sugar
- 4 lemons
- ⅔ cup/20 g celery leaves
- ½ cup/15 g flat-leaf parsley leaves
- 1 cup/15 g cilantro leaves
- 4 tbsp capers
- 2 green chiles, seeded and finely sliced
- 2 tbsp olive oil, plus extra to finish
- 4 eggs
- 7 oz/200 g feta, broken into ¾-inch/2-cm chunks (1 cup)
- salt and black pepper

SERVES FOUR
as a starter

WATERCRESS SALAD WITH QUAIL EGGS, RICOTTA, AND SEEDS

12 quail eggs
2 small cloves garlic, crushed
1½ tbsp lemon juice
3½ tbsp/50 ml olive oil, plus extra to finish
1 cup/15 g dill leaves
½ cup/15 g basil leaves, torn
1 cup/15 g cilantro leaves
1 cup/30 g watercress leaves
3½ tbsp/50 g ricotta
salt and black pepper

Seeds
1½ tbsp sliced almonds
1½ tbsp pumpkin seeds
2 tsp sesame seeds
scant ½ tsp nigella seeds
¼ tsp chile flakes
¼ tsp olive oil
salt

The seeds sprinkled over this salad at the end give it a real boost in look, texture, and flavor. Make more of the mix than you need and keep it in a jar ready for your next creation that's lacking crunch.

Many an Ottolenghi salad has benefited from the addition of these seeds over the years, so one day we decided to start selling them in jars labeled "Sami's Seeds," alongside a new range of spicy nuts that were also going to bear Sami's name in a similar fashion. Lisa Reynolds, a sassy ex-Ottolenghi shift manager, rightly pointed out that these names might not necessarily enhance the eating experience we were hoping to give our customers and, luckily, got us to change the names before too many labels were printed.

Start with the seeds. Place all the ingredients in a small pan with a pinch of salt and cook over medium heat, stirring frequently, for 3 to 5 minutes, until the sesame seeds take on color. Remove from the heat and set aside to cool.

Place the quail eggs in a saucepan, cover with cold water, and bring to a boil. Simmer for 30 seconds for semisoft, or 2 minutes for hard-boiled. Refresh in cold water, then peel.

For the dressing, place the garlic, lemon juice, olive oil, ¼ teaspoon salt, and some black pepper in a small bowl. Whisk to combine and set aside.

To assemble the salad, mix the herbs and watercress together and then divide half of the salad among 4 starter plates. Halve the quail eggs and put a few halves on every plate. Use a teaspoon to deposit tiny dollops of ricotta over the salad and drizzle the dressing on top. Pile the remaining salad leaves over each portion, giving it as much height as possible. Carefully dot the salad with any remaining egg halves and cheese and drizzle with a tiny amount of oil. Finish with a sprinkle of the seeds on top and serve at once.

SERVES FOUR

RAW VEGETABLE SALAD

⅓ head cauliflower
 (7 oz/200 g), broken
 into small florets
7 oz/200 g radishes
 (long variety if possible),
 thinly sliced lengthwise
6 asparagus spears
 (7 oz/200 g), thinly
 sliced lengthwise
1 cup/30 g watercress
 leaves
⅔ cup/100 g fresh or frozen
 green peas, blanched for
 1 minute and refreshed
⅔ cup/20 g basil leaves
scant ⅔ cup/75 g pitted
 Kalamata olives

Dressing
1 small shallot, finely
 chopped (2 tbsp/20 g)
1 tsp mayonnaise
2 tbsp champagne vinegar
 or good-quality white
 wine vinegar
1½ tsp Dijon mustard
6 tbsp/90 ml good-quality
 sunflower oil
salt and black pepper

Certain vegetables—cauliflower, turnip, asparagus, and zucchini are all good examples—are hardly ever eaten raw in the UK. When I travel back home to visit my parents, I always enjoy a crunchy salad like this one, where the vegetables of the season are just chopped and thrown into a bowl with a fine vinaigrette. The result is stunning; it properly captures the essence of the season and is why I would make this salad only with fresh, seasonal, top-notch vegetables. This is really crucial. Ditto the dressing: if you can use a good-quality sunflower oil—one that actually tastes of sunflower seeds—it will make a real difference. The best way to cut the asparagus into strips is with a vegetable peeler.

First make the dressing. Mix together the shallot, mayonnaise, vinegar, mustard, and some salt and pepper in a large bowl. Whisk well as you slowly pour in the oil, along with ¾ teaspoon salt and a good grind of black pepper.

Add all the salad ingredients to the dressing, use your hands to toss everything together gently, and serve.

CRUNCHY ROOT VEGETABLES

SERVES TWO TO FOUR

Narrowing down the raw vegetable salads for this book was a very meaty task: beet, carrot, and red cabbage slaw, beet and celery root slaw, Fancy Coleslaw (page 8), Raw Vegetable Salad (opposite), Tart Apple and Celery Root Salad (page 22). A great many vegetables were sacrificed (to our tummies) for you, in pursuit of the perfected and very prized short list. A mandoline or food processor with the appropriate attachment will aid you still further in limiting hassle and preserving time.

Place the sliced vegetables in a large bowl and add the chile, lemon juice, vinegar, sugar, oil, and a scant ½ teaspoon salt. Mix well and set aside.

Place the almonds in a small pan and toast for 1 minute, stirring all the time. Add the poppy seeds and fry for another minute, taking care not to overcolor the almonds. Remove from the pan and set aside.

Just before serving, add the almonds, poppy seeds, cilantro, and dill to the vegetables and mix together. Transfer to serving bowls or a large platter, spoon the pomegranate seeds over the top, and serve.

1 small kohlrabi, peeled and cut into very fine strips roughly 2-inches/ 5-cm long and paper-thin (¾ cup/100 g)

¼ small rutabaga, peeled and cut into very fine strips roughly 2-inches/ 5-cm long and paper-thin (¾ cup/100 g)

1 small turnip, peeled and cut into very fine strips roughly 2-inches/ 5-cm long and paper-thin (⅔ cup/80 g)

1 small carrot, peeled and cut into very fine strips roughly 2-inches/ 5-cm long and paper-thin (½ cup/60 g)

1 red chile, finely chopped

1 tbsp lemon juice

1 tbsp cider vinegar

1½ tsp superfine sugar

1½ tbsp canola oil

scant ¼ cup/25 g sliced almonds

2 tsp poppy seeds

1¼ cups/20 g cilantro leaves

1 cup/15 g dill leaves

scant ⅓ cup/50 g pomegranate seeds (seeds from about ½ small pomegranate)

salt

SERVES FOUR
as a starter

FIG SALAD

2 small red onions
 (7 oz/200 g)
3 tbsp olive oil
⅓ cup/50 g hazelnuts,
 with skin
2 oz/60 g radicchio leaves
 (about 7), coarsely torn
1⅓ cups/40 g basil leaves
1⅓ cups/40 g watercress
 leaves
6 large ripe figs
 (10½ oz/300 g)
1 tbsp balsamic vinegar
¼ tsp ground cinnamon
salt and black pepper

Late summer and early autumn are peak time for figs. At any other time of the year, you will probably be getting fruit from great distances and, as figs don't ripen after picking, this normally means bland and dry. A great fig should look as if it's just about to burst its skin. When squeezed lightly, it should give a little and not spring back. It must be almost unctuously sweet, soft, and wet. Once you've managed to find a fig that meets all these criteria, I guarantee a heavenly experience. Assemble this salad at the last minute and serve as a starter.

Preheat the oven to 425°F/220°C.

Peel the onions, halve lengthwise, and cut each half into wedges 1¼-inches/3-cm wide. Mix together the wedges with 1½ teaspoons of the olive oil, a pinch of salt, and some black pepper and spread out on a baking sheet. Roast in the oven for 20 to 25 minutes, stirring once or twice during cooking, until the onions are soft and golden and turning crispy in parts. Remove and set aside to cool before pulling the onions apart with your hands into bite-size chunks.

Turn down the oven temperature to 325°F/160°C. Scatter the hazelnuts in a small roasting pan and toast for 20 minutes. Remove from the oven and, when cool enough to handle, roughly crush with the flat side of a large knife.

Assemble the salad on 4 individual plates. Mix the radicchio, basil, and watercress together and place a few on the bottom of each plate. Cut each fig lengthwise into 4 or 6 pieces. Place a few fig pieces and some roasted onion on the leaves. Top with more leaves and continue with the remaining fig and onion. You want to build up the salad into a small pyramid.

In a small cup, whisk together the remaining 2½ tablespoons olive oil, the vinegar, and cinnamon with a pinch of salt and some black pepper. Drizzle this over the salad, finish with the hazelnuts, and serve.

POMELO SALAD

SERVES FOUR

Once in a while, not very often, my mother brought home a pomelo. This used to just sit there, on the kitchen counter, a massive old thing, and we, the children, couldn't do much with it. It took an adult to peel off the thick skin with a serious knife and then get the juicy flesh out of the tight, bitter membrane. It was a proper ceremony that my mum used to conduct after dinner. We would all sit and wait, like chicks in a nest, for the precious pieces to come our way, never quite fast enough.

These days I think of pomelo as one of the most underappreciated of fruit. Oranges and grapefruits are almost mundane staples, yet many people don't have a clue about the third party in this citrusy trio. Well, I am happy to champion its bittersweet, sharpish flavor and firm yet juicy texture to anyone who is willing to listen. It is refreshing, delicious, and worth a bit of peeling effort.

Pomelos vary in size. Here you'll need at least two, if they are grapefruit size, or only one of the large standard pomelos.

This salad is perfect alongside some grilled shrimp or calamari, and if you're already willing to go nonvegetarian, add a few drops of fish sauce to give the fruit extra depth. Cold cooked rice noodles will bulk up the salad and turn it into a fresh vegetarian main course.

First make the marinade. Place the vinegar and sugar in a small saucepan and warm gently, stirring, until the sugar dissolves. Remove from the heat, add the orange blossom water, star anise, cinnamon, ginger, and chiles and set aside.

Use a sharp knife to peel the pomelo skin. Divide into segments and use the knife to remove and discard the pith and membrane. Break the fruit segments into 1 or 2 bite-size chunks, put in a shallow dish, and pour in the marinade. Leave for at least 30 minutes—the longer, the better.

Remove and discard the star anise and cinnamon. Drain and save the marinade. Place the pomelo, ginger, and chiles in a large bowl and add 3 tablespoons of the reserved marinade along with the mango, cilantro, mint, shallots, watercress, peanut oil, lime juice, and ¼ teaspoon salt. Gently toss, add more marinade, if needed, and then sprinkle with the sesame seeds and peanuts and serve.

Marinade
5 tbsp/75 ml rice wine vinegar
¼ cup/40 g palm (or superfine) sugar
1 tbsp orange blossom water
2 star anise pods
1 cinnamon stick, broken in two
1¼-inch/3-cm piece fresh ginger (about ⅓ oz/10 g), peeled and cut into thin strips
2 red chiles, seeded and cut into thin strips

Salad
1 large (or 2 small) pomelo (2¼ lb/1 kg in total; 2 cups/350 g once peeled and segmented)
1 small green or regular mango, peeled and cut into thin strips (scant 1 cup/140 g)
⅔ cup/10 g cilantro leaves
⅓ cup/10 g mint leaves
4 baby red or regular shallots, thinly sliced (⅓ cup/40 g)
2 cups/60 g watercress leaves
2 tsp peanut oil
2 tsp lime juice
2 tsp black sesame seeds (or white, if unavailable)
¼ cup/40 g roasted peanuts, coarsely chopped
salt

SERVES FOUR

PINK GRAPEFRUIT AND SUMAC SALAD

6 pink or red grapefruits (5 lb/2.2 kg)
2 tbsp superfine sugar
1 small dried red chile (use less if it is very hot)
4 tbsp/60 ml olive oil
1½ tbsp lemon juice
1 tbsp sumac
½ medium red onion, very thinly sliced (about ⅔ cup/70 g)
2 or 3 small heads red Belgian endive, leaves separated and any large leaves cut in half on the diagonal (about 3 cups/280 g)
scant 3 cups/80 g watercress leaves
⅔ cup/20 g basil leaves
salt

Something about the word or connotations of grapefruit often stops people from ordering it from a menu, but I urge you to give this a go: its astringency is more than balanced here by the sweetness of the basil and the dressing. It works as a palate-awakening starter or between courses, and it is also a nice side dish served along fried firm tofu pieces or a spicy roasted chicken. Preparing the grapefruit takes a little time but can be done well in advance.

Using a small, sharp knife, slice off the top and tail of 5 of the grapefruits. Cut down the side of each grapefruit, following its natural line, to remove the skin and white pith. Over a small bowl, cut between the membranes to remove the individual segments. Place in a colander to drain and gently squeeze any remaining juices into a small saucepan.

Squeeze enough juice from the last grapefruit to bring the juice in the pan up to 1¼ cups/300 ml. Add the sugar and chile and bring to a boil. Turn down the heat to medium and simmer until the sauce thickens and you have about 5 tablespoons left, about 30 minutes. Set aside to cool down, then whisk in the olive oil, lemon juice, sumac, and ¼ teaspoon salt.

To assemble the salad, put the grapefruit segments, onion, endive, watercress, and basil in a large bowl. Pour over three-quarters of the dressing and toss very gently. Add the remainder of the dressing if the salad seems dry; otherwise, keep in the fridge for another leafy salad. Serve immediately.

SERVES FOUR TO SIX

TART APPLE AND CELERY ROOT SALAD

¾ cup / 120 g quinoa
3 tbsp white wine vinegar
2 tbsp superfine sugar
1 medium red onion, thinly sliced (rounded 1 cup / 130 g)
¼ cup / 60 ml canola oil
½ large celery root (10½ oz / 300 g)
¼ cup / 60 ml lemon juice
2 or 3 Granny Smith apples (14 oz / 400 g)
2 tsp poppy seeds
1 red chile, thinly sliced on the diagonal
1 cup / 15 g cilantro leaves, coarsely chopped
salt

This salad hits you on the head with its sharp sweetness and oniony heat, and it's exactly what I'd prescribe to shake you up a little on a drowsy wintry night. Serve it alongside a seasonal stew, and you'll get a perfect balance. When serving it on its own, try adding a handful of chopped walnuts and a few baby leaves. Use a mandoline for the celery root and apple, if you have one.

Bring a saucepan of water to a boil. Add the quinoa and simmer for 9 minutes. Drain, refresh under cold water, and then set aside to dry completely.

Place the vinegar, sugar, and 1 teaspoon salt in a bowl and whisk to combine. Add the onion and rub the liquids into it using your hands. Add the oil, stir, and set aside for 30 minutes to marinate.

Peel the celery root, cut into very thin strips, and place in a bowl with the lemon juice to prevent discoloration. Quarter the apples, remove the cores, and cut each quarter into similarly thin strips. Add to the celery root and mix well. Add the onion along with the quinoa, poppy seeds, chile, and cilantro. Mix well and taste to see if you need any more salt, sugar, or vinegar: you are aiming for a pungent, sweet-and-sour flavor.

SERVES FOUR

PARSLEY, LEMON, AND CANNELLINI BEAN SALAD

⅔ cup / 100 g red quinoa
⅔ cup / 20 g flat-leaf parsley leaves, finely shredded
⅔ cup / 20 g mint leaves, finely shredded
1¾ oz / 50 g green onions (3 to 4), green and white parts, thinly sliced
1⅓ cups / 250 g cooked cannellini beans, drained
½ large lemon, skin and seeds removed, flesh finely chopped (about ⅓ cup / 70 g)
½ tsp ground allspice
¼ cup / 60 ml olive oil
salt and black pepper

I ate a lot of this sort of salad when traveling around the southern and eastern Mediterranean filming for my first series of Mediterranean Feast. *It's super-simple, ready in minutes, and absolutely delicious. The red quinoa looks great against the cannellini, but use regular white, which needs a minute or two less cooking, if that's what you have on hand.*

Bring a saucepan of water to a boil. Add the quinoa and simmer for 11 minutes. Drain, refresh under cold water, and set aside to dry completely. Transfer the cooked quinoa to a large bowl. Add the parsley, mint, green onions, beans, lemon, allspice, olive oil, ¾ teaspoon salt, and some black pepper. Stir together and serve.

ORANGE AND DATE SALAD

SERVES FOUR

For one logistical reason or another, this heavenly salad didn't make it to the final cut of my Morocco episode of Mediterranean Feast. *Budget and pressures on timing aside, the crew were delighted to keep reshooting it in different locations—on* riad *rooftops and in the kitchens of kind strangers—if only to devour the offerings once the "wrap" was called.*

To make the dressing, whisk together the lemon juice, garlic, orange blossom water, cinnamon, and fennel seeds. Add the olive oil, ½ teaspoon salt, and a generous grind of pepper and whisk until well combined. Set aside.

Using a small, sharp serrated knife, slice off the top and tail of each orange. Cut down the sides of each orange, following its natural curve, to remove the skin and white pith. Cut crosswise into slices ¼ inch/5 mm thick and remove the seeds.

Put the oranges, dates, radishes, onion, arugula, lettuce, cilantro, parsley, and mint in a large salad bowl. Stir the dressing and pour it over the salad. Gently stir everything together, pile into a large but shallow bowl, and serve.

5 medium oranges (2¼ lb/ 1 kg in total; about 3 cups/500 g after peeling and slicing)
3 large Medjool dates, pitted and quartered lengthwise (2 oz/60 g)
4 oz/120 g radishes, sliced paper-thin
⅓ small red onion, very thinly sliced into rings (⅓ cup/30 g)
3 cups/60 g arugula
1 oz/30 g Lollo Rosso lettuce (2 to 3 leaves), torn into 1¼-inch/ 3-cm pieces
1 cup/15 g cilantro leaves, coarsely chopped
½ cup/15 g flat-leaf parsley leaves, coarsely chopped
½ cup/15 g mint leaves, coarsely torn

Dressing
2 tbsp lemon juice
1 clove garlic, crushed
1 tsp orange blossom water
½ tsp ground cinnamon
2 tsp fennel seeds, toasted and lightly crushed
3 tbsp olive oil
salt and black pepper

SPROUT SALAD

SERVES FOUR

1½ tbsp cumin seeds
1 lb/450 g mixed sprouts (such as mung bean, chickpea, aduki bean, and lentil)
1 daikon, peeled and thinly sliced (about 2 cups/250 g), or common radishes or kohlrabi if unavailable
2 large carrots, peeled and thinly sliced (about 2 cups/250 g)
⅔ cup/20 g flat-leaf parsley leaves, coarsely chopped
⅔ cup/10 g cilantro leaves, coarsely chopped
2 cloves garlic, crushed
3 tbsp sunflower oil
2 tbsp canola oil
2 tbsp white wine vinegar
2 tbsp cider vinegar
2 cups/300 g baby plum tomatoes, halved lengthwise
scant 3 cups/80 g baby spinach leaves
salt and black pepper

My Camden test kitchen is an autonomous unit, separate from our shops and restaurants by distance and pervading atmosphere. Calm and collected is how I'd describe it, nothing like the frenzied air of the "professional" kitchens we run; those can become pretty mad at times, churning out tons of food at a heart-stopping pace. Still, when Cornelia, Noam, or Sami pop over from one of the shops to have chats and, invariably, sample the day's recipes, things can turn a bit thorny, even in my little paradise. Few words are minced by my discerning and hard-to-please business partners. Praise is rarely without qualification; improvements are often suggested.

Sami is quick to disqualify; Noam to reject anything white; but Cornelia who, generally, would always prefer a piece of minced raw steak over anything, is the hardest to please. So, as you can probably imagine, bets were not placed on her rooting for this virtuous-sounding salad. We were all wrong. She absolutely loved it. And when Cornelia loves something, she makes it over and over again. This salad has made it into her all-time top ten, the biggest accolade imaginable!

Different oils and vinegars are used here to add a certain richness, but you can use just one of each, and the daikon can be substituted with common radishes or kohlrabi. Walnuts and chunks of creamy blue cheese would move this away from the land of the virtuous and turn it into a sumptuous main course.

Place the cumin seeds in a small sauté pan. Toast over high heat for a minute or two, shaking the pan to move the seeds around, until they give off their aroma and begin to pop. Transfer to a mortar and crush with a pestle until powdery.

Put the sprouts, daikon, and carrots in a large bowl. Add the herbs, garlic, oils, vinegars, ground cumin seeds, 1 teaspoon salt, and some black pepper. Stir well, taste, and adjust the seasoning if you need. Add the tomatoes and spinach leaves, stir gently, and serve.

See picture on the following right-hand page

SPROUT SALAD, PART TWO

SERVES FOUR

I'm not entirely sure of the etiquette surrounding sequels to recipes, but three years on from the January when the first sprout salad was devised, I found myself in a similar state of post-festive-season excess, in need of a detox. This was the result, and, again, for a while it will make not eating cheese and drinking red wine seem like a very good idea indeed. The salty-sour umeboshi purée, made from pickled plums, can be found either in large supermarkets with other Japanese ingredients or in Japanese or specialty food stores.

Preheat the oven to 325°F/170°C.

Place the sunflower seeds and almonds on a small baking sheet and roast for 15 to 20 minutes, until golden. Remove from the oven and set aside to cool.

To make the dressing, put all the ingredients in a small bowl along with a scant ½ teaspoon salt. Whisk well until combined and set aside.

Bring a saucepan of water to a boil, add the edamame, bring back to a boil, and then immediately drain and refresh under cold water. Shake well to dry before transferring them to a large bowl. Add the radishes, kohlrabi, carrot, sprouts, avocados, cilantro, and toasted sunflower seeds and almonds to the edamame. Pour the dressing over the salad, mix to combine and serve.

See picture on the following left-hand page

---

3 tbsp/20 g sunflower seeds
3 tbsp/20 g sliced almonds
1 cup/150 g frozen shelled edamame (soybeans)
15 medium radishes, cut into paper-thin rounds (1¼ cups/140 g)
1 small kohlrabi, peeled and cut into thin strips
1 medium carrot, peeled and cut into thin strips
scant 1¼ cups/120 g mung bean sprouts
2 large ripe avocados, peeled, pitted, and cut into ⅔-inch/1.5-cm dice (2 cups/280 g)
1⅓ cups/20 g cilantro leaves, chopped

Dressing
1½ tsp umeboshi purée
1 tbsp rice vinegar
1½ tbsp lime juice
1 tbsp soy sauce
½ tsp sesame oil
2 tsp superfine sugar
1 small shallot (1 oz/30 g), finely chopped (2½ tbsp/25 g)
3 tbsp sunflower oil
salt

SERVES FOUR TO SIX

SPRING SALAD

10 asparagus spears (12 oz/350 g), trimmed and each spear sliced on a sharp diagonal into 3 or 4 thin pieces
7 oz/200 g haricots verts, trimmed
2¾ cups/300 g shelled fresh or frozen fava beans
1⅔ cups/50 g baby spinach leaves
1 banana shallot, or 2 regular shallots, very thinly sliced (½ cup/50 g)
1 red chile, finely diced
½ tsp sesame oil
2 tbsp olive oil
1 tbsp lemon juice
1 tbsp/10 g mixed black and white sesame seeds, toasted
1 tsp nigella seeds
salt

I love dishes that feature the various shades of a single color, making you stop to check what's in there. Spring and early summer are the time to do this with green, with artichoke, arugula, asparagus, fava beans, watercress, peas, cabbage, all kinds of lettuce, and many, many more vegetables to choose from. When you put a few of these in one bowl, you get the most glorious celebration of color and spring.

Bring a large pan of water to a boil, add the asparagus, and blanch for 3 minutes. Use a slotted spoon to transfer the asparagus to a bowl of ice-cold water. Add the haricots verts to the boiling water and blanch for 5 minutes. Use the slotted spoon to transfer them to the bowl with the asparagus, drain both, and then set aside to dry. Add the fava beans to the boiling water and blanch for 2 minutes. Drain, refresh under cold water, and then remove and discard the skins by pressing each bean gently between your finger and thumb.

Place both beans and the asparagus in a large bowl. Add the spinach, shallot, chile, oils, lemon juice, sesame seeds, nigella seeds, and ½ teaspoon salt, stir gently, and serve at once.

DAKOS

SERVES FOUR

I sometimes worry that my mild obsession with these Cretan barley rusks is in excess of their status as, essentially, some dried crisp bread. I fell in love with them over a summer in Crete, and with apologies to Turkey's apple tea, these flings don't always stand the test of time once the holiday bags have been unpacked. The second I snack on dakos *though, piled high with sweet chopped tomatoes and dotted with feta cheese and wrinkly black olives, I'm more convinced than any smitten seventeen-year-old that this is a relationship that will last. The barley in the rusks makes them sweeter, nuttier, crunchier (and more utterly addictive) than their wheat-only counterparts. If you can't find the Greek* dakos, *other rusks are fine here: I particularly like the whole-grain Swedish Krisprolls, which are widely available.*

As with all simple tomato-based salads, the quality of the tomatoes is key. If yours are anything other than bursting with flavor, a pinch of sugar or a few drops of balsamic vinegar will help to draw out their natural sweetness.

---

6 large tomatoes, cut into ⅜-inch/1-cm dice (2¾ cups/500 g)
½ red onion, cut into ¼-inch/5-mm dice (⅓ cup/50 g)
1½ tbsp red wine vinegar
3 tbsp olive oil
½ tsp ground allspice
5 oz/150 g Cretan dakos or other rusks, coarsely broken
½ cup/70 g coarsely crumbled feta
⅓ cup/40 g black olives, pitted and halved
3½ tbsp/30 g capers, whole or very coarsely chopped
2 tbsp/5 g chopped flat-leaf parsley, to serve
salt and black pepper

Place the tomatoes, onion, vinegar, 2 tablespoons of the oil, the allspice, a scant ½ teaspoon salt, and a good grind of black pepper in a large bowl. Stir gently and set aside.

Spread out the dakos on a serving platter and spoon the tomato mixture on top. Sprinkle the feta, olives, and capers over the tomato mixture, followed by the parsley and the remaining 1 tablespoon olive oil. Leave to sit for 5 minutes before serving.

SERVES FOUR

CARAMELIZED FIG, ORANGE, AND FETA SALAD

½ cup / 100 g superfine sugar

16 ripe figs, cut in half lengthwise

4 medium oranges, topped and tailed, peeled, and sliced into rounds ⅜-inch / 1-cm thick (about 4½ cups / 750 g)

2 tbsp lemon juice

1½ tbsp raki, Pernod, or another aniseed-flavored liqueur

1 tsp aniseeds or fennel seeds, lightly toasted

1 clove garlic, crushed

⅓ cup / 80 ml olive oil

7 oz / 200 g feta, broken into ⅜-inch / 1-cm chunks

1 tbsp oregano leaves, small leaves whole and larger ones chopped

3 cups / 60 g arugula

coarse sea salt and black pepper

Bringing caramel to just the right point of caramelization while trying to look good for a camera is no mean feat—one I didn't manage to pull off, I hasten to add, while filming in Majorca for Mediterranean Feast. *I was granted the benefit of three takes to get the dish (and myself) looking right for the shoot, but I suggest you keep focused on the dish alone. This was the first-ever dish that Esme tested for me in Camden. In classic day-one madness, her attempts to caramelize were impeded by the fact that she had reached for the salt, rather than the sugar, to add to the pan!*

Working with caramel may seem intimidating, but you needn't worry: the juicy fruit will be fine even if the caramel is slightly crystallized or lumpy. It won't be thanking you, though, if the caramel burns, so you need to work fast when the caramel reaches the desired color and not to worry if you add the fruit before all of the sugar has melted. If you can look cute and talk to the camera at the same time, then all credit to you. There is nothing strictly "tossed" about this recipe, I know, but the other salads insisted on taking it under their wing.

Place a large sauté pan over medium heat and add half the sugar. Leave for 2 to 3 minutes, or until it turns a golden caramel color; don't stir the sugar at this stage. Once nice and golden, add half the figs, cut side down. Cook for 2 minutes, until starting to soften, before turning to cook for a minute more. Remove from the pan and add the second batch of figs and repeat the cooking process. You might need to add a tablespoon or two of water to the pan if the figs aren't very juicy.

Add the remaining sugar to the pan, return to the heat, and let the sugar start to caramelize before adding the oranges and leaving for 1 minute on each side. They should take on a rich caramel color. Remove and add to the plate of figs.

Take the caramel off the heat and whisk in the lemon juice, liqueur, aniseeds, garlic, ¾ teaspoon coarse sea salt, and a generous grind of black pepper. Once combined, whisk in the olive oil and set aside.

Arrange the oranges and figs on a large platter and dot with the feta pieces. Drizzle any juices left on the fruit plate over the top, followed by the dressing. Sprinkle with the oregano and arugula and serve.

See pictures on the following pages

STEAMED

SERVES FOUR

STEAMED EGGPLANT WITH SESAME AND GREEN ONION

2 medium eggplants, topped and peeled (scant 1½ lb/650 g)
5 green onions, white and green parts, thinly sliced on the diagonal (¾ cup/70 g)
1 tbsp/10 g mixed black and white sesame seeds, toasted

Dressing
2½ tsp mirin
½ tsp sesame oil
1½ tbsp light soy sauce
2½ tsp rice vinegar
1½ tsp maple syrup
2 tsp peeled and finely chopped fresh ginger
1 clove garlic, crushed
salt

That rare Ottolenghi combination: an eggplant without olive oil, due only to the Japanese heritage of the dish. Steaming maintains some of the texture of the vegetable flesh, which doesn't happen if you cook it any other way, giving the dish a particular substantial quality. It's suitable to serve as a main course with just plain rice or fried tofu. The black sesame seeds look fantastic, but use white if that's all you have on hand.

Fill a large pot (for which you have a lid) with water to a quarter of the way up the sides and bring to a boil. Place the eggplants in a steamer or a colander hovering over the water, making sure the water doesn't touch the base of the steamer. Cover tightly, using foil to seal the edges if you need to, and steam for 30 minutes, turning the eggplants once. When the eggplants are cooked, remove the steamer from the pot and leave the eggplants to cool and drain inside the steamer. Shred the flesh by hand into long, thin strips ¼ inch/5 mm wide, then continue to drain for another 20 minutes.

Meanwhile, make the dressing. Mix together the mirin, sesame oil, soy sauce, vinegar, maple syrup, and ¼ teaspoon salt. Stir in the ginger and garlic and set aside.

Once the eggplant strips are completely cool, gently toss them with the dressing before adding the green onions and sesame seeds. Leave to marinate for at least 10 minutes and then serve.

SERVES SIX TO EIGHT

RICE SALAD WITH NUTS AND SOUR CHERRIES

scant 1 cup/150 g wild rice
scant 1¼ cups/220 g basmati rice
5½ tbsp/80 ml olive oil
⅔ cup/100 g quinoa
6½ tbsp/60 g almonds, skins on, coarsely chopped
7 tbsp/60 g pine nuts
¼ cup/60 ml sunflower oil
2 medium onions, thinly sliced (about 3 cups/320 g)
1 cup/30 g flat-leaf parsley leaves, coarsely chopped
⅔ cup/20 g basil leaves, coarsely chopped
⅓ cup/10 g tarragon leaves, coarsely chopped
2 cups/40 g arugula
⅔ cup/80 g dried sour cherries
¼ cup/60 ml lemon juice, plus the grated zest of 1 lemon
2 cloves garlic, crushed
salt and black pepper

Forgive me for all the pots and pans here. They are all left fairly clean, so a good wipe with a towel between uses will save some washing up. The sour cherries have a welcome bite, which sweet raisins lack, so they are worth seeking out in larger shops. You could substitute chopped dried cranberries soaked in a little lemon juice, if need be. This salad makes a satisfying meal-in-a-bowl and will keep in the fridge for a day at least. Just remember not to serve it cold and to readjust the seasoning before serving.

Place the wild rice in a saucepan, cover with plenty of water, bring to a boil, and then turn down to a gentle simmer and cook for 35 minutes, until the rice is cooked but still firm. Drain, rinse under cold water, and set aside to dry.

Mix the basmati rice with 1 tablespoon of the olive oil and ½ teaspoon salt. Place in a saucepan with 1⅓ cups/330 ml of boiling water, cover, and cook over the lowest possible heat for 15 minutes. Remove from the heat, place a tea towel over the pan, replace the lid, and set aside for 10 minutes. Uncover and allow to cool down completely.

Bring a small saucepan of water to a boil and add the quinoa. Cook for 9 minutes, then drain into a fine sieve, refresh under cold water, and set aside.

Place the almonds and pine nuts in a small pan with 1 tablespoon of the olive oil and a pinch of salt. Cook over medium-low heat for about 5 minutes, stirring frequently. Transfer to a small plate as soon as the pine nuts begin to color and set aside.

Heat the sunflower oil in a large sauté pan and add the onions, ¼ teaspoon salt, and some black pepper. Cook over high heat for 5 to 8 minutes, stirring often, so that parts of the onion get crisp and others just soft. Transfer to paper towels to drain.

Place all the grains in a large bowl along with the chopped herbs, arugula, fried onion, nuts, and sour cherries. Add the lemon juice and zest, the remaining 3½ tablespoons olive oil, the garlic, ½ teaspoon salt, and some pepper. Mix well and set aside for at least 10 minutes before serving.

LEMON AND CURRY LEAF RICE

SERVES FOUR

This will be a revelation to those who tend toward plain steamed basmati. The method is fail-safe, and the result is stunning. Serve this rice with an Asian savory pickle to make a vegetarian meal, or next to a freshly roasted chicken. Try to look for fresh curry leaves for this dish, using them on the stem. They freeze well, so don't worry if you end up getting a large bunch.

5 short cinnamon sticks, each about 2-inches/5-cm long
10 whole cloves
shaved rind of 1 lemon, plus 1 tbsp lemon juice
3 stems fresh curry leaves (about 25 leaves), or 35 dried curry leaves
rounded 2 cups/400 g basmati rice, rinsed, soaked in water for 15 minutes, and drained well
¼ cup/60 g unsalted butter
salt and white pepper

Preheat the oven to 400°F/200°C.

Put the cinnamon sticks, cloves, lemon rind, curry leaves, 1½ teaspoons salt, and ½ teaspoon pepper in a saucepan. Cover with 2¾ cups/680 ml water and place over high heat. As soon as the water boils, remove the pan from the heat.

Spread the rice out in a baking dish or roasting pan approximately 9½ by 12-inches/24 by 30-cm, cover with the boiled water and aromatics, and stir well. Lay a piece of waxed paper over the surface of the water and cover the dish with aluminum foil. Cook in the oven for 25 minutes, then remove and leave to sit, covered, for 8 to 10 minutes.

Just before serving, melt the butter in a small saucepan. Once it's melted and very hot, carefully add the lemon juice and swirl together to mix. Pour this over the hot rice and fluff up the rice with a fork. Transfer to a serving bowl and serve at once (you can remove the curry stems and cinnamon sticks or keep for the look).

See pictures on the following pages

SAFFRON, DATE, AND ALMOND RICE

SERVES FOUR

I have been having a long literary love affair with Claudia Roden, instigated initially by my crippling dependence on her The Book of Jewish Food, *which I consulted whenever I needed to cook anything typically Jewish. Later I met my idol in the flesh and immediately fell for her charm, captivating modesty, and endless stream of stories. It is a real honor to count her as a friend.*

Apart from her Jewish cookery bible, Claudia has written several masterpieces covering the cuisines of Italy and Spain and many other illuminating recipe collections. Her A Book of Middle Eastern Food, *in particular, has paved the way for many writers on the subject and still feels as current as it did when it was first published in 1968. This recipe is inspired by a marvelous Iranian dish from that book.*

I have said it before and I am happy to repeat myself: Iranians make the best rice. Their technique of washing and parboiling the rice and then allowing it to steam in the residual moisture makes it worthy of being included in this chapter much more than other rice cooking methods that, technically, are more about absorption than steaming. The result is light rice, every grain perfectly defined from the rest of the clan. Don't be alarmed by the amount of salt called for in the water before the rice is drained and rinsed, and also don't worry about some rice sticking to the bottom and burning a little: it makes it nice and crunchy, just like the Iranians like it. The rice will go fantastically well with the Indian Ratatouille (page 128) or the Iranian Vegetable Stew with Dried Lime (page 134).

rounded 2 cups / 400 g basmati rice
½ cup / 110 g unsalted butter
⅔ cup / 100 g whole blanched almonds, coarsely chopped
4 large Medjool dates, pitted and coarsely chopped (3 oz / 80 g)
¼ tsp saffron threads, soaked in 2 tbsp hot water
salt and white pepper

Rinse the rice well under running cold water. Put it in a large bowl, cover with plenty of lukewarm water, and stir in 2 tablespoons salt. Allow the rice to sit for 1 to 2 hours, then drain and wash with lukewarm water.

Bring a pot of water to a boil and add 2 tablespoons salt, then the rice. Gently boil the rice for 3 to 4 minutes, until the rice is almost cooked. Check this by removing a grain and biting into it: it should still have a tiny bit of bite. Drain the rice and rinse under lukewarm water. Set aside to drain.

In the same saucepan, melt 5½ tablespoons / 80 g of the butter and sauté the almonds for 4 minutes, until they turn slightly golden. Add the dates and cook for a few more minutes. Stir in ½ teaspoon white pepper, ¼ teaspoon salt, and half the rice. Gently flatten this rice and then layer the remaining rice on top. Melt the remaining 2½ tablespoons butter and drizzle this over the top along with 3 tablespoons water. Cover the pan tightly with a lid and cook on the lowest heat possible for 35 minutes. Remove from the heat and spoon the saffron and its soaking water over the top. Cover the pan immediately with a kitchen towel, seal with the lid, and set aside for 10 minutes.

To serve, don't stir the rice, just use a large serving spoon to remove portions with the distinct two layers kept separate. Serve at once.

MISO VEGETABLES AND RICE WITH BLACK SESAME DRESSING

SERVES FOUR

1½ cups/300 g sushi (short-grain white) rice
1½ tsp dashi stock powder or a light vegetarian stock powder
1½ tbsp tamari soy sauce
1½ tbsp mirin
scant 2 tbsp/30 g dark red or brown miso paste
1½ tsp superfine sugar
7½ oz/220 g broccolini, trimmed and cut in half crosswise (about 2 cups/180 g); if thick, halved, lengthwise as well
6 oz/165 g buna-shimeji (brown beech) mushrooms, separated into small clusters
1 large carrot, peeled and cut into ¼ by 2½-inch/5 mm by 6-cm batons (1 cup/140 g)
scant 2 oz/50 g snow peas, cut into fine matchsticks
1 baby cucumber, cut into ¼ by 2½-inch/5 mm by 6-cm batons (¾ cup/100 g)
⅔ cup/10 g cilantro leaves

Black sesame dressing
4½ tbsp/40 g peanuts, toasted and coarsely chopped
1½ tbsp/15 g black or white sesame seeds
1 tbsp rice vinegar
1 tsp maple syrup
1 tsp peanut oil
½ tsp chile flakes

This is my go-to dish for winter-evening comfort food. You can buy dashi stock powder in Asian or health food shops, but most varieties are not suitable for vegetarians. A decent vegetarian dashi can be made by boiling kombu (which your Asian or health food shop should sell), an edible kelp, for just 5 minutes. Use the boiling liquid, instead of the water specified in the recipe, omitting the stock powder but still adding the soy, mirin, miso, and sugar.

Soak the rice for 15 minutes in cold water, drain, place in a saucepan for which you have a lid, and cover with 1½ cups/375 ml water. Cover the pan, bring to a boil, then turn down the heat to the lowest setting. Cook for 10 minutes, remove from the heat, and leave, covered, for a further 15 minutes.

Meanwhile, place all of the ingredients for the black sesame dressing in a small bowl and mix together well.

Pour another 1½ cups/375 ml water into a separate pan and add the dashi powder, soy sauce, mirin, miso paste, and sugar. Bring to a boil, stirring occasionally, and then turn down the heat to medium. Add the broccolini and simmer for 4 minutes. Using a slotted spoon, transfer the broccolini to a large bowl. Add the mushrooms to the stock mixture, cook for 3 minutes, remove, and add to the bowl with the broccolini. Repeat with the carrots—they need 2 minutes; snow peas, 1 minute; cucumber, just 15 seconds. When all the vegetables have been cooked and set aside, increase the temperature under the stock and reduce the liquid until there is about ¼ cup/60 ml left: this should take about 10 minutes.

Divide the rice among 4 bowls and place the vegetables on top. Spoon the reduced cooking liquid over the top, followed by the black sesame dressing. Finish with the cilantro leaves and serve at once.

BLANCHED

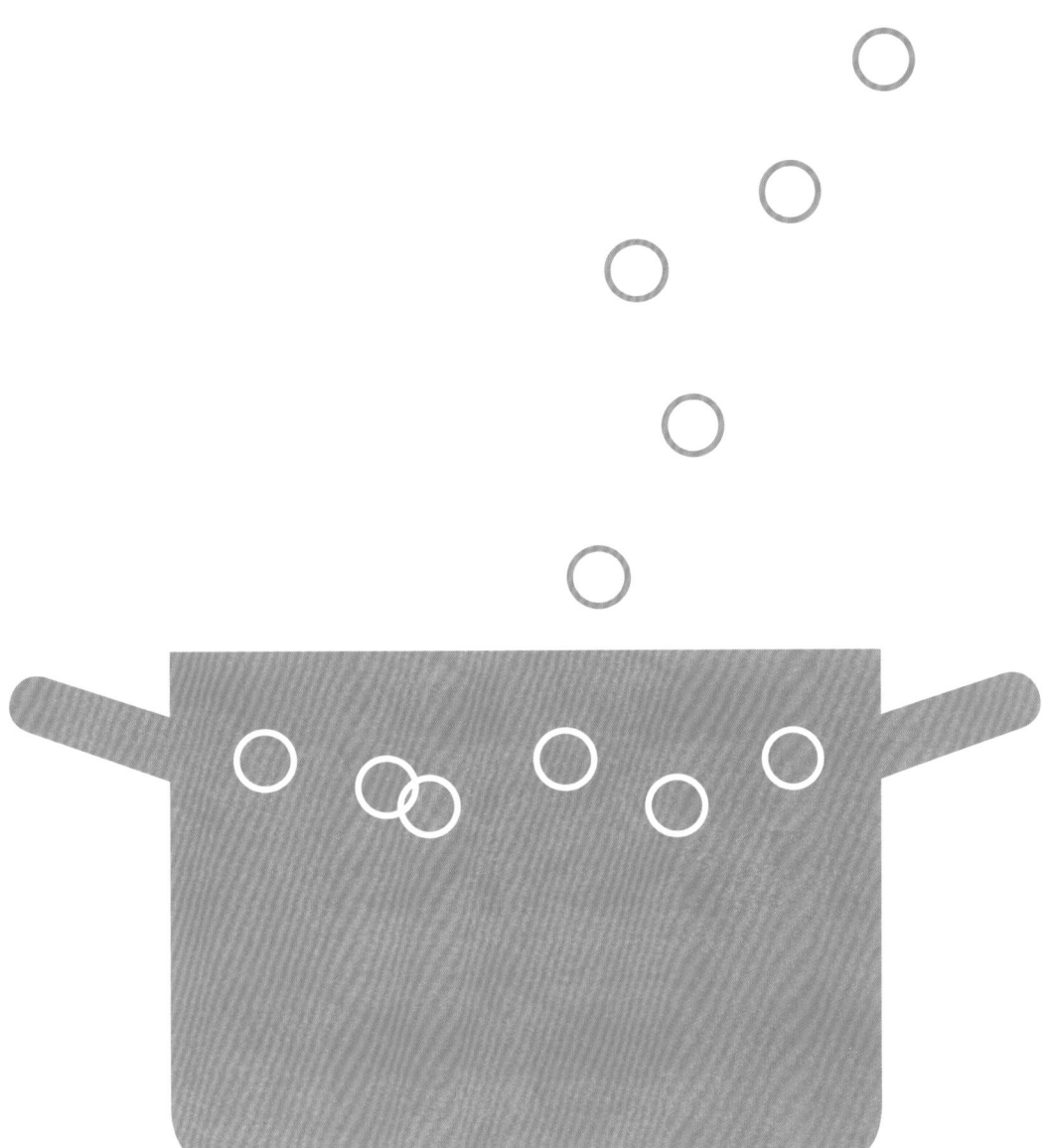

TOMATO AND ROASTED LEMON SALAD

SERVES FOUR

2 medium lemons, halved crosswise, seeds removed, and cut into paper-thin slices (9 oz/260 g)
3 tbsp olive oil
½ tsp superfine sugar
8 sage leaves, finely shredded
2⅔ cups/400 g baby tomatoes, yellow or red or a mixture of both, halved
scant ½ tsp ground allspice
⅓ cup/10 g flat-leaf parsley leaves
½ cup/15 g mint leaves
seeds of 1 small pomegranate (⅔ cup/120 g)
1½ tbsp pomegranate molasses
½ small red onion, thinly sliced (about ½ cup/50 g)
salt and black pepper

I cooked a recipe similar to this in Sardinia when I shot my Mediterranean Island Feast *series last year. I was performing in front of two cameras and our small crew when suddenly a bunch of chirpy Aussie ladies arrived to check into the tiny hotel of my host, Robert Flore, in the remote Monte Ferru mountains. By coincidence, they had come straight from London, which they had visited especially in order to eat in the restaurants of their favorite chef; that chef turned out to be your humble servant. The raucous exhilaration was hard to contain, but it did, I must admit, seriously boost my performance. There's nothing like a noisy home crowd!*

Seek out the sweetest tomatoes you can for this salad in order to balance the bitterness of the lemon. You can bulk it up, as I did in Sardinia, by adding lots more leaves and fresh herbs and some cooked fregola. *This will turn the salad into a whole meal. Otherwise, serve it with oven-roasted potatoes or panfried fish.*

Preheat the oven to 325°F/170°C.

Bring a small saucepan of water to a boil, add the lemon slices, and blanch for 2 minutes. Drain well, place the lemon in a bowl, and add 1 tablespoon of the oil, ½ teaspoon salt, the sugar, and the sage. Gently mix and then spread the lemon mixture out on a baking sheet lined with parchment paper. Place in the oven and cook for 20 minutes, until the lemons have dried out a little. Remove and set aside to cool.

In a bowl, combine the tomatoes, allspice, parsley, mint, pomegranate seeds, pomegranate molasses, onion, the remaining 2 tablespoons oil, ¼ teaspoon salt, and some freshly ground pepper. Add the lemon slices, stir gently, and serve.

RICE NOODLES WITH GREEN ONIONS AND EDAMAME

SERVES FOUR

These noodles are unchallenging in the best sense of the term: they are easy to make and very comforting. As they are they'd be lovely with the Steamed Eggplant with Sesame and Green Onion (page 40), omitting the green onion from the eggplant recipe. Or, as a stand-alone dish, adding 4 oz/120 g of picked crabmeat with some lime juice at the final stage is a delicious upgrade.

Bring a large pot of salted water to a boil and cook the noodles for about 5 minutes, or as instructed on the package, until al dente. Drain well, rinse under hot water, and set aside in a large bowl with 1½ teaspoons of the sunflower oil stirred through. Keep the bowl somewhere warm, covered, until ready to use.

Heat the remaining 2 tablespoons sunflower oil in a large wok or sauté pan over high heat. Add the green onions and chiles and cook for 2 to 3 minutes over high heat, stirring frequently, until the onions soften a little but don't turn mushy. Add the edamame and heat them for about 30 seconds.

Give the noodles a quick rinse under warm water if they have become stuck together and then, when drained, pour the contents of the wok over them, followed by the sesame oil, sesame seeds, vinegar, cilantro, and ¾ teaspoon salt. Stir well, sprinkle the lime zest over the top, and serve at once, with the wedges alongside.

8 oz/250 g dried wide rice noodles
2½ tbsp sunflower oil
1 lb/450 g green onions (about 35 small ones), white and green parts, trimmed and cut on the diagonal into slices 1¼-inches/3-cm long
2 or 3 green chiles, depending on heat, seeded and thinly sliced
1⅔ cups/250 g frozen shelled edamame (soybeans), blanched for 3 minutes, refreshed, and left to dry
1 tbsp sesame oil
3 tbsp sesame seeds (a mix of black and toasted white or just toasted white)
2 tbsp rice vinegar
1 cup/15 g cilantro leaves, coarsely chopped
1 lime, zest finely grated and then cut into 6 wedges
salt

SERVES SIX

SEAWEED, GINGER, AND CARROT SALAD

1½ oz/40 g dried sea spaghetti or another dried seaweed
2-inch/5-cm piece fresh ginger (about 1½ oz/40 g), peeled and cut into very thin strips
3 medium carrots, peeled and cut into very thin matchsticks (1½ cups/200 g)
5 tbsp/80 ml rice vinegar
1 tbsp superfine sugar
1 large cucumber, peeled, quartered lengthwise, seeded, and cut into very thin strips (about 2 cups/275 g)
1 large mango, peeled and cut into very thin strips (1½ cups/260 g)
⅔ cup/100 g peanuts, toasted and salted, then coarsely chopped
2 tbsp sesame seeds, toasted
2 tsp lime juice
1 tbsp peanut oil
1⅓ cups/20 g cilantro leaves, chopped
⅔ cup/20 g mint leaves, shredded
salt

I originally made this using hijiki seaweed, which looked and tasted great, but as I was about to press the "send" button and email it to the Guardian, *I received an urgent note from Tara pointing out that the government agency responsible for food safety had advised against eating hijiki because of high levels of inorganic arsenic. This was after I had already eaten buckets of the stuff (!) and enjoyed it thoroughly. Luckily, for my readers at least, the salad tastes just as good and looks striking with sea spaghetti (harvested in the North Sea and eastern Atlantic) or other varieties of seaweed. Look for a range of varieties in Asian stores or online.*

Start by rinsing the seaweed in cold water, drain, and then cover generously with cold water. Set aside for 30 minutes.

Bring a large pot of water to a boil. Drain the seaweed and add it to the boiling water along with the ginger. Boil for 2 minutes and then add the carrots. Boil for another 2 minutes, drain, and immediately pat dry. Transfer everything to a large bowl and immediately add the vinegar, sugar, and 1¼ teaspoons salt. Mix well and leave aside to cool.

Once the mixture is cool and you are ready to serve, add the cucumber, mango, peanuts, sesame seeds, lime juice, oil, cilantro, and mint and stir to mix well, then serve.

SERVES SIX

SPICY TURNIP

1 ancho chile (⅔ oz / 20 g), stem and seeds removed
½ tsp Aleppo chile flakes, or just a pinch if using other very hot chile flakes
2 small cloves garlic, coarsely chopped
½ tsp ground cumin
⅛ tsp ground cardamom
1 tsp caraway seeds, toasted
1½ tbsp olive oil
1½ tbsp sunflower oil
1½ tsp superfine sugar
3 tbsp cider vinegar
2 tbsp lemon juice
5 or 6 small turnips, stems removed but unpeeled (1½ lb / 700 g)
3 oz / 90 g preserved lemon, halved, flesh and skin thinly sliced, seeds removed
1 cup / 15 g cilantro leaves, chopped
salt

For all turnips in need of a makeover, this is the dish. Sassy and scene-stealing, this heady condiment is everything that people won't expect of the plain Jane of the root vegetable world. A bit like pickle, this can be stored in the fridge for a few days, ready to eat with grilled meat or fish, to add to sandwiches and salads, or even just to serve alongside steamed rice. Ancho chile is mild on heat, big on aroma, and well worth seeking out. Supermarkets are beginning to stock a range of dried chiles, but you can also buy them very easily online.

Place the ancho chile in a small heatproof bowl and pour in boiling water just to cover. Leave to soak for 30 minutes, until soft. Remove the chile from the water and squeeze out some of the moisture. Set aside 2 tablespoons of the chile water and discard the rest.

Place the ancho in the bowl of a small food processor and add the chile flakes, garlic, cumin, cardamom, caraway, oils, sugar, vinegar, lemon juice, and 1 teaspoon salt. Add the reserved chile water and blitz to form a rough paste. Transfer to a medium bowl and set aside.

Bring a pan of water to a boil, add the turnips, and blanch for 3 minutes. Drain and refresh under cold water, pat dry, and cut into wedges ⅜ inch / 1 cm wide. Add these to the chile paste, along with the preserved lemon, and mix well. Cover and leave to marinate for at least 1 hour. Sprinkle with the cilantro and serve.

SOBA NOODLES WITH QUICK-PICKLED MUSHROOMS

SERVES FOUR
as a starter or light lunch

Cold noodles are a Japanese art form. On a trip to Tokyo a few years ago, I queued with a bunch of suited businessmen to have lunch in one of the city's most renowned soba noodle restaurants. It was incredibly humbling to watch a bunch of very busy people putting aside time to sit quietly for half an hour and completely immerse themselves in appreciation of the profound subtlety of the noodles. Enlightenment still escapes me, but I've had my own little "life moments" in various London noodle bars in recent months.

....

In a small saucepan, mix together the vinegar, sugar, ginger, and ¾ teaspoon salt. Gently warm to dissolve the sugar, remove from the heat, and add the mushrooms. Set aside to cool, stirring occasionally.

Blanch the carrots in a small saucepan of boiling water for 30 seconds. Drain, refresh under cold water, drain again, and dry well.

Throw the noodles into a pan with plenty of boiling salted water and cook for about 7 minutes, or as instructed on the package, until al dente. Drain, refresh under cold water, and set aside in a colander to drain.

Just before serving, in a large bowl, combine the mushrooms and their liquid, carrots, noodles, radishes, cress, green onion, chile, cilantro, nori, oil, sesame seeds, and snow peas. Toss together gently and serve.

¼ cup/60 ml rice vinegar
2½ tsp superfine sugar
1¼-inch/3-cm piece fresh ginger (⅓ oz/10 g), peeled and cut into very thin strips
5 oz/150 g buna-shimeji (brown beech) mushrooms, separated into individual mushrooms
2 small carrots, peeled and cut into very thin matchsticks (¾ cup/100 g)
3 oz/80 g dry soba noodles
3½ oz/100 g radishes, thinly sliced
½ cup/20 g salad cress or another cress or tender leaf
1 green onion, white and green parts, trimmed and very thinly sliced (2½ tbsp/15 g)
1 red chile, finely diced
2 tbsp chopped cilantro
5 nori (dried seaweed) sheets (8 inches/20 cm square) cut into ⅜ by 1½-inch/1 by 4-cm strips
1 tsp peanut oil
1 tbsp sesame seeds, toasted
1¾ oz/50 g snow peas (about 15), finely shredded
salt

SPROUTING BROCCOLI AND EDAMAME SALAD WITH CURRY LEAVES AND COCONUT

SERVES FOUR

14½ oz/420 g purple sprouting broccoli, trimmed, or 12 oz/350 g broccolini
7½ oz/220 g haricots verts, trimmed
1⅓ cups/200 g shelled frozen edamame (soybeans)
3 tbsp olive oil, plus 1 tbsp to finish
1 medium onion, finely diced (1 cup/150 g)
2½ tsp black mustard seeds
30 fresh curry leaves, or 40 if using dried curry leaves
3 whole dried chiles (or fewer, depending on how hot they are)
shaved rind of 1 lime, plus 1½ tbsp lime juice
⅔ cup/10 g cilantro leaves
⅔ cup/50 g coarsely grated fresh coconut
salt

This salad works just as well without the coconut; it's your call, although the chewy texture of the freshly grated flakes contrasts brilliantly with the more yielding beans. Cracking open a coconut is a fun family challenge that children love to get involved in (from a distance, please!). For the non-thrill-seekers, small containers of fresh coconut pieces are available in some shops and supermarkets. As ever, I urge you to look for fresh curry leaves, as they make a world of difference. If you find yourself with an abundance, it wouldn't be overkill to serve this with Lemon and Curry Leaf Rice (page 45). The leaves also freeze well.

Bring a large pot of salted water to a boil. Add the broccoli and haricots verts and blanch for 3 to 4 minutes, until they are cooked but still have bite. Use a slotted spoon to transfer the vegetables to a colander and run them under cold water. Drain, pat dry well, transfer to a large bowl, and set aside.

Return the pan of water to a boil, add the edamame, and blanch for 2 minutes. Transfer to the colander, run under cold water, pat dry, and add to the broccoli and beans. Sprinkle ½ teaspoon salt over the vegetables, stir, and set aside.

Heat the olive oil in a sauté pan over medium-high heat. Add the onion and ¼ teaspoon salt and cook for about 4 minutes, until soft. Add the black mustard seeds and, when they begin to pop, add the curry leaves, chiles, and lime rind. Fry for a final 2 minutes before pouring everything over the vegetables. Stir and set aside for 10 minutes.

Just before serving, add the lime juice, cilantro, and coconut. Give everything a very gentle stir and serve.

BEET, AVOCADO, AND PEA SALAD

SERVES FOUR TO SIX

The possibility of blanching beets could do with some championing to those who always incline toward the hour-long boil or roast: keeping a bite on the purple root adds another layer of texture in a salad. Prepare everything in advance (keep the herbs in the fridge), combine when you're ready, and serve with something substantial, like Bread and Pumpkin "Fondue" (page 264).

Bring a large pot of water to a boil and add the beets. Blanch for 3 to 5 minutes, until semicooked but still retaining a bite. Refresh under cold water and pat dry before transferring to a large bowl. Add the onion, vinegar, oil, sugar, chile sauce, 1 teaspoon salt, and some freshly ground black pepper. Toss gently and then leave aside for 15 minutes.

When ready to serve, spread half of the beet mixture on a large platter or shallow bowl. Top with half the avocado, cilantro, mint, pea shoots, and peas. Add the rest of the beet mixture and arrange the remaining ingredients on top. Finish with a drizzle of oil and serve.

See pictures on the following pages

4 medium beets, peeled and cut into paper-thin slices (about 3 cups/400 g; if the beets are large, halve them after peeling)
1 small red onion, thinly sliced (scant 1 cup/100 g)
3 tbsp sherry vinegar
¼ cup/60 ml olive oil, plus extra to finish
½ tsp superfine sugar
1 to 3 tsp savory chile sauce or paste such as Tabasco or Mexican Cholula Hot Sauce
2 medium avocados, peeled, pitted, and thinly sliced (1⅓ cups/200 g)
⅔ cup/10 g cilantro leaves
⅓ cup/10 g mint leaves
⅔ cup/20 g pea shoots, or mâche if you can't get them
1 cup/150 g fresh or frozen green peas, quickly blanched and refreshed
salt and black pepper

SPROUTING BROCCOLI WITH SWEET TAHINI

SERVES FOUR

This is my take on a Japanese favorite, goma-dare *(sweet sesame sauce), using another much-loved seasonal ingredient, purple sprouting broccoli. I mix it here with other greens for a refreshing blend of textures, but you can also use it solo. Please forgive me for the unorthodox mix of tahini and soy; my only defense is that it works perfectly.*

In a small bowl, whisk together all the ingredients for the sauce along with ½ teaspoon salt. You want the consistency to be smooth and thick but pourable, a bit like honey; add a tiny bit of extra water or tahini paste if needed and whisk well.

Trim off the broccoli leaves. If the stems are thick, cut them lengthwise in half or in quarters so you are left with long, thinner stems, similar in proportion to the haricots verts.

Bring a pot filled with plenty of unsalted water to a boil. Blanch the haricots verts for about 4 minutes, until just cooked but still retaining a bite. Using a slotted spoon, transfer the haricots verts to a colander, run under plenty of cold water, and then dry well with a tea towel. In the same water, blanch the snow peas for 2 minutes. Use the slotted spoon to remove them from the water, then refresh and dry as before. Repeat the same process with the broccoli, blanching it for 2 to 3 minutes.

Once all the vegetables are cooked and dry, mix them together in a bowl with the oil. You can now serve the salad in two ways. Mix most of the cilantro and seeds with the vegetables and pile up on a serving dish. Pour the sauce on top and finish with the remaining cilantro and seeds. Alternatively, pile the vegetables on a serving plate, dotting them with cilantro leaves and sprinkling with seeds as you go, and serve the sauce in a bowl on the side.

10½ oz/300 g purple sprouting broccoli, or 9 oz/250 g broccolini
4 oz/120 g haricots verts, trimmed
6½ oz/180 g snow peas, trimmed
1 tbsp peanut oil
1⅓ cups/20 g cilantro leaves
2½ tbsp sesame seeds, toasted
1 tsp nigella seeds

Sauce
about 3½ tbsp/50 g tahini paste
about 2 tbsp water
1 small clove garlic, crushed
½ tsp tamari soy sauce
1½ tsp honey
1 tbsp cider vinegar
salt

SERVES FOUR
as a side dish

PEAS WITH SORREL AND MUSTARD

2 cups / 300 g fresh or defrosted frozen green peas
2 tsp Dijon mustard
1½ tsp dry mustard
¾ tsp superfine sugar
2 tbsp olive oil
8 oz / 220 g green onions, white and green parts, trimmed and sliced on the diagonal into ⅜-inch- / 1-cm-thick slices (2 cups / 180 g)
2 cloves garlic, thinly sliced
1 tbsp black mustard seeds, toasted
6 tbsp / 75 g Greek yogurt
3½ oz / 100 g sorrel leaves and stems, coarsely shredded
salt

I once said that I look for "drama in the mouth" when eating. I don't need every spoonful to make a statement, but I am always on the lookout for bursts of pronounced flavor and mouthfuls that surprise and delight. These can come in many forms: preserved lemon skin, barberries, thin-stem ginger in syrup. Give any of these a mellow background and they'll shine. Sorrel is another ingredient with this in-built "wow" factor. When paired with more evenly balanced flavors, this sour leaf can turn even the most frugal of meals into something very special.

I hope that more supermarkets will begin to stock sorrel when it's in season in the summer months. A few do, but it's still hard to find, so you'll need to hunt it down at good grocery stores and farmers' markets.

This dish snuck into the book at the eleventh hour, when things were being wrapped up and new recipes were being developed for future Guardian *columns. One bite secured its late entry to the book, and it will always be the recipe that heralded the end of the shoot, the beginning of spring, and a celebration of all good things. It's delicious by itself but goes very well with some simply cooked fish or chicken and plain rice or bread.*

Bring a pan of water to a boil, add the peas, and blanch for just 30 seconds. Drain into a colander, refresh under cold water, and set aside.

Place both mustards in a small bowl with the sugar, 3 tablespoons water, and ½ teaspoon salt. Mix together to form a smooth paste and set aside.

Place a large sauté pan over medium-high heat and add the oil. Once hot, add the green onions and garlic and fry for 8 minutes, stirring frequently, until golden brown. Turn down the heat to low and add the mustard sauce, peas, 2 teaspoons of the mustard seeds, and the yogurt. Stir for 1 minute until everything is well mixed and the yogurt is warmed through. Remove from the heat, stir in the sorrel, and serve at once, with the remaining 1 teaspoon mustard seeds sprinkled on top.

SIMMERED

TAGLIATELLE WITH WALNUTS AND LEMON

SERVES TWO

When this recipe was first published in the Guardian, *it sparked a short discussion between two readers about the ideal quantity of pasta in a single portion. This debate demonstrates a point we always discuss at length in my test kitchen: how many people does the recipe serve? This question is almost as redundant as "how long is a piece of string?" yet all food writers engage in it seriously every time we write a recipe, because that's the convention: a good recipe must indicate the number of servings.*

When I mentioned in my article that a main course should have 3½ to 5 oz/100 to 150 g of dried pasta per person, one reader accused me of greediness—though not in so many words—and claimed 2½ oz/75 g is absolutely enough, while another justified my estimate. If I am totally honest, I can eat anywhere between 3½ and 10½ oz/100 and 300 g of pasta, depending on how hungry I am and, more important, how delicious it is. I am sure this applies to most people.

This is why I would like to suggest a new system of portion indication, which will take these two factors into consideration. So a recipe may "serve two people with a medium level of hunger but who are absolutely in love with white truffles," or "serve a single diner with a massive appetite but only when expertly prepared," or "will satisfy ten little stomachs when the cook is pressed for time." I think my system will illuminate the subject and both prevent food going to waste and people going hungry.

On a more serious note, this recipe is pretty simple and quick to prepare yet delivers an unexpected richness of flavors. Make sure you use fresh walnuts, without any bitterness in them.

⅔ cup/60 g walnuts, roughly broken up
2 tbsp/30 g unsalted butter
⅓ cup/10 g sage leaves, finely shredded
grated zest of 1 medium lemon
3 tbsp heavy cream
10½ oz/300 g tagliatelle or tagliolini
1¾ cups/50 g Parmesan, shaved
½ cup/15 g flat-leaf parsley leaves, chopped
2 tbsp lemon juice
salt and black pepper

....

Preheat the oven to 325°F/160°C.

Spread out the walnuts on a baking sheet and toast in the oven for 15 minutes. Remove and set aside to cool.

Place a sauté pan over high heat and add the butter. Cook for 1 minute, add the sage, and fry for about 2 minutes, until the butter starts to brown. Add the lemon zest, cream, ½ teaspoon salt, and plenty of black pepper and stir and cook for just a few seconds to thicken the sauce a little. Remove from the heat at once so the cream doesn't separate. Set aside until ready to use.

Bring a large pan of salted water to a boil and add the pasta. Cook for 8 minutes, or according to the package instructions, until al dente. Drain, reserving a few tablespoons of the cooking liquid, and place in a large bowl.

Warm the sauce, adding some cooking liquid if it has become very thick, then add it to the pasta along with the walnuts, Parmesan, and parsley. Toss the mix, stir in the lemon juice, and serve at once.

BRUSSELS SPROUT RISOTTO

SERVES FOUR

- 2 tbsp/30 g unsalted butter
- 2 tbsp olive oil
- 2 small onions, finely chopped (1⅓ cups/200 g)
- 2 large cloves garlic, crushed
- 2 tbsp thyme leaves
- 2 lemons, rind shaved in long strips from one, finely grated zest from the other
- 1½ cups/300 g Arborio or another risotto rice
- 18 oz/500 g trimmed brussels sprouts, 7 oz/200 g shredded and 11 oz/300 g quartered lengthwise
- scant 1 cup/200 ml dry white wine
- scant 4 cups/900 ml hot vegetable stock
- about 1⅔ cups/400 ml sunflower oil
- 1½ cups/40 g coarsely grated Parmesan
- 2 oz/60 g Dolcelatte, broken into ¾-inch/2-cm chunks
- ⅓ cup/10 g tarragon leaves, chopped
- 2 tsp lemon juice
- salt and black pepper

If you wonder about a risotto full of brussels sprouts, please trust me and set your doubts aside. My recipe tester, Claudine, said she had similar misgivings but totally loved it. The fried sprout quarters add a layer of texture and crunch which risottos often lack: they are so good that you'll quickly be figuring out other dishes they can be sprinkled over.

I was lucky enough to be able to get hold of some kale-sprout hybrids to fry—the little purple-stemmed vegetables you can see in the photo at right. They're not quite established enough to have a name that everyone can agree on—BrusselKale, Kalettes, and Flower Sprouts are a few options out there—but do pick some up if you see them to use instead of the 11 ounces/300 grams of quartered sprouts listed below. You'll still need the 7 ounces/200 grams of shredded brussels sprouts, though, for the heart of the risotto, reminding us to never neglect the old-timers.

Place the butter and olive oil in a large sauté pan over medium-high heat. Add the onions and fry for 10 minutes, stirring occasionally, until soft and lightly caramelized. Add the garlic, thyme, and lemon rind strips and cook for a further 2 minutes. Add the rice and shredded sprouts and cook for another minute, stirring frequently. Pour in the wine and let it simmer for a minute before you start adding the stock, 1 teaspoon salt, and a good grind of pepper. Turn down the heat to medium and carry on adding the stock in ladlefuls, stirring often, until the rice is cooked but still retains a bite and all the stock is used up.

While the rice is cooking, pour the sunflower oil into a separate large saucepan; it should rise ¾-inch/2-cm up the sides. Place over high heat and, once the oil is very hot, use a slotted spoon to add a handful of the quartered sprouts. (Take care that they are completely dry before you add them; they will still splatter, so be careful.) Fry the sprouts for less than 1 minute, until golden and crispy, then transfer them to a plate lined with paper towels. Keep them somewhere warm while you fry the remaining sprouts.

Add the Parmesan, Dolcelatte, tarragon, and half the fried sprouts to the cooked risotto and stir gently. Serve at once with the remaining sprouts spooned on top, followed by the grated lemon zest and the lemon juice.

See pictures on the following pages

LEGUME (NOODLE) SOUP

SERVES EIGHT

- ⅔ cup / 125 g dried chickpeas, soaked in water overnight with 2 tbsp baking soda
- ⅔ cup / 125 g dried lima beans, soaked in water overnight with 1 tbsp baking soda
- 5½ tbsp / 80 g clarified butter
- 2 large onions, thinly sliced (4 cups / 400 g)
- 10 cloves garlic, thinly sliced
- 1½ tsp ground turmeric
- rounded 1 cup / 225 g yellow split peas
- 8½ cups / 2 liters vegetable stock
- about 1 cup / 35 g flat-leaf parsley leaves, chopped
- about 2 cups / 35 g cilantro leaves, chopped
- 1 cup / 15 g dill leaves, chopped
- rounded 1 cup (100 g) thinly sliced green onions, white and green parts
- 5 cups / 150 g baby spinach leaves
- 3½ oz / 100 g reshteh or linguine
- ⅔ cup / 150 g sour cream, plus 1 tsp per portion to finish
- 1½ tbsp white wine vinegar
- 4 limes, halved
- salt and black pepper

My previous life must have been somewhere in old Persia. I am absolutely convinced of this. I am completely infatuated with the richness of Persian cuisine, by its clever use of spices and herbs, by the ingenuity of its rice making, by pomegranate, saffron, and pistachios, by yogurt, mint, and dried limes. It seems that my palate is just naturally honed for this set of flavors.

Unfortunately, I have never been able to travel to Iran, but my love affair with its food has been abundantly fed in recent years by the inspirational books of Najmieh Batmanglij. These are where I go to for a peek into a sweet, yet forbidden, culinary world.

This heartwarming thick soup, called ash-e reshteh, *is the Iranian answer to minestrone. It is wonderfully wholesome and nourishing and leaves a real smile on your face. I found* reshteh *noodles at an Iranian grocery near me, but linguine would do the job just as well. As suggested by the parentheses in the recipe name, you can dispense with the noodles altogether if you like. There is plenty going on, body-wise, without them.*

Drain and rinse the chickpeas and lima beans and place them in 2 separate saucepans with plenty of water. Place over medium heat, bring to a simmer, and cook until just tender. This should take anywhere between 20 and 40 minutes. Drain and set aside.

Put the butter, onions, and garlic in a large pan and place over medium heat. Cook for 20 minutes, stirring occasionally, until soft and golden brown. Stir in the turmeric, ½ teaspoon salt, and some black pepper and remove one-third of this mix from the pan to use later.

Add the chickpeas and lima beans to the pan, then add the split peas and stock. Simmer for about 35 minutes, skimming the froth occasionally, until the peas are tender.

Add the herbs, green onions, and spinach, stir well, and cook for another 15 minutes; add more stock or water if the soup is very thick. Add the noodles and cook for about 10 minutes, until they are just done. Stir in the sour cream and vinegar and serve at once, garnished with 1 teaspoon of sour cream per portion and the reserved cooked onion. Serve lime halves to squeeze over each portion.

SERVES FOUR

FREGOLA AND ARTICHOKE PILAF

3 globe artichokes (2 lb/ 900 g), or 10½ oz/300 g artichoke hearts
2 tbsp lemon juice
2 tbsp olive oil
2 medium onions, thinly sliced (3 cups/300 g)
4 tsp/20 g unsalted butter
9 oz/250 g fregola, rinsed well under cold water and left in a colander to drain
2½ cups/600 ml boiling vegetable stock
1½ tbsp red wine vinegar
scant ½ cup/60 g pitted black Kalamata olives, torn in half
½ cup/60 g sliced almonds, toasted
⅓ cup/10 g flat-leaf parsley leaves, chopped
salt and black pepper

Green chile sauce
3 green chiles, seeded and coarsely chopped
1 clove garlic, coarsely chopped
1 small preserved lemon (1½ oz/40 g), seeded, flesh and skin coarsely chopped
1 tbsp lemon juice
3 tbsp olive oil
1 cup/30 g flat-leaf parsley leaves, chopped

Unlike many of my dishes, this one doesn't excel on the visual front. What it has going for it is its surprisingly fresh set of flavors and wonderfully warm and comforting texture; I am quite happy to scoff this down every day of the week. Fregola is a type of pasta from Sardinia, similar to giant couscous. Couscous, giant couscous, fregola, mograbiah, maftoul—confused? Don't be! Although springing from different countries and going by various names, they are all variations on the theme of very little (or quite little), round (or pretty-much-round) balls of pasta. They are happiest when supporting flavorful ingredients in soups, stews, salads, or sauces, but they are also great simply served alongside meat and fish.

Use commercial frozen, canned, or jarred artichoke hearts here if you like to save yourself time and labor.

Place all the ingredients for the chile sauce in the bowl of a small food processor. Blitz to form a rough paste and set aside until ready to use.

Cut most of the stalk off the artichokes and remove the tough outer leaves by hand. Once you reach the softer leaves, cut ¾-inch/2-cm off the top and trim the base around the stalk. Cut in half lengthwise, so that you can reach the heart, scrape it clean of hairs, and cut each half into 3 triangular segments. Put the artichokes in a saucepan, pour over enough water to cover (around 2 cups/500 ml), and add the lemon juice. Bring to a boil, turn down the heat to medium, and simmer gently for about 8 minutes, until the artichokes are semicooked but still firm. Drain, season with ¼ teaspoon salt, and set aside.

Place the oil in a large sauté pan for which you have a lid and place over medium-high heat. Add the onions and ¾ teaspoon salt and cook for 10 minutes, stirring often, until the onion is brown and caramelized. Add the butter and stir until it melts, then add the semicooked artichoke, fregola, stock, and a good grind of black pepper. Stir once, cover the pan, and cook over low heat for about 18 minutes, until the fregola is cooked and all of the liquid has been absorbed. Avoid the temptation to stir, as this will lead to a starchy dish.

Remove the pan from the heat and leave to sit, covered, for 10 minutes. Remove the lid, add the vinegar, olives, and almonds, and stir gently. Sprinkle with the parsley and serve warm or at room temperature, with a generous spoonful of the chile sauce on top.

HOT-AND-SOUR MUSHROOM SOUP

SERVES SIX

This takes its inspiration from Asian soups, such as Thai tom yum or Vietnamese pho. The key to these is a rich and hearty stock, with many layers of flavor hitting the palate at different stages, a bit like a great aged wine. This is why my list of ingredients—please forgive me for it—is so long here. I have a hunch you will find it worthwhile. This soup is intentionally light, but it can be bulked up with cooked rice noodles. Add more tamarind paste if you like this super-sharp. Cilantro roots, available in many Indian and other Asian stores, have a deeper and more intense flavor than the leaves. If you can't get hold of any, tie together a small bunch of cilantro stems with a piece of string, gently bruise them with a rolling pin to help release their flavor, and use them instead.

Heat the sunflower oil in a large saucepan over high heat and add the onions, carrots, celery, garlic, and ginger. Cook for about 5 minutes, until the edges of the vegetables begin to color. Pour in 2½ quarts/2.2 liters water and add the lemongrass, prunes, chile, star anise, soy, lime leaves, and cilantro roots. Bring to a boil, then turn down the heat to a low simmer, add the tamarind paste, followed by the enoki and white mushrooms, and cook for 45 minutes.

Strain the stock and return it to the pan. You can discard the vegetables and prunes, though I love eating the carrot and celery. Bring the stock back to a very low simmer, add the enoki and white mushrooms, and cook for 1 minute. Then add the buna-shimeji mushrooms, lime juice, cilantro leaves, basil, bean sprouts, green beans, tamarind, and 1½ teaspoons salt and cook for 1 minute to heat through. Ladle into warmed bowls and finish with a little drizzle of sesame oil, no more than a few drops in each bowl.

See pictures on the following pages

- 1 tbsp sunflower oil
- 3 small onions, coarsely chopped (3 cups/350 g)
- 3 medium carrots, peeled and coarsely chopped (2 cups/250 g)
- 6 celery stalks, coarsely chopped (3½ cups/350 g)
- 6 cloves garlic, left whole
- 4-inch/10-cm piece fresh ginger (2½ oz/75 g), peeled and coarsely chopped
- 3 lemongrass stalks, coarsely chopped (¾ cup/50 g)
- 12 prunes (4 oz/120 g)
- 3 red chiles, coarsely chopped
- 6 star anise pods
- 2 tbsp tamari soy sauce
- 6 lime leaves
- 1 oz/30 g cilantro roots, chopped
- 2 tbsp tamarind paste
- 5 oz/150 g enoki mushrooms
- 5 oz/150 g white mushrooms, sliced
- 5 oz/150 g buna-shimeji (brown beech) mushrooms
- ¼ cup plus 1 tsp/65 ml lime juice (about 2 limes)
- 1⅓ cups/20 g cilantro leaves, plus extra to garnish
- ⅔ cup/20 g Thai basil leaves
- 1½ cups/160 g bean sprouts
- 5½ oz/160 g green beans, trimmed, cut crosswise into thirds, boiled for 4 minutes, and refreshed
- salt
- toasted sesame oil, to finish

SPICY CHICKPEA AND BULGUR SOUP

SERVES FOUR

2 tbsp olive oil
2 small onions, cut into ⅜-inch/1-cm dice (1½ cups/180 g)
4 cloves garlic, crushed
2 large carrots, peeled and cut into ⅜-inch/1-cm dice (2 cups/250 g)
4 celery stalks, cut into ⅜-inch/1-cm dice (2½ cups/250 g)
2 tbsp harissa paste (less if you don't like things very hot)
1 tsp ground cumin
1 tsp ground coriander
1½ tsp caraway seeds
2½ cups/500 g drained cooked chickpeas (canned are fine)
5 cups/1.2 liters vegetable stock
¾ cup/100 g coarse bulgur wheat
salt and black pepper

Creamed feta paste (optional)
3½ oz/100 g feta, broken into large chunks
¼ cup/60 g crème fraîche
1 cup/15 g cilantro leaves, coarsely chopped
½ cup/15 g mint leaves
salt

This simple and soothing soup, minus the optional feta paste, can most likely be made with ingredients you already have in your cupboards and fridge (and if you don't have some celery stalks and a couple of carrots regularly lying around in your fridge, plus a jar of good harissa, I highly recommend that you do; they form the base of some of my favorite sauces). The dairy-free soup works well without the paste, but a spoonful on top elevates a midweek supper into something pretty special.

Put the oil in a saucepan over medium heat. Add the onions and sauté for 5 minutes, stirring from time to time, until translucent. Add the garlic, carrots, and celery and continue cooking for another 8 minutes. Add the harissa, cumin, coriander, and caraway seeds and cook for a further 2 minutes, stirring well. Gently mix the chickpeas into the vegetable mixture—you don't want them to break down—along with 1 teaspoon salt and plenty of black pepper. Add the stock and bring to a boil. Turn down the heat and simmer gently for 10 minutes.

Meanwhile, rinse the bulgur, put in a small saucepan, and cover generously with cold water. Bring to a boil and immediately remove from the heat. Drain, refresh under cold water, drain again, and set aside.

To make the feta paste, put the feta, crème fraîche, cilantro, mint, and ⅛ teaspoon salt in the bowl of a small food processor and blitz for a couple of minutes, until a smooth, creamy paste forms. Keep in the fridge until needed.

Before serving, add the cooked bulgur to the soup and bring to a gentle simmer. Divide the soup among bowls, add a spoonful of feta paste to each bowl, and serve at once.

GREEN ONION SOUP

SERVES FOUR TO SIX

Kashk is a relatively recent addition to my pantry, and it has become an absolute favorite. Kashk, kash, and kishk signify different things throughout the Middle East, Turkey, and Greece, but they are often used to name foodstuffs produced by the process of fermentation and then drying of yogurt or curdled milk and turning them into a powder that can later be reconstituted. Iranian kashk is used to bulk up soups and stews and gives them a wonderfully deep and sharp aroma: a bit like feta but in runny form. You can get it from specialized Iranian shops, but don't worry if you cannot get hold of it. I'm aware it's not easy to come by, and a mixture of crème fraîche and grated Parmesan or another mature cheese makes a perfectly good substitute.

Cut the white part of the green onions into slices ⅔-inch/1.5-cm wide, the green part into segments 1-inch/2.5-cm wide, and keep them separate.

Melt the butter in a large saucepan over medium heat. Add the olive oil, the white parts of the green onions, the garlic cloves, ½ teaspoon salt, and some black pepper and sauté for 10 to 15 minutes, until the vegetables are soft and have lost some of their harshness. Add the green parts of the green onions and the bay leaves and continue cooking for about 10 minutes. Add the peas and zucchini and cook for another 5 minutes.

Remove half the vegetables from the pan and set aside. Cover the remaining vegetables with the stock, bring to a boil, and simmer for 3 minutes. Remove the bay leaves, add the parsley, and blitz in a food processor or with a handheld blender. Return the reserved vegetables to the pan and warm them up before stirring in the kashk.

Transfer the soup to individual bowls and sprinkle with the mint and lemon zest. If you are not using the kashk, spoon a teaspoon of crème fraîche into each bowl. Finish each serving with a drizzle of oil.

- 2 lb/900 g green onions, white and green parts, if possible a large variety with a thick bulb
- 3½ tbsp/40 g unsalted butter
- 3½ tbsp/50 ml olive oil, plus extra to finish
- 2 medium heads garlic, cloves peeled and halved lengthwise (2 oz/60 g)
- 3 bay leaves
- 2 cups/300 g fresh or defrosted frozen green peas
- 1 medium zucchini, cut into ⅜-inch/1-cm dice (1½ cups/200 g)
- 5½ cups/1.3 liters vegetable stock
- ⅔ cups/80 g flat-leaf parsley leaves, coarsely chopped
- ¼ cup/60 g kashk (or mix a scant 3 tbsp/40 g crème fraîche and a generous 3 tbsp/20 g grated Parmesan, with extra crème fraîche to serve)
- ⅔ cup/20 g mint leaves, chopped
- finely grated zest of ½ lemon
- salt and black pepper

SIMMERED

THAI RED LENTIL SOUP WITH AROMATIC CHILE OIL

SERVES FOUR

Fresh, creamy, and loaded with flavors, this soup would be the first thing I'd make when the arrival of autumn is officially announced. If you like your soup totally smooth, with no "interruptions," forget the sugar snaps. Thanks to the brilliant Leith's Vegetarian Cookery Book for the chile oil: you'll make more than you need for the soup, but keep it in a sealed jar in the fridge for up to a month, for drizzling over other soups, salads, or grilled dishes. You can also do without the oil, and drizzle the soup with a good savory sauce instead.

4 oz / 120 g sugar snap peas
3 tbsp sunflower oil
1 medium onion, thinly sliced (1½ cups / 160 g)
1½ tbsp vegetarian red curry paste
2 lemongrass stalks, gently bashed with a rolling pin
4 fresh Kaffir lime leaves (or 12 dried)
1¼ cups / 250 g red lentils
1 cup / 250 ml coconut milk
1½ tbsp lime juice
1½ tbsp soy sauce
1 cup / 15 g cilantro leaves, coarsely chopped
salt

Chile-infused oil
¾ cup / 180 ml sunflower oil
1 banana shallot, or 2 regular shallots, coarsely chopped (½ cup / 50 g)
1 clove garlic, coarsely chopped
1 tsp peeled and coarsely chopped fresh ginger
½ red chile, coarsely chopped
½ star anise pod
2 tsp curry powder
1 tsp tomato paste
grated zest of ½ small lemon

First make the chile oil. Heat 2 tablespoons of the sunflower oil in a small saucepan. Add the shallot, garlic, ginger, chile, star anise, and curry powder and fry over low heat for 5 minutes, stirring from time to time, until the shallot is soft. Add the tomato paste and cook gently for 2 minutes. Stir in the remaining oil and the lemon zest and simmer very gently for 30 minutes. Leave to cool and then strain through a cheesecloth-lined sieve.

For the soup, bring a small pan of water to a boil and throw in the sugar snap peas. Cook for 90 seconds, drain, refresh under cold water, and set aside to dry. Once cool, cut them on the diagonal into slices 1/16-inch / 2-mm thick.

Heat the sunflower oil in a large pot and add the onion. Cook over low heat, with a lid on, for 10 to 15 minutes, stirring once or twice, until the onion is completely soft and sweet. Stir in the red curry paste and cook for 1 minute. Add the lemongrass, lime leaves, red lentils, and 3 cups / 700 ml water. Bring to a boil, turn down the heat to low, and simmer for 15 minutes, until the lentils are completely soft.

Remove the soup from the heat and take out and discard the lemongrass and lime leaves. Use a blender to process the soup until it is completely smooth. Add the coconut milk, lime juice, soy sauce, and ½ teaspoon salt and stir. Return the soup to medium heat, and once the soup is almost boiling, ladle into bowls. Scatter the snap peas on top, sprinkle with the cilantro, and finish with ½ teaspoon chile oil drizzled over each portion.

SERVES SIX

TOMATO AND WATERMELON GAZPACHO

4½ lb/2 kg tomatoes (about 20), blanched, peeled, and coarsely chopped (10½ cups/1.9 kg)
5 cloves garlic, coarsely chopped
6 celery stalks, white parts and leaves finely chopped (about 3 cups/450 g)
1 small onion, finely chopped (1 cup/140 g)
2⅔ cups/400 g seeded and coarsely chopped watermelon flesh
3½ oz/100 g crustless white bread (about 4 slices), broken into small chunks
⅔ cup/150 ml passata (tomato purée) or tomato juice
½ cup/15 g basil leaves
2 tbsp red wine vinegar
scant 1 cup/200 ml olive oil, plus extra to finish
salt and black pepper
coarse sea salt, to serve

Croutons
5 oz/150 g crustless white bread (about 5 slices), broken into ¾ to 1¼-inch/ 2 to 3-cm chunks
3 tbsp olive oil
1½ tbsp red wine vinegar
salt

I first made this during my sun-drenched days in Majorca. The sweet, red Ramallet tomatoes were out of this world, and the group of old ladies who taught me how to thread them together into a fine bunch were the most animated and amusing seventy-something crew I've ever met. My offering in return was this wonderfully sweet and refreshing soup. Forgive my slipping it into the "simmered" section; I know there is no mention of things bubbling away gently on the stove, but it wanted to be with its fellow soups.

First make the croutons. Preheat the oven to 400°F/200°C. Place the bread in a bowl along with the oil, vinegar, and ½ teaspoon salt. Place a grill pan over high heat, add the croutons, and cook for 2 minutes, turning until all sides are slightly charred and starting to crisp. Transfer the croutons to a baking sheet and place in the oven for about 12 minutes, until golden brown and crispy. Set aside to cool.

Place the tomatoes, garlic, celery, onion, watermelon, bread, passata, and two-thirds of the basil in a blender (or large bowl, if using a handheld blender) along with ¾ teaspoon salt and a good grind of black pepper. Blend until smooth and then, with the blender still going, add the vinegar and olive oil. Refrigerate until needed.

To serve, pour the soup into individual bowls and top with the croutons. Scatter the remaining basil leaves over each portion, along with a final drizzle of oil. Finish with a little coarse salt and serve at once.

ALPHONSO MANGO AND CURRIED CHICKPEA SALAD

SERVES FOUR

Unlike the large, often hard mangoes available year-round, the Alphonso and other Indian and Pakistani varieties (look out for Kesar, Banganpali, Langra, and Chaunsa) are fiberless, fragrant, small, and sublime. People get pretty evangelical about the Alphonso mango: the Bangladeshi national anthem mentions the fruit by name, newspaper headlines in India announce the arrival of the fruit's short season, and courier companies in Mumbai advertise specialist "mango delivery services" to transport boxes around the city. It might all seem a bit much to those who have not held out for the short but intensely sweet Alphonso mango season, which lasts through May and June. Cargo logistics mean that large supermarkets don't tend to stock them, so head to your local produce market or open market stall and look out for the bright-yellow boxes of the fruit, whose subcontinental labels, tissue paper, and tinsel poking out make them the ready-made presents that they are.

Drain and rinse the chickpeas and place them in a saucepan with plenty of water. Place over medium heat, bring to a very gentle simmer, and cook for 45 minutes to 1 hour, until the chickpeas are completely soft. Drain, transfer to a large bowl, and leave somewhere warm.

Place the coriander, mustard, and cumin seeds in a large sauté pan and dry roast them until they begin to pop. Use a spice grinder or pestle and mortar to crush them to a powder and then mix them with the curry powder, turmeric, sugar, and ½ teaspoon salt; set aside.

In the same pan, heat half the oil over high heat. Add the onion and cook for 5 minutes, stirring occasionally, until it starts to gain some color. Add the spice mix, turn down the heat to medium, and cook, stirring, for another 5 minutes, until the onion is completely soft. Transfer to the bowl with the warm chickpeas and keep aside.

Bring a large pot of water to a boil, throw in the cauliflower, and blanch for just 1 minute. Drain, pat dry, and set aside to dry thoroughly. Once the cauliflower is completely dry, heat the remaining oil in the same pan you cooked the onion in (you don't need to clean it), add the cauliflower and ¼ teaspoon salt, and fry for 3 to 4 minutes, just to give it color.

Add the hot cauliflower and any oil from the pan to the onion and chickpeas and stir well. Leave for 5 minutes if you want the salad warm or longer for room temperature. Add the mangoes, chile, cilantro, lime juice, and spinach. Stir well and serve at once, or chill and serve within 24 hours.

¾ cup/150 g dried chickpeas, soaked in water overnight with 2 tsp baking soda
1 tsp coriander seeds
1 tsp black mustard seeds
½ tsp cumin seeds
1 tsp curry powder
½ tsp ground turmeric
1 tsp superfine sugar
5½ tbsp/80 ml sunflower oil
1 large onion, thinly sliced (2 cups/200 g)
1 small cauliflower, broken into 1½-inch/4-cm florets (4 cups/400 g)
2 or 3 Alphonso mangoes or 1 large, ripe regular mango, peeled and cut into ¾-inch/2-cm dice (about 3¼ cups/570 g)
1 medium-hot green chile, seeded and finely chopped
1⅓ cups/20 g cilantro leaves, chopped
3 tbsp lime juice
1⅔ oz/50 g baby spinach leaves
salt

SERVES FOUR

CANDY BEETS WITH LENTILS AND YUZU

8 medium candy beets or a variety of beets (1⅔ lb/750 g)
rounded 1 cup/225 g Puy lentils
2 to 4 tbsp yuzu juice, depending on intensity
3 tbsp/50 ml olive oil, plus extra to finish
½ small red onion, thinly sliced (½ cup/50 g)
2 tsp maple syrup
1½ tbsp lemon juice
1⅓ cups/40 g watercress
1⅓ cups/40 g baby chard or baby spinach leaves
1 tsp yuzu powder (optional)
salt and black pepper

The aptly named candy beet (aka Chioggia) is as sweet as candy and its flesh is made up of beautiful alternating red and white rings. You can slice it thinly and use it raw in salads; once cooked, it turns a uniform mellow pink. If you can't find it, search for golden beets or normal red beets. A combination of all three is stunning, but just one will work absolutely fine.

Yuzu is a citrus fruit originating in East Asia whose flavor is close to a combination of lime and mandarin. Its zest and juice are commonly used to add a fresh aroma to various Japanese dishes, including fresh soups. As it's almost impossible to get hold of fresh yuzu, you'll have to rely on bottled juice. The intensity of the flavor varies considerably from brand to brand, however, so you'll need to check this before adding it to the dish. Look for the juice in Japanese markets or online. If you're not able to find it, use a bit of lime juice in its place.

Place all but 1 of the beets in a saucepan and cover with plenty of water. Bring to a boil, turn down the heat to a gentle simmer, and cook for about 1 hour, adding more boiling water as needed to keep covered, until cooked. Remove from the heat, take the beets out of the water, and leave to cool down (you can now keep them refrigerated for a day or two). Peel the beets, halve them, and cut into wedges about ⅜-inch/1-cm thick at the base.

Place the lentils in a small saucepan and cover with plenty of water. Bring to a boil, then simmer for 15 to 20 minutes, until cooked but retaining a bite. Drain well, transfer to a bowl, and immediately stir in 1 tablespoon each of the yuzu juice and olive oil, ½ teaspoon salt, and some black pepper. Set aside to cool down (the lentils can also be kept in the fridge for a couple of days).

Peel the remaining uncooked beet and, using a mandoline, if you have one, cut into paper-thin slices.

To put the salad together, add 1 tablespoon of the yuzu juice and the remaining 2 tablespoons oil to the lentils. Add the cooked and raw beets, onion, maple syrup, and lemon juice and toss gently. Taste for seasoning, adding more yuzu depending on the intensity. Transfer the salad to a shallow bowl, dotting it with the watercress and chard. Finish with a sprinkle of powdered yuzu and a final drizzle of oil.

GLOBE ARTICHOKE SALAD WITH PRESERVED LEMON MAYONNAISE

SERVES FOUR
as a starter

You think you know how to do something until you witness the pros at work. My summer spent filming the first series of Mediterranean Feast *made me question my right to be calling myself a pastry chef after my day spent with kids a quarter of my age making sheets of* warka *pastry. My relationship with vegetables was similarly challenged upon witnessing the speed and dexterity with which artichokes were cleaned by weathered hands in the markets (without even using a chopping board; just hands up in the air). Seemingly effortless, the immaculate chokes produced within seconds by a few strikes of the knife were astounding and in a completely different league from anything I've seen before. Still, even if it costs you a good half hour and a bunch of blackened fingertips, it is an effort well worth making. Fresh artichokes are heavenly!*

The mayonnaise makes more than you need, but any left over will keep in a sealed jar in the fridge for a few days.

---

4 large globe artichokes (3½ lb/1.6 kg)
5 tbsp/75 ml lemon juice
1 medium russet potato, peeled and cut into 12 wedges similar in size and proportion to the artichoke pieces (9 oz/250 g)
1 large thyme sprig, plus 1 tbsp leaves
⅔ cup/10 g dill leaves, chopped
1 tbsp tarragon leaves, chopped
1½ cups/50 g pea shoots
1 tbsp olive oil
salt and black pepper

Mayonnaise
1 egg yolk
¼ tsp Dijon mustard
1 small clove garlic, crushed
1½ tsp white wine vinegar
¼ tsp superfine sugar
1 small preserved lemon (1 oz/30 g), chopped flesh and skin
5 tbsp/75 ml sunflower oil

To clean the artichokes, cut off most of the stalk and start removing the tough outer leaves by hand. Once you reach the softer leaves, trim off ¾ to 1¼-inches/2 to 3-cm from the tops of the leaves with a sharp, serrated knife. Trim the base and around the stalk. Cut the artichoke in half lengthwise so you can reach the heart and scrape it clean of the hairs with a small knife. Dip the clean heart halves in 1 to 2 tablespoons lemon juice mixed with some water to prevent discoloring, and cut each into 3 triangular segments.

Put the artichokes in a saucepan along with the potato. Add the remaining lemon juice (about 3 tablespoons), the thyme sprig, and ¾ teaspoon salt and top with enough water just to cover the artichokes, approximately 3⅓ cups/800 ml. Bring to a boil, turn down the heat to a gentle simmer, and cook for 10 to 15 minutes, until a knife is easily inserted into both the potato and the artichokes. Remove from the heat and allow the vegetables to cool in the liquid.

For the mayonnaise, put the egg yolk, mustard, garlic, vinegar, sugar, and preserved lemon in the bowl of a small food processor. With the motor running, slowly pour in the oil until a glossy and firm mayonnaise forms. Refrigerate until needed.

To assemble, drain the artichokes and potatoes and mix together in a large bowl with the thyme leaves, dill, tarragon, pea shoots, olive oil, ¼ teaspoon salt, and some black pepper. Gently toss together and serve with a dollop of mayonnaise and a good grind of black pepper.

GLOBE ARTICHOKE AND MOZZARELLA WITH CANDIED LEMON

SERVES FOUR

4 large globe artichokes (3½ lb/1.6 kg)
3 lemons, halved
2 bay leaves
4 thyme sprigs
1 medium onion, quartered
4 oz/120 g Little Gem lettuce leaves, cut crosswise into strips ⅜-inch/1-cm wide
7 oz/200 g buffalo mozzarella
⅓ cup/10 g flat-leaf parsley leaves, chopped
⅓ cup/10 g mint leaves, chopped
⅓ cup/10 g basil leaves, chopped
½ cup/120 ml olive oil
1 clove garlic, crushed
salt and black pepper

Candied lemon
1 lemon
scant 3 tbsp/35 g superfine sugar

As our hands are not all as adept as those mentioned on page 97, shortcuts are always possible with artichokes: instead of cleaning and cooking them, you can always use frozen or jarred artichoke hearts or bases (I do prefer frozen to jarred though). Also, while the candied lemon looks and tastes fantastic, the juice and grated zest of a fresh lemon will work fine instead.

Working with 1 artichoke at a time, remove and discard the stem and hard outer leaves. Continue removing the leaves until you reach the heart and then cut the heart in half lengthwise. Use a small, serrated knife to clear the heart of all the inedible bits—tough leaves and hairs—so you are left with a clean shell. As you do this, use the juice of 1 lemon to smear the artichokes so they don't discolor. When all the artichoke hearts are trimmed, put them in a large saucepan, squeeze in the juice of the remaining 2 lemons, and throw in 2 of the squeezed halves, as well. Cover with water, add the bay leaves, thyme, onion, and ½ teaspoon salt and simmer for 10 to 15 minutes, until tender. Drain the artichokes and lemon, discarding the onion, bay, and thyme, and set aside to cool.

To prepare the candied lemon, use a vegetable peeler to shave off wide strips of lemon rind; avoid the white pith. Cut the rind into long, paper-thin strips and place them in a small saucepan. Squeeze the lemon, measure the juice, and add water as needed to total 7 tablespoons/100 ml. Pour over the lemon rind, add the sugar, and bring to a light simmer. Cook for about 15 minutes, until the syrup is reduced to about one-third of its original volume. Set aside to cool down.

To assemble the dish, cut the artichoke halves into wedges ¾ inch/2 cm thick and arrange them on a serving platter together with the lettuce. With your hands, break the mozzarella into large, uneven chunks and dot the salad with them. Stir together the herbs, olive oil, and garlic and season with ¼ teaspoon salt; spoon this over the vegetables and cheese. Use a fork to scatter some candied rind on top and drizzle with a tiny amount of the syrup. Finish with a sprinkle of black pepper.

SERVES FOUR
as a main course

CURRY LAKSA

8 baby shallots, peeled and coarsely chopped (⅔ cup/100 g)
8 cloves garlic, peeled and roughly chopped
1½-inch/4-cm piece fresh ginger (1 oz/30 g), peeled and sliced
1 large lemongrass stalk, soft white stem only, sliced (about ⅓ cup/20 g)
2 tsp ground coriander
3 large dried red chiles
2 tbsp sambal oelek or another savory chile paste
4 tbsp/60 ml vegetable oil
1½ oz/40 g cilantro, leaves and stems (about 18 sprigs)
5 cups/1.2 liters vegetable stock
3 branches laksa leaves or fresh curry leaves or a mixture of both
2 tsp curry powder
2 tbsp superfine sugar
1⅔ cups/400 ml coconut milk
3 cups/300 g bean sprouts
5 oz/150 g haricots verts, trimmed and halved
3½ oz/100 g rice vermicelli
9 oz/250 g fried tofu puffs (optional)
2 limes, halved
salt

The term laksa *is used to describe two different types of spicy noodle soup: curry* laksa *and Assam* laksa. *Each has many variants, but broadly speaking, curry* laksa *sees its noodles served in a coconut curry soup, and Assam* laksa *has its noodles in a sour fish version. I love the tamarind and shrimp paste often found in an Assam, but for comfort and sustenance in equal measure, you can't beat the Malaysian aromatic, coconutty curried kind. My version is a heart-and-limb-warming soup with quite a kick, so tone down the heat if you're not a fan of chile.*

Tofu puffs are squares of bean curd that have already been deep-fried and are sold in bags in Asian markets. They're a great addition to soups and stews, absorbing tons of flavor and liquid. If you can't get tofu puffs, cut some firm tofu into large chunks, coat generously with cornstarch, and deep-fry.

Place the shallots, garlic, ginger, lemongrass, coriander, chiles, and sambal oelek in the bowl of a small food processor. Add half the oil and the stems of the cilantro and process to form a semismooth paste. Coarsely shred the cilantro leaves and set aside for later.

Heat the remaining 2 tablespoons oil in a saucepan over medium-low heat and fry the spice paste for 15 to 20 minutes, stirring very frequently. You want to cook it slowly without burning. Add the stock, laksa leaves, curry powder, sugar, coconut milk, and 1½ teaspoons salt. Increase the heat, bring to a gentle simmer, and leave to cook for 30 minutes.

Throw the bean sprouts into a pan of boiling water, drain at once, and refresh. Cook the haricots verts in boiling water for 3 minutes, drain, and refresh. Once your broth is ready, steep the rice noodles in boiling water for 3 minutes and drain. Just before serving, remove the laksa branches and discard (the leaves can stay in the soup). Add the haricots verts, noodles, and half the bean sprouts and heat through. Spoon the soup into large bowls and top with the remaining bean sprouts, the tofu puffs, and the cilantro leaves. Squeeze ½ teaspoon lime juice on top—or more, if you want—and throw a squeezed lime half into each bowl. Serve at once.

See pictures on the following pages

QUINOA PORRIDGE WITH GRILLED TOMATOES AND GARLIC

SERVES FOUR

Quinoa as comfort food is not quite the oxymoron some might initially think. The cooking method here is opposite to the way I normally cook quinoa, where, like pasta, I throw it into boiling water for 9 minutes, then drain it and refresh it under cold water. Whereas that method encourages every grain to remain separate and distinct, the porridge-like consistency of this recipe, enriched with butter and feta, is more the method you'd follow to cook polenta. The result is satisfying and comforting in a way that will appeal to both signed-up converts to the seed and those still in need of some convincing. You don't want the quinoa to sit once it's cooked, or it will set, so make sure the tomatoes and herb oil are ready as soon as the quinoa is done.

1½ cups / 250 g quinoa
about 4⅔ cups / 1.1 liters vegetable stock
4 tsp / 20 g unsalted butter
⅓ cup / 10 g flat-leaf parsley leaves, chopped
3½ oz / 100 g feta, broken into ¾-inch / 2-cm chunks
1 tsp olive oil
1⅔ cups / 250 g baby plum tomatoes
4 cloves garlic, thinly sliced
⅓ cup / 10 g mint leaves
salt and black pepper

Herb oil
1 green chile, seeded and coarsely chopped
½ cup / 15 g flat-leaf parsley leaves
½ cup / 15 g mint leaves
7 tbsp / 100 ml olive oil
salt

To make the herb oil, place the chile, parsley, mint, oil, and ½ teaspoon salt in the bowl of a small food processor and process to form a smooth sauce with a thick pouring consistency.

Place the quinoa in a medium saucepan, add the stock, and bring to a boil. Turn down the heat to medium and cook gently, uncovered, for about 25 minutes, stirring from time to time, until a porridge-like consistency is formed. You might need to add a bit more stock if the quinoa is sticking to the pan. At the very end, fold in the butter until it melts, followed by the parsley and then the feta, making sure the feta stays in chunks.

While the quinoa is cooking, place a large sauté pan over high heat and add the oil. When the oil is hot, add the tomatoes and cook for about 5 minutes, shaking the pan once or twice so that all sides get some good charred color. Add the garlic and cook for 30 seconds, so that it turns golden brown without burning. Transfer to a bowl and sprinkle with ¼ teaspoon salt and some black pepper. Chop the mint and fold it into the tomatoes just before serving, as it will start to blacken once chopped.

Spoon the warm quinoa porridge into shallow bowls, top with the tomatoes, finish with a drizzle of the herb oil, and serve at once.

See pictures on the following pages

SERVES FOUR

IRANIAN-STYLE PASTA

3 large eggplants
  (2¾ lb/1.2 kg)
scant 1 cup/200 g kashk,
  or mix a scant ⅔ cup/
  140 g crème fraîche and a
  scant ⅔ cup/60 g grated
  Parmesan
5 tbsp/75 ml olive oil, plus
  extra to finish
1 large onion, finely
  chopped (1⅓ cups/200 g)
2 tsp cumin seeds
3 cloves garlic, crushed
2 tbsp lime juice
¾ cup/150 g Greek yogurt
2 tsp dried mint
about 1 lb/500 g reshteh
  or linguine
½ tsp saffron threads,
  soaked in 1½ tsp
  lukewarm water
⅓ cup/10 g mint leaves,
  shredded
salt and black pepper

As in the case of pizza, I always get slightly indignant that because of the term pasta, *Italians end up dominating a scene that includes a vast set of dishes made all over the planet. There just isn't a good alternative word in English to "pasta," as there isn't to "pizza," even though this particular Iranian dish is as about as far removed from Italian pasta as it is from pad Thai. So I am just stuck with "pasta" (though I could think of worse things to be "stuck" with).*

Kashk, the fermented Iranian yogurt I've raved about elsewhere (see the Green Onion Soup headnote on page 87), is a good way of giving vegetarians who don't eat Parmesan the umami-rich taste inherent in the cheese. If kashk *is not available, a good alternative here for anyone who does eat Parmesan is a mixture of crème fraîche and grated Parmesan.*

For more about reshteh *noodles, see page 80.*

Preheat the oven to 450°F/230°C.

Pierce the eggplants in a few places with a sharp knife, place on a baking sheet lined with parchment paper, and roast in the oven for about 1 hour, until the flesh is completely soft. Set aside until cool enough to handle, then cut in half and spoon out the flesh into a colander. Let drain for at least 30 minutes. Discard the skin.

Place the kashk in a small saucepan with 5 tablespoons/75 ml water. Bring to a simmer over medium heat, stir, and then set aside until ready to use.

Heat 2 tablespoons of the oil in a sauté pan over medium-high heat. Add the onion and cumin seeds and cook for 12 minutes, stirring occasionally, until soft. Add the eggplant flesh, garlic, 1 teaspoon salt, and some black pepper. Cook for another 2 minutes before adding the lime juice. Stir through for a final minute and then remove from the heat.

Add the yogurt to the kashk pan and heat over low heat for 5 minutes, stirring from time to time. Keep an eye on the mixture, as you don't want the yogurt to separate.

Mix the dried mint with 1 tablespoon of the oil and set aside.

Bring a large pan of salted water to a boil and add the pasta. Cook for 8 minutes, or according to the package instructions, until cooked but still retaining a bite. Stir the remaining 2 tablespoons oil through the pasta, mix, and then divide among shallow bowls or plates. Drizzle the mint oil over the top, followed by the eggplant. Top this with the kashk mixture, followed by the saffron water, fresh mint, and a final drizzle of oil. Serve at once.

STUFFED ZUCCHINI

SERVES SIX

It is not by mere coincidence that this recipe doesn't come with a picture. These zucchini, once cooked for a good two hours, are just not that handsome any more: the vibrant green turns dull gray, the firm flesh becomes limp and tired. Still, this is one of my favorite recipes, so I put zucchini vanity aside and forgive my green heroes their unfortunate transformation (with the help of some yogurt foundation and some mint paste mascara).

These zucchini—stuffed with rice and cooked in a sweet and slightly sour liquor that reduces to an unctuous sauce—only get better with time. You can serve them as soon as they cool down, but I prefer to refrigerate them and have them the next day, slightly above fridge temperature. The flesh you scoop when preparing the zucchini can be shallow-fried with garlic, diced red pepper, chile, and fresh herbs and then spooned over pasta or rice.

6 medium zucchini (scant 3 lb / 1.3 kg)
1 cup / 30 g mint leaves
¼ cup / 60 ml olive oil
scant ½ cup / 90 g Greek yogurt
salt

Filling
1½ tbsp sunflower oil
1 small onion, finely chopped (⅔ cup / 100 g)
1½ cups / 300 g short-grain white rice
1 tsp ground cumin
2 tsp ground allspice
1 tbsp dried mint
1 small tomato, finely chopped (½ cup / 80 g)
grated zest of 1 lemon
1 cup / 15 g cilantro leaves, chopped
salt and black pepper

Cooking liquid
about 2 cups / 450 ml vegetable stock
1 tsp ground allspice
1½ tbsp pomegranate molasses
1 tbsp superfine sugar
1 tbsp dried mint
3 cloves garlic, crushed
2 tbsp lemon juice
salt and black pepper

Start with the filling. Select a large sauté pan with a tight-fitting lid and heat the oil over medium heat. Add the onion and sauté for 5 minutes, stirring occasionally, before adding the rice, ground spices, and dried mint. Continue to cook and stir for another 8 minutes. Remove from the heat and stir in the tomato, lemon zest, cilantro, 1½ teaspoons salt, and some black pepper.

Cut the zucchini in half lengthwise and use a teaspoon to scoop out the flesh (see the headnote, above). Fill one half of each generously with the rice mixture. Place the other halves back on top and tie tightly with string in a few places to secure the filling inside. Wipe the sauté pan clean and place the zucchini inside, sitting snugly side by side.

For the cooking liquid, put all the ingredients in a medium saucepan, adding 1 teaspoon salt and some black pepper. Bring to a boil and then pour over the zucchini. The juices need to rise roughly ¾-inch / 1-cm up the sides of the pan; add more stock if needed. Place the pan over medium heat and, as soon as the liquid comes to a simmer, press the zucchini down with a heatproof plate so they won't float when cooking. Cover the pan with the lid and simmer gently for 1½ to 2 hours. At this point, both the zucchini and the rice should be completely soft and about 3 tablespoons liquid should remain in the pan. Remove from the heat, uncover, and allow the zucchini to cool to room temperature. If serving these the next day, refrigerate overnight but leave at room temperature for 30 minutes before serving.

Put the fresh mint, oil, and a pinch of salt in the bowl of a small food processor and blitz until smooth. Place a zucchini on each plate and spoon some yogurt on top. Drizzle with the mint sauce and serve at once.

SERVES FOUR

SLOW-COOKED CHICKPEAS ON TOAST WITH POACHED EGG

rounded 1 cup/220 g dried chickpeas, soaked in water overnight with 2 tsp baking soda
1 tbsp olive oil, plus 1 tbsp to finish
1 medium onion, coarsely chopped (about 1 cup/ 140 g)
3 cloves garlic, crushed
1½ tsp tomato paste
¼ tsp cayenne pepper
¼ tsp smoked paprika
2 medium red peppers, cut into ¼-inch/5-mm dice (about 1¼ cups/180 g)
1 beefsteak tomato, peeled and coarsely chopped (1⅔ cups/300 g)
½ tsp superfine sugar
4 slices sourdough bread, brushed with olive oil and grilled on both sides
4 eggs, freshly poached (see page 198 for poaching instructions)
2 tsp za'atar
salt and black pepper

This recipe was tested among card-carrying skeptics—"5 hours' cooking for beans on toast?!"—they couldn't see how it could possibly be justified when a variation on the theme can be made in 15 minutes (or even 15 seconds, for those inclined to opening a well-known brand of beans and popping bread in the toaster). The result more than won over my fellow recipe testers—the chickpeas are impossibly soft and yielding and the flavor is rich and deep in a way that only slow cooking can bring about. So, having won over two skeptics, I ask you to take a leap of faith.

Notwithstanding the cooking time, it's a very low-maintenance and highly comforting dish: one to simmer away on the stove some weekend when you are puttering about in slippers at home. It tastes fantastic the next day and the day after that, so you might want to double the quantities and keep a batch in the fridge. A spoonful of Greek yogurt can be served alongside each portion, if you like.

Drain and rinse the chickpeas and place them in a large saucepan with plenty of water. Place over high heat, bring to a boil, skim the surface, and boil for 5 minutes. Drain and set aside.

Place the oil, onion, garlic, tomato paste, cayenne, paprika, red peppers, 1 teaspoon salt, and some black pepper in a food processor and blitz to form a paste.

Wipe out the chickpea saucepan, return it to the stove over medium heat, and add the paste. Fry for 5 minutes (there's enough oil there to allow for this), stirring occasionally, before adding the tomato, sugar, chickpeas, and a scant 1 cup/200 ml water. Bring to a low simmer, cover the pan, and cook over very low heat for 4 hours, stirring from time to time and adding more water when needed to retain a sauce-like consistency. Remove the lid and cook for a final hour: the sauce needs to thicken without the chickpeas becoming dry.

Place a piece of warm grilled bread on each plate and spoon the chickpeas over the bread. Lay a poached egg on top, followed by a sprinkle of za'atar and a drizzle of oil. Serve at once.

QUINOA AND FENNEL SALAD

SERVES FOUR

Adding freshly chopped lime or lemon flesh to a salad will be a revelation to those who haven't tried it before. Against the mild and nutty quinoa, it makes a simple salad sing. This is a small meal in its own right but can be fortified further by adding nigella or pumpkin seeds, toasted walnuts, goat cheese, and oven-dried tomatoes.

Pour 3 tablespoons of the olive oil into a large sauté pan, place over high heat, add the fennel, and sear for 5 minutes, stirring once, to get some color. Turn down the heat to medium and cook for another 10 minutes, stirring occasionally, until the fennel is completely soft and golden. Add the sugar, vinegar, and ¾ teaspoon salt and cook for another 2 minutes. Remove from the heat and set aside.

Pour the quinoa into a pot of boiling water and cook for 9 minutes. Drain into a fine sieve and refresh under cold water. Shake well to dry and then add to the fennel along with the fava beans, chile, cumin, herbs, currants, ½ teaspoon salt, and a good grind of black pepper. Stir gently and set aside.

Using a small, sharp serrated knife, slice off the top and tail of each lime. Cut down the sides of each lime, following its natural line, to remove the skin and white pith. Over a small bowl, remove the segments from the limes by slicing between the membranes. Squeeze out any remaining juice from the membranes over the segments and discard the rest. Cut each segment into thirds and add them, along with the juice and the remaining 2 tablespoons olive oil, to the salad. Give everything a final stir and serve.

---

5 tbsp/75 ml olive oil
3 large fennel bulbs, trimmed and thinly sliced (about 1½ lb/700 g)
1 tbsp superfine sugar
3 tbsp cider vinegar
scant 1 cup/150 g quinoa
2¾ cups/300 g fresh or frozen shelled fava beans, blanched and skins removed
1 green chile, seeded and finely chopped
1½ tsp ground cumin
scant 1 cup/25 g mint leaves, chopped
1⅔ cups/25 g cilantro leaves, chopped
1⅔ cups/25 g dill leaves, chopped
4½ tbsp/40 g dried currants
3 limes
salt and black pepper

GREEN BEANS WITH FREEKEH AND TAHINI

SERVES FOUR

½ cup/70 g cracked freekeh, rinsed and drained
1½ lb/700 g haricots verts, trimmed
1 cup/20 g chervil leaves
½ cup/50 g walnuts, coarsely chopped (optional)
½ tsp Aleppo chile flakes
salt

Sauce
5 tbsp/75 g tahini paste
3 tbsp olive oil
2 tbsp lemon juice
1½ tsp dried mint
1 large clove garlic, crushed
1 tsp maple syrup
salt

Scully would say that anything with freekeh shows my hand at work in the kitchen, but the credit for this salad is his. When NOPI opened in 2011, there were all sorts of ways in which we thought it would be different from the existing Ottolenghi shops. Meringues and window displays would not feature. Try as we did, however, we could not resist the pull of a salad counter. Seeing the vast array of colors, textures, and layers upon entering the restaurant is a treat we just couldn't keep from our customers.

The quality of the beans is important here: if they are old or overcooked, they will lose their vibrancy and the dish just won't be the same. The walnuts add another layer of texture and flavor, but there is plenty going on if you want to leave them out.

Place all the ingredients for the sauce, along with ½ teaspoon salt, in a bowl. Whisk until combined and set aside.

Fill a saucepan with plenty of water—it should be two-thirds full—and bring to a boil. Add the freekeh and ½ teaspoon salt, turn down the heat to medium, and simmer, uncovered, for 15 minutes, until the freekeh is cooked through but still retains a bite. Drain and refresh well under cold water. Transfer the freekeh to a large bowl and set aside.

Fill a large saucepan with plenty of cold water and add 2 teaspoons salt. Place over high heat, bring to a boil, then add the beans. Boil rapidly for 4 minutes, until the beans are just cooked, then drain and refresh under cold water. Pat the beans dry well before adding them to the freekeh. Pour the tahini sauce over the freekeh and beans and mix gently so that the beans are completely coated. Just before serving, mix in the chervil and the walnuts along with the chile flakes.

URAD DAL WITH COCONUT AND CILANTRO

SERVES FOUR

This is all about the texture of the urad dal, also known as black gram or black lentil. The texture—which retains a bite even after its long cooking—is more like that of a mung bean than that of your usual lentil. The difference between black and white urad dal is that the white version has had its skin removed. I prefer to use the black—the skin helps the dal keeps its shape and gives the dish a pleasing bite—but the white, which you won't need to soak overnight, works just as well. The inspiration for this I owe to Aasmah Mir, whose website, crackingcurries.com, is a treasure trove of Pakistani family cooking.

Drain the dal, rinse under cold water, and set aside.

Place the butter in a large sauté pan over medium-high heat. When it starts to sizzle, add the onion and fry for 15 minutes, stirring from time to time, until soft and golden brown. Add the garlic, ginger, chile, and garam masala and fry for another 2 minutes, stirring constantly. Add the tomatoes and cook for a further 4 minutes. Add the dal, 4½ cups/1 liter water, and 1 teaspoon salt. Turn down the heat to medium and simmer for 40 minutes, stirring every 5 minutes or so, until the sauce has the consistency of thick soup and the dal is cooked but still holding its shape. Bring to a rapid boil for a few minutes toward the end of cooking if the sauce needs reducing.

Turn the heat down to low, then stir in the coconut cream, lime juice, and black mustard seeds. Remove from the heat and serve, accompanied with the toppings in 3 separate bowls, for diners to sprinkle on top of their portion as they like.

1⅓ cups/250 g black urad dal, soaked overnight in plenty of water
¼ cup/60 g clarified butter or ghee
1 large onion, finely chopped (1⅓ cups/200 g)
3 cloves garlic, crushed
4-inch/10-cm piece fresh ginger (2½ oz/75 g), peeled and coarsely grated
1 green chile, flesh and seeds finely chopped
1 tbsp garam masala
5 medium tomatoes, peeled and coarsely chopped (3½ cups/600 g)
⅔ cup/160 g coconut cream
2 tbsp lime juice, plus 1 lime, cut into wedges, to serve
1½ tbsp black mustard seeds, toasted
salt

Toppings
1¼ cups/100 g coarsely grated fresh coconut
1¾ oz/50 g crispy fried shallots (store-bought)
2 cups/30 g cilantro leaves, coarsely chopped

BRAISED

SERVES FOUR

LENTILS WITH MUSHROOM AND PRESERVED LEMON RAGOUT

⅓ cup / 10 g dried porcini mushrooms
½ medium onion (3½ oz / 100 g)
4 thyme sprigs
2 bay leaves
2 medium carrots (8 oz / 240 g), peeled; one cut in half crosswise, the other cut into ⅜-inch / 1-cm dice
scant 1 cup / 175 g Puy lentils
¼ small celery root, peeled and cut into ⅜-inch / 1-cm dice (¾ cup / 100 g)
5 tbsp / 75 ml olive oil
2 cups / 30 g cilantro leaves, chopped
1 large leek, white part only, cut in half lengthwise and sliced into 2-inch / 5-cm chunks (2½ cups / 230 g)
7 oz / 200 g fresh porcini mushrooms, cut into slices ¼-inch / 5-mm thick
7 oz / 200 g mixed fresh wild mushrooms, coarsely torn
3 tbsp heavy cream
1¼ oz / 35 g preserved lemon skin, finely diced
about ¾ cup / 160 g Greek yogurt
salt and white pepper

I've talked previously about looking for "drama in the mouth" when I eat. Finely chopped preserved lemon skin delivers this drama in spades in this recipe, as it does in various stews and salads. Cooking with preserved lemons spreads a mellow aroma throughout, while chopping and folding it in at the end gives you a more intense yet sporadic experience. Serve this any time of the day, and that's all you'll need, really.

Soak the dried porcini in a scant 1 cup / 200 ml of boiling water for 1 hour. Strain the water through cheesecloth into a fresh bowl—it can be gritty—and set aside; rinse the porcini in fresh water and add to the strained water.

Fill a medium saucepan half full with water. Place over high heat and add the onion, thyme, bay, halved carrot, and ½ teaspoon salt. Bring to a boil and then add the lentils. Turn down the heat to medium and boil gently for 15 to 20 minutes, until the lentils are cooked but still retain a bite. Drain, remove and discard the vegetables and herbs, and set the lentils aside.

Preheat the oven to 425°F / 220°C.

Place the diced carrot and celery root in a small bowl with 2 tablespoons of the oil, ½ teaspoon salt, and ¼ teaspoon white pepper. Spread out on a baking sheet and place in the oven for 30 minutes, gently stirring once during cooking, until the vegetables are cooked and starting to caramelize. Remove from the oven and transfer to a bowl, along with the lentils and two-thirds of the cilantro. Keep warm.

Place a large sauté pan over high heat with 1 tablespoon of the oil. Add the leek and ½ teaspoon salt and fry for 2 minutes on each side, until soft and caramelized. Remove from the pan, add the fresh porcini, another 1 tablespoon oil, and a pinch of salt, and fry for 3 minutes, until caramelized. Add these to the leek and then repeat with the wild mushrooms, another 1 tablespoon oil, and a pinch of salt, before returning all the seared mushrooms and the leek to the pan. Add the cream, preserved lemon, and the rehydrated dried porcini and strained water. Increase the heat and boil for 5 minutes, until the sauce has thickened and reduced by half.

To serve, divide the lentils among 4 plates and spoon the mushrooms over the top. Finish with the yogurt, sprinkle with the remaining cilantro, and serve at once.

LIGHTLY STEWED FAVA BEANS, PEAS, AND GEM LETTUCE WITH PARMESAN RICE

SERVES FOUR

This quick stew of fresh seasonal vegetables is comfort personified, particularly when served with the cheesy rice. For those who like their comfort served alongside a healthy conscience, the rice can be swapped for pearled barley or spelt, boiled and mixed with olive oil and some garlic. For those of the opposite persuasion, more Parmesan than recommended can happily be added.

¼ cup/60 ml olive oil, plus extra to finish
3 cloves garlic, sliced
10 green onions, white and green parts, cut on the diagonal into slices ¾-inch/2-cm long (¾ cup/75 g)
3½ cups/375 g fresh or frozen shelled fava beans, blanched and skins removed
1¾ cups/250 g fresh or defrosted frozen green peas
about 1½ cups/350 ml vegetable stock
4 thyme sprigs
3 Little Gem lettuces, ends removed and quartered lengthwise (10½ oz/300 g)
⅔ cup/20 g mint leaves, chopped
grated zest of 1 lemon
salt and black pepper

Rice
1⅓ cups/250 g basmati rice
3½ tbsp/50 g unsalted butter
¾ cup/80 g grated Parmesan
1½ tbsp lemon juice
salt

Start with the rice. Place the rice, one-third of the butter, and ¼ teaspoon salt in a saucepan over high heat and stir as the butter melts and the rice heats up. Add 2 cups/480 ml boiling water, turn down the heat to the lowest setting, and simmer, covered, for 15 minutes. Remove from the heat and leave covered for another 10 minutes.

While the rice is cooking, take a large sauté pan, pour in the oil, and place over medium heat. Add the garlic and green onions and sauté for 4 minutes, stirring occasionally, until they start to take on some color. Add the fava beans and cook for another 4 minutes. Add the peas, stock, thyme, ½ teaspoon salt, and a generous grind of black pepper. The vegetables should be well covered, so add more stock if needed. Bring to a light simmer and cook for 5 minutes. Add the lettuce and cook for another 7 minutes, stirring from time to time. The dish is ready when the lettuce hearts have softened but aren't soggy and you are left with about half the stock.

To serve, add the Parmesan and the remaining butter to the hot rice and fluff it up with a fork. Add the lemon juice before spooning the rice onto serving plates. Remove and discard the thyme from the vegetables and stir in the mint before spooning the vegetables over the rice. Finish with a drizzle of oil, a bit more black pepper, and the lemon zest.

SERVES SIX
as a starter

FAVA BEANS WITH LEMON AND CILANTRO

¼ cup / 60 ml olive oil
1 large onion, finely diced
   (1⅓ cups / 190 g)
5 cloves garlic, crushed
about 3⅓ cups / 50 g cilantro leaves, chopped
5½ cups / 600 g fresh or frozen shelled fava beans, thawed if frozen
1 tsp sweet paprika
¼ tsp ground allspice
2 tsp lemon juice
salt and black pepper

This doesn't look half as exquisite as it tastes, but love really is blind with this Lebanese classic. You don't need to skin the fava beans, so the temptation to fall for this low-maintenance dish is even greater. With very young beans, you could even cook and eat them in the pods, as they do in Lebanon. Serve with rice or plain quinoa, or with lots of other Middle Eastern mezze such as Zucchini "Baba Ghanoush" (page 151) and Batata Harra (page 280).

Pour the oil into a large sauté pan and place over medium heat. Add the onion and cook for 8 minutes, stirring occasionally, until translucent. Add the garlic and about four-fifths of the cilantro and sauté for another minute. Add the fava beans, paprika, allspice, ½ teaspoon salt, plenty of black pepper, and a scant 1 cup / 200 ml water and stir well. Cover the pan and simmer gently for about 25 minutes, stirring occasionally, until the beans are very soft. A lot of the water will have evaporated, but the mixture should be wet, with the beans still immersed in liquid. Remove from the heat, take off the lid, and leave to cool. Add the lemon juice, stir in the remaining cilantro, and serve.

BRAISED KALE WITH CRISPY SHALLOTS

SERVES FOUR

If vegetables were strutting their stuff on the catwalk, kale would get the award for "exponential surge in popularity throughout recent years." Wherever you look, it's being braised, blitzed, blanched, and seared. I have even seen a kale Popsicle. The combination of it being exceptionally tasty and obscenely healthy might have something to do with it.

For a nonvegetarian option, oyster sauce can be used instead of the kecap manis, *which is an Indonesian sweet soy sauce, available in Asian markets and some supermarkets; if you use oyster sauce, you'll need to add a tablespoon more. With thanks to Sarah Joseph for this recipe.*

1¼ lb/550 g kale, stems removed and leaves coarsely shredded (6½ cups/450 g)
1 tbsp olive oil
3 cloves garlic, thinly sliced
1½ tbsp kecap manis
1 tsp sesame oil
1 tbsp sesame seeds, toasted
2 tbsp all-purpose flour
8 shallots, thinly sliced (1⅓ cups/140 g)
½ cup/120 ml sunflower oil
salt

Bring a large pan of water to a boil. Add 2 teaspoons salt and then the kale and blanch for 4 minutes. Drain and set aside to dry.

Heat the olive oil in a large sauté pan over medium heat. Add the garlic and cook for 2 minutes, until golden and crispy. Add the blanched kale and stir well. Pour in the kecap manis and sesame oil and cook for a couple of minutes, until the kale has softened and any liquid reduced. Remove from the heat and stir in the sesame seeds and ¼ teaspoon salt. Cover the pan with a lid and set aside somewhere warm.

Place the flour and shallots in a bowl and mix well, coating the shallots evenly. Heat the sunflower oil in a small saucepan over medium-high heat. When hot, add one-third of the shallots and cook for 5 minutes, until golden and crispy. Use a slotted spoon to transfer them to a plate lined with paper towels. Sprinkle with ⅛ teaspoon salt and repeat with the remaining shallots in two batches.

To serve, either arrange the warm kale on a serving dish and scatter the crispy shallots over the top, or mix together the kale and shallots. Serve at once.

SWEET-AND-SOUR LEEKS WITH GOAT'S CURD AND CURRANTS

SERVES FOUR

I have done it before, and I am doing it again here, that is, placing leek right in the center of a substantial stand-alone dish. This is not trivial for a vegetable that is normally given the side job of flavoring other things, like stocks and soups. I find the creaminess of leeks and their sweet oniony flavor very satisfying. This dish, with its jewel-like currants, makes an elegant starter. Use long, relatively thin leeks if you can find them; otherwise, just halve their number.

8 small leeks, white part only
2 bay leaves
2 cloves garlic, thinly sliced
scant 1 cup/200 ml dry white wine
3 tbsp olive oil
1 small red onion, finely chopped (⅔ cup/100 g)
scant 2½ tbsp/20 g dried currants
1 tbsp cider vinegar
2 tsp superfine sugar
2 tbsp sunflower oil
3½ oz/100 g goat's curd or a creamy goat cheese
1 tbsp chervil or flat-leaf parsley leaves
salt and black pepper

Cut the leeks crosswise into two segments, each about 4-inches/10-cm long, and wash well. Lay all the leeks on the bottom of a large, shallow pan and add the bay leaves, garlic, wine, olive oil, and about 1 cup/250 ml water, so that the leeks are half covered in liquid. Add ¾ teaspoon salt and some black pepper, place over medium heat, and simmer gently for about 30 minutes, until a knife can be inserted into the leeks without any resistance. Turn the leeks over once or twice during cooking so that they are cooked evenly.

Using a slotted spoon, remove the leeks from the pan and place on a plate to one side. Strain the remaining cooking liquid into a small saucepan and reduce over high heat until you are left with just 3 tablespoons. This should take between 12 and 15 minutes. Remove from the heat and add the onion, currants, vinegar, sugar, ¼ teaspoon salt, and some black pepper. Set aside to soften and marinate.

Heat the sunflower oil in a large sauté pan over medium-high heat. Carefully add the leeks and fry for 2 minutes on each side, until lightly golden. Transfer to a plate and set aside to cool.

To serve, divide the leeks among 4 plates. Dot with the cheese, spoon the onion and currant dressing over the top, and finish with the chervil.

BUTTERNUT SQUASH WITH BUCKWHEAT POLENTA AND TEMPURA LEMON

SERVES SIX

Butternut
1 large butternut squash (3 lb/1.3 kg)
3 tbsp olive oil
1½ tbsp/25 g unsalted butter, diced
1¼ cups/300 ml vegetable stock
3 oregano sprigs (⅓ oz/10 g)
15 black peppercorns
8 allspice berries
6 cardamom pods, crushed
6 bay leaves
6 thyme sprigs
rind of 1 large orange shaved in long, narrow strips
8 cloves garlic, lightly cracked with the skin on
salt

Polenta
3 tbsp/30 g roasted buckwheat (kasha) or buckwheat groats
⅔ cup/150 ml whole milk
3¾ cups/900 ml vegetable stock
⅓ cup/10 g oregano leaves, coarsely chopped
1 bay leaf
1 tbsp thyme leaves
Shaved rind of ½ lemon
¾ cup/120 g polenta
¼ cup/60 g unsalted butter
salt and white pepper

Tempura lemon
4½ tbsp/35 g flour
3 tbsp plus 1 tsp/25 g cornstarch
5 tbsp/75 ml cold soda water
sunflower oil, for frying
1 lemon, cut crosswise into 6 slices ⅛-inch/3-mm thick
salt

Karl and I spent a few months in Boston working our way, among other things, around the city's eateries. One of our top five memories is the tempura Meyer lemon skin we had at restaurant Toro on Washington Street. It was sublime. A squeeze of fresh lemon can be used as an alternative, but for those with the time or inclination, it makes the dish special.

Preheat the oven to 400°F/200°C. Trim the top and bottom off the butternut and halve lengthwise. Scoop out and discard the seeds and cut each half into 3 long wedges, skin on. Place the wedges in a large roasting pan with all the remaining squash ingredients and ¾ teaspoon salt, coating the butternut well with the aromatics. Bake for 50 minutes, turning the butternut pieces every 10 minutes or so and spooning the juices over them, until the squash is cooked, golden brown, and starting to crisp on top. Add a little stock during cooking if the pan is drying out.

Meanwhile, to make the polenta, put the kasha in a small baking pan and toast in the oven at the same time as the squash for 5 minutes, or 10 minutes for plain groats. Remove and crush lightly with a pestle and mortar.

In a large saucepan over high heat, combine the milk, stock, herbs, lemon rind strips, ¾ teaspoon salt, and a pinch of white pepper. Bring to a boil and then turn the heat to low and whisk in the polenta and buckwheat. Using a wooden spoon, stir every few minutes for 35 to 40 minutes, until the polenta is thick and cooked. If it is getting too thick, add a little water. At the end of the cooking, stir in the butter. The polenta should be thick but runny enough to fall off the spoon easily. Cover the top of the polenta with plastic wrap to stop a skin from forming and leave somewhere warm.

To make the tempura, mix together the flour and cornstarch, then whisk in the soda water until the mixture is smooth and runny. Sit the bowl over ice for 45 minutes.

Pour oil to a depth of 1¼-inches/3-cm into a saucepan and heat to about 320°F/160°C. Dip the lemon slices into the batter and fry for 2 to 3 minutes, until golden and crispy. Remove with a slotted spoon and sprinkle immediately with salt.

Place a spoonful of warm polenta on each plate and lay a squash wedge across it, adding a mix of the baked aromatics on top. Finish with a tempura lemon slice and serve at once.

LENTILS, RADICCHIO, AND WALNUTS WITH MANUKA HONEY

SERVES FOUR

1 cup / 200 g Puy lentils
2 bay leaves
scant 5 tbsp / 100 g manuka honey
¼ tsp chile flakes
½ tsp ground turmeric
1 cup / 100 g walnuts
3 tbsp red wine vinegar
6 tbsp / 90 ml olive oil
½ medium head radicchio, or 2 heads red Belgian endive (4 oz / 120 g)
2 oz / 60 g pecorino fiore sardo or another mature sheep or goat cheese, shaved
⅔ cup / 20 g basil leaves, coarsely chopped
1⅓ cups / 20 g dill leaves, coarsely chopped
⅔ cup / 20 g flat-leaf parsley leaves, coarsely chopped
salt and black pepper

I got a thorough introduction to manuka honey on a trip to New Zealand, where it appears repeatedly on restaurant menus and cocktail lists. Aside from its famous healing properties, manuka has a strong, woodsy flavor that colors a whole dish with a unique aroma. Still, manuka is expensive and not available everywhere, so you can substitute Scottish heather honey or another good strong variety. Radicchio's bitterness offers the right balance to the rich sweetness of honey, but if this isn't to your taste, you can leave it out or replace it with red Belgian endive, if you like. While, technically, there is no braising going on in this recipe I have decided, nonetheless, to include it in this section. As when you braise large chunks of vegetables, the lentils are slowly infused with flavor as they cool down, using their residual heat and steam.

Preheat the oven to 325°F / 170°C.

Place the lentils in a saucepan, cover with plenty of water, add the bay leaves, and simmer for about 20 minutes, until tender. Drain well and return to the pan.

While the lentils are cooking, prepare the walnuts. Put half the honey, the chile flakes, the turmeric, and ¼ teaspoon salt in a small bowl. Mix well, adding just enough water to create a thick paste—about 1 teaspoon. Add the walnuts and stir until well coated. Spread the walnuts out on a baking sheet lined with parchment paper and roast in the oven for about 20 minutes, stirring once, until golden and crunchy but still a little sticky. Remove from the oven and set aside, removing them from the parchment paper as soon as they are cool enough to touch.

Whisk together the vinegar, half the oil, the remaining honey, ¾ teaspoon salt, and some black pepper until the honey dissolves. Stir into the lentils while they are still hot, then leave to cool down a little, discarding the bay leaves.

To cook the radicchio, pour the remaining oil into a sauté pan and place over high heat. Cut the radicchio into 8 long wedges (or quarter each Belgian endive lengthwise) and place the wedges in the hot oil. Cook them for about 1 minute on each side and transfer to a large bowl. Add the lentils, walnuts, pecorino, and herbs. Stir gently and serve warmish or at room temperature.

SERVES FOUR TO SIX

INDIAN RATATOUILLE

about ½ cup / 120 ml sunflower oil, for frying
2 medium red onions, cut into 1¼-inch/3-cm dice (about 2½ cups/300 g)
2¼ lb/1 kg Yukon gold potatoes, peeled and cut into 1¼-inch/3-cm dice
3 large red peppers, cut into 1¼-inch/3-cm dice (2 cups/300 g)
1½ tbsp *panch phoran*
¼ tsp ground turmeric
5 cardamom pods
1 lb/450 g okra, trimmed, or haricots verts if you remain unconvinced
2 tomatoes, peeled and chopped (5½ oz/160 g)
3 green chiles, seeded and finely chopped
about 24 fresh curry leaves
2 tsp superfine sugar
1 to 3 tbsp tamarind paste, depending on acidity
6 tbsp/50 g pumpkin seeds, lightly toasted
1 tbsp chopped cilantro, to serve
salt

Okra is to grown adults what brussels sprouts are to ten-year-olds: those subjected to the overcooked, soggy, or slimy version will just never, point-blank, try them again. Having done my bit for brussels sprouts in the form of advocating roasting over boiling every time, I now urge all okra-phobes to give them one more go in this version of a ratatouille, based on a Bengali vegetable curry. Panch phoran *is a whole-seed mix from eastern India. It can be bought or made by mixing equal amounts of fenugreek, fennel, black mustard, nigella, and cumin seeds. Making your own tamarind paste from pulp is ideal, but ready-made pastes are widely available. The difference between one brand and the next is great, so you'll need to taste and assess—the vinegar levels can be high—before adding it to the pot. Remember, you can always add more. For more on tamarind, see page 232. Serve this with white or brown rice with a dollop of yogurt, if you like.*

Preheat the oven to 425°F/220°C.

Heat the oil in an extra-large sauté pan over medium-high heat. Add the onions and potatoes and fry for 10 minutes, stirring occasionally. Lift the vegetables out with a slotted spoon and set aside.

Top up the oil, if needed, so you have 2 tablespoons in the pan. Add the peppers and spices and fry over high heat for 3 minutes, stirring often. Add the okra, tomatoes, chiles, and curry leaves and fry over high heat for 5 minutes.

Return the onions and potatoes to the pan. Add the sugar, tamarind paste, a scant 1 cup/200 ml water, and ¾ teaspoon salt and simmer for 5 minutes.

Spread the vegetables out on a large baking sheet, sprinkle with the pumpkin seeds, and bake for 12 minutes. Serve warm, sprinkled with cilantro.

FENNEL WITH CAPERS AND OLIVES

SERVES FOUR
as a starter

If there were one ingredient I could "magic" onto all supermarket and grocery store shelves, it would be verjuice. Common in Australia thanks, largely, to Maggie Beer's championing of the product, it's a mystery to me why it hasn't yet taken hold here. Made from the juice of semiripe wine grapes, it has the mildly sweet tartness of lemon juice and acidity of vinegar, without the harshness of either. It's used, as you would both of these more common ingredients, to heighten other flavors and as a base for sauces and dressings. If you can't get hold of verjuice, a mixture of two-thirds lemon juice to one-third red wine vinegar works well as an alternative. And, no, the 15 garlic cloves isn't a typo: once scorched, they add a mellowing sweetness to an otherwise sharp dressing. The ricotta isn't essential, if you'd rather keep this dairy-free, but it helps to balance the acidity.

4 medium fennel bulbs, trimmed (1⅔ lb/750 g)
about 3 tbsp olive oil, plus extra to finish
15 large cloves garlic, skin on (2½ oz/75 g)
¼ cup/60 ml verjuice, or a mixture of ¼ cup/60 ml lemon juice and 2 tbsp red wine vinegar
1 small tomato, cut into ⅜-inch/1-cm dice (about ⅓ cup/70 g)
about 1 cup/250 ml vegetable stock
2½ tbsp/20 g capers
3½ tbsp/30 g black wrinkly olives, pitted and cut in half
1 tbsp chopped thyme leaves
2½ tsp superfine sugar
6½ tbsp/100 g ricotta (optional)
1 tsp grated lemon zest
salt and black pepper

Cut the trimmed fennel from top to bottom along the longest side into slices ¾-inch/2-cm thick.

Place 2 tablespoons of the olive oil in a large sauté pan for which you have a lid and place over medium-high heat. Add half of the fennel along with a pinch of salt and a good grind of black pepper. Cook for 5 to 6 minutes, turning once, so that both sides are nice and browned. Remove from the pan and repeat with the remaining fennel, adding more oil, if needed, and seasoning as you go.

Once all the fennel is seared and removed from the pan, add the garlic cloves and a tiny bit of oil, if needed (a thin film of oil is enough here), and fry for about 3 minutes, tossing occasionally, so that the garlic skin gets scorched all over. Turn down the heat to medium before carefully (it spits!) adding the verjuice. Let it reduce for a couple of minutes to about 2 tablespoons liquid. Add the tomato, 7 tablespoons/100 ml of the stock, the capers, olives, thyme, sugar, ¼ teaspoon salt, and some black pepper. Bring to a simmer for 2 minutes before returning the fennel to the pan. Add the remainder of the stock, cover the pan, and simmer for about 12 minutes, turning once during the cooking, until the fennel is completely soft and the sauce has thickened. You might need to remove the lid and increase the heat for the final 2 or 3 minutes of cooking, to reduce and thicken the sauce.

Place 2 slices of fennel on each plate, spoon the sauce over the slices, and serve with a spoonful of ricotta, if using, and some lemon zest. Finish with a drizzle of olive oil and serve warm or at room temperature.

MUSHROOMS, GARLIC, AND SHALLOTS WITH LEMON RICOTTA

SERVES TWO TO FOUR

If you are not put off by peeling lots of shallots and garlic cloves, you are in for a winter treat: hearty, oniony mushroom stew, topped with fresh ricotta. You don't need much more, though a chunk of sourdough will not go amiss. To help with the peeling, soak the shallots and garlic in water for half an hour.

Put the olive oil in a large sauté pan with a scant 3 tablespoons/40 g of the butter and place over medium heat. Add the shallots, garlic, thyme, and cinnamon and sauté gently for about 12 minutes, until the onions are beginning to soften. Increase the temperature to medium-high, add the portobello and chestnut mushrooms, mix well, and cook for 2 minutes more. Add the buna-shimeji mushrooms and the chile flakes and cook for another minute. Pour in the stock and simmer rapidly for 8 to 10 minutes, stirring gently once or twice, until the liquid has almost disappeared and the shallots and garlic are cooked through. Pour in the Pernod, 1¼ teaspoons salt, and a good grind of black pepper. Cook for 1 to 2 minutes to allow the alcohol to evaporate, before stirring in the remaining butter and the chopped herbs.

Mix together the ricotta and lemon zest in a small bowl. Divide the warm mushrooms among individual plates and top each serving with equal portions of the ricotta mixture. Finish with a drizzle of oil and serve.

2 tbsp olive oil, plus extra to finish
4 tbsp/60 g unsalted butter
about 1 lb/470 g peeled baby shallots (about 35)
scant 3 oz/80 g peeled garlic cloves (about 24)
2 thyme sprigs
2 cinnamon sticks
7 oz/200 g portobello mushrooms, quartered
8 oz/250 g cremini mushrooms, halved
3½ oz/100 g buna-shimeji (brown beech) or wild mushrooms
¼ tsp chile flakes
scant 1 cup/200 ml vegetable stock
7 tbsp/100 ml Pernod
3 tbsp/5 g tarragon leaves, chopped
⅓ cup/10 g flat-leaf parsley leaves, chopped
⅓ cup/10 g mint leaves, chopped
1 cup/250 g ricotta
grated zest of 1 lemon
salt and black pepper

SERVES SIX

IRANIAN VEGETABLE STEW WITH DRIED LIME

- 3½ tbsp/50 g clarified butter
- 1 large onion, finely diced (1½ cups/220 g)
- ½ tsp ground turmeric
- 1½ tsp cumin seeds
- 1 tbsp tomato paste
- ¾ oz/20 g cilantro sprigs
- ⅓ oz/10 g tarragon sprigs
- ⅓ oz/10 g dill sprigs
- 2¼ lb/1 kg Yukon gold potatoes or another waxy variety, peeled and cut into 1½-inch/4-cm chunks
- 1 medium butternut squash (about 2½ lb/1.1 kg), peeled, seeded, and cut into 1½-inch/4-cm chunks (1⅔ lb/760 g)
- 3 Iranian limes, pierced 2 or 3 times
- 1 green chile, slit on one side from stem to tip
- 4 medium tomatoes, quartered (14 oz/400 g)
- 5 cups/150 g spinach leaves
- 2 tbsp/15 g barberries
- 1½ cups/300 g Greek yogurt (optional)
- salt

Small dried limes (or lemons) are a regular feature in Iranian cooking, adding a sharp tang and sweetish aroma to marinades, stews, and salads. They are rock hard and not easy to grind (although you can do so, in a coffee or spice grinder), so puncture them a couple of times and then put them in whole. You can also buy them in powder form, although this isn't as pungent. Sumac or grated lemon zest can be used as an alternative, but if you are passing a Middle Eastern grocery or you shop online, they are well worth seeking out. For information on barberries, see page 241. Serve this sweet and sharp stew with steamed rice, that's all.

Preheat the oven to 400°F/200°C.

Place a large Dutch oven over medium heat and sauté the butter, onion, turmeric, and cumin for 10 minutes. Add the tomato paste and cook, stirring, for another 2 minutes. Bundle the herbs together and use some string to tie them into a bunch. Add these to the dish along with the potatoes, squash, limes, chile, 1½ teaspoons salt, and 4½ cups/1 liter water and bring to a boil. Turn down the heat and boil gently for 15 minutes, until the potatoes are semicooked. Stir in the tomatoes, spinach, and barberries, crushing the limes gently to release some of the juice inside, and transfer everything to a large roasting pan. Bake uncovered for 20 minutes, until the sauce has thickened a little and the vegetables are soft. Remove from the oven, discard the herb bundle, and allow to sit for 5 minutes before serving with a dollop of yogurt on the side.

GRILLED

GRILLED LETTUCE WITH FARRO AND LEMON

SERVES TWO TO FOUR

You want to serve this salad quite soon after the romaine hearts are grilled so they retain their fresh color and texture. The farro has a great texture—like, but not to be confused with, spelt—and the mixture of lemon, Parmesan, tarragon, and the smoky romaine is a twist on a Caesar salad.

Preheat the oven to 475°F/240°C.

Bring a small saucepan with plenty of water to a boil, add the farro, and simmer over medium heat for 14 minutes, until the farro is cooked but still has a little bit of bite. Drain, refresh under cold water, and leave aside to dry.

While the farro is cooking, make the dressing. Using a small, sharp serrated knife, slice off the top and tail of the fresh lemon. Cut down the sides of the lemon, following its natural line, to remove the skin and white pith. Over a bowl, remove the segments from the lemon by slicing between the membranes. Chop the segments coarsely and return to the bowl, along with any juices left in the membrane or on your chopping board. Next, add the preserved lemon, garlic, shallot, 2 tablespoons of the olive oil, the Pernod, maple syrup, ¼ teaspoon salt, and a generous grind of black pepper. Gently whisk and set aside.

Brush the slices of bread with 2 tablespoons of the olive oil, place on a small baking sheet, and put in the oven for 8 to 10 minutes, turning them over halfway. Remove them from the oven once they have started to brown and are completely crisp, allow to cool down, then break into rough 1¼-inch/3-cm croutons.

When you are ready to serve, place a ridged grill pan over high heat. While you wait for it to heat up, put the romaine quarters in a large bowl with the remaining 1 tablespoon olive oil and ¼ teaspoon salt. Gently mix and, when the pan is smoking hot, place the lettuce wedges in the pan for about 30 seconds, turning them over once, so they get char marks all over. Return to the bowl and add the cooked farro, tarragon, and dressing. Gently mix with your hands and then finally add the croutons and Parmesan, giving the salad a final toss before serving.

---

6 tbsp/75 g farro
1 medium lemon
1 medium preserved lemon (1½ oz/45 g), cut in half and thinly sliced, seeds removed
1 small clove garlic, crushed
1 shallot, finely chopped (2 scant tbsp/15 g)
5 tbsp/75 ml olive oil
2 tsp Pernod or another anise-flavored alcohol, such as raki or pastis
¾ tsp maple syrup
2 slices crusty white bread (2 oz/60 g)
2 romaine hearts, outer leaves removed and quartered lengthwise (9 oz/250 g)
½ cup/15 g tarragon leaves, coarsely chopped
1¾ oz/50 g Parmesan, shaved
salt and black pepper

SERVES FOUR
as a starter

ZUCCHINI AND FENNEL WITH SAFFRON CRUMBS

¼ tsp saffron threads
4 oz/120 g ciabatta bread, crust removed (2 oz/60 g)
sunflower oil, for frying
3 cloves garlic, thinly sliced
2 medium zucchini, cut lengthwise into slices ¼-inch/5-mm thick (12 oz/350 g)
2 tbsp olive oil
2 small fennel bulbs, trimmed and cut lengthwise into slices ¼-inch/5-mm thick (scant 3 cups/250 g)
2 tbsp lemon juice
3 tbsp/10 g chopped dill
salt and black pepper

Something resembling a crumb obsession took hold of the test kitchen at one point, where few soups, salads, or grilled dishes escaped the additional crunch and layer of taste brought about by flavored crumbs. Mustard or chile croutons, saffron crumbs, sumac-sprinkled fried pita—they are a great and versatile way of bringing color and luxury to otherwise simple dishes. Cook more crumbs than you need here, omitting the garlic, and keep them in an airtight jar for a week or so, to elevate midweek meals.

Preheat the oven to 325°F/170°C.

Pour ⅓ cup/80 ml boiling water over the saffron and leave to infuse for 10 minutes. Tear the ciabatta into small but not uniformly sized pieces, up to ¾-inch/2-cm long. Place them in a small bowl, then pour the saffron water in slowly, as you stir the bread with your other hand, so that all the pieces evenly soak up the liquid. Spread the bread out on a baking sheet lined with parchment paper and put in the oven for 10 to 15 minutes, until the bread has dried out completely, then remove.

Pour sunflower oil to a depth of ⅜-inch/1-cm into a saucepan and place over medium heat. When the oil is hot, carefully drop in the saffron "crumbs" and garlic. Fry for just 30 seconds, until the garlic is golden. With a slotted spoon, transfer to paper towels and sprinkle with ⅛ teaspoon salt.

Place a ridged grill pan over high heat and leave for a few minutes. Mix the zucchini with 1½ teaspoons of the olive oil and ¼ teaspoon salt and grill lightly for about 1 minute on each side, until lightly charred. Repeat with the fennel, again mixing it with 1½ teaspoons of the olive oil and ¼ teaspoon salt before grilling on both sides. Put all the vegetables in a bowl, pour in the lemon juice and the remaining 1 tablespoon olive oil, and add a good grind of black pepper. Mix gently and leave to marinate for 15 to 20 minutes.

Spread the vegetables out on a platter, sprinkle with the dill, followed by the saffron crumbs and garlic, and serve at once.

SQUASH WITH LABNEH AND PICKLED WALNUT SALSA

SERVES FOUR

3½ oz / 100 g pickled walnuts
½ medium red onion, cut into ¼-inch / 5-mm dice (½ cup / 80 g)
1½ tbsp cider vinegar
1 tsp superfine sugar
1 mild red chile, seeded and finely chopped
¼ tsp ground allspice
2 tbsp olive oil, plus extra to finish
1 Crown Prince squash or another variety of squash or pumpkin (about 2½ lb / 1.1 kg)
1½ cups / 30 g arugula
5 oz / 150 g labneh or a very fresh goat cheese
⅔ cup / 10 g dill leaves
salt and black pepper

A few years ago, I went to visit Opie's pickle factory in Kent, where I was shown the process of pickling fresh, green walnuts. If I am completely frank, I had more than a doubt or two about the idea of pickling walnuts, a process exclusive to Britain and New Zealand, I hear. It seemed pretty esoteric. Well, I still think they are somewhat of an oddity, but I do love pickled walnuts now and use them regularly in various salsas and sauces. If you can't get pickled walnuts, try making the salsa for Red Onions with Walnut Salsa (page 164) and using it here instead of the pickled walnut salsa.

Labneh, thick strained yogurt, is available from many Middle Eastern markets as small white balls marinated in olive oil. You can make your own by hanging natural yogurt in cheesecloth for a couple of days. Alternatively, use a very fresh goat cheese.

Start by making the salsa. Rinse the walnuts briefly to remove the outer black skin, pat dry, and cut into ¼-inch / 5-mm dice. Place in a small bowl and add the onion, vinegar, sugar, chile, allspice, 1 tablespoon of the oil, and ⅛ teaspoon salt. Mix and set aside.

Preheat the oven to 425°F / 220°C.

Cut the squash in half lengthwise (there is no need to peel it), remove the seeds, and cut crosswise into slices ⅔-inch / 1.5-cm thick. Place in a large bowl, add the remaining 1 tablespoon oil, ¼ teaspoon salt, and a good grind of black pepper. Mix with your hands to coat in the oil.

Place a ridged grill pan over high heat and let it turn red-hot. Cook the squash pieces in batches for 2 to 3 minutes on each side, to get good grill marks all over.

Transfer to a baking sheet lined with parchment paper and place in the oven for 15 minutes, until tender. Remove from the oven and leave to cool.

To assemble, arrange the squash wedges and arugula leaves on a serving plate, dotting with dollops of labneh as you go. Spoon over the walnut salsa and sprinkle with dill. Finish with a drizzle of olive oil and serve.

SERVES SIX TO EIGHT

GRILLED ZITI WITH FETA

- 3 tbsp olive oil, plus extra to finish
- 1½ tbsp cumin seeds
- 1 tbsp caraway seeds
- 2 tsp dried oregano
- 2 small onions, cut into ⅜-inch/1-cm dice (1⅓ cups/210 g)
- 2 celery stalks, cut into ⅜-inch/1-cm dice (1 cup/110 g)
- 1½ tsp superfine sugar
- 2 tbsp tomato paste
- 8 large ripe tomatoes, coarsely chopped (4½ cups/800 g)
- 1 red chile, finely chopped
- ½ cup/15 g basil leaves, chopped
- ⅓ cup/10 g oregano leaves, chopped
- 2 cloves garlic, crushed
- about 1 lb/500 g long ziti (broken into uneven smaller segments) or penne rigate
- 5 oz/150 g Parmesan, coarsely grated
- 5 oz/150 g mature Cheddar, coarsely grated
- 5 oz/150 g feta, broken into ¾-inch/2-cm chunks
- salt and black pepper

I always preferred my father's pasta the next day, when it was thrown into the oven with heaps of cheese and ended up slightly burnt and completely crisp on top. To maximize this effect, make sure the surface of your baking dish is large enough to accommodate the pasta in a shallow layer. This is a wonderful main course, no matter what age you are.

Place the oil in a saucepan over medium-high heat. Add the cumin and caraway seeds, dried oregano, onion, and celery and cook for 6 minutes, stirring from time to time, until the onion is soft but not colored. Add the sugar and tomato paste and cook for another minute before adding the tomatoes, chile, 1½ teaspoons salt, and a good grind of black pepper. Turn down the heat to medium and let the sauce simmer for 20 minutes, stirring occasionally. Add the basil, fresh oregano, and garlic; stir and set aside.

Bring a large pan of water to a boil with 1 tablespoon salt, add the pasta, and cook for 10 to 12 minutes, or according to the package instructions, until al dente. Drain and add to the tomato sauce along with one-third of the Parmesan and one-third of the Cheddar. Stir and then transfer to a shallow ovenproof dish, roughly 12-inches/30-cm square. Dot the feta on top, sprinkle over the remaining Parmesan and Cheddar, and place under the broiler for 8 to 15 minutes (oven broilers tend to vary a lot), until the cheese melts and the top layer of pasta dries out and turns crisp.

Allow to cool for 5 minutes before serving with a final drizzle of oil.

CORN SLAW

SERVES SIX

Most sweet things will benefit from a bit of smoke here and there. For this you can set up your kitchen with some seriously geeky and expensive kit; you can smoke casually in a wok or a saucepan (see Smoked Beets with Yogurt and Caramelized Macadamias on page 173), or you can use my preferred method and just cook whatever it is you are smoking on a hot ridged grill pan, with a bit of oil. Corn on the cob is ideal this way because the kernels are protected on one side so they don't dry out.

This slaw was originally made to go with my Southern fried chicken, but it is also a welcome addition alongside anything cooked on the grill, under the broiler, or roasted in the oven.

7 tbsp/100 ml white wine vinegar
¼ white cabbage, shredded (4¼ cups/300 g)
3 small carrots, peeled and cut into fine strips (1½ cups/175 g)
1 medium red onion, thinly sliced (scant 1½ cups/140 g)
4 ears corn (1⅓ lb/600 g), lightly brushed with olive oil
2 red chiles, finely chopped
1⅓ cups/20 g cilantro leaves
⅔ cup/20 g mint leaves
olive oil
salt and black pepper

Dressing
3½ tbsp/50 g mayonnaise
2 tsp Dijon mustard
1½ tsp sunflower oil
1 tbsp lemon juice
1 clove garlic, crushed

Place the vinegar and a scant 1 cup/200 ml water in a small saucepan along with 1 tablespoon salt. Bring to a boil and then remove from the heat. Place the cabbage and carrots in a bowl and pour in two-thirds of the salty liquid. In a separate bowl, pour the remaining liquid over the onion and set both bowls aside for 20 minutes. Rinse the vegetables and onion well, pat dry, place together in a large bowl, and set aside.

Place a ridged grill pan over high heat, and when it starts to smoke, lay the corn on it. Grill for 10 to 12 minutes, turning so that all sides get some color (this will create quite a lot of smoke, so put the exhaust fan on, if you have one). Remove from the heat and, when cool enough to handle, use a large knife to shave off the corn in clumps and add to the salad bowl.

Whisk together all the dressing ingredients, pour over the salad, and stir gently. Add the chile, cilantro, and mint, along with a grind of black pepper, give everything another gentle stir, and serve.

See picture on the following right-hand page

BUTTERNUT TATAKI AND UDON NOODLE SALAD

SERVES FOUR

½ cup/120 ml rice vinegar
1½ tbsp superfine sugar
1⅓-inch/3.5-cm piece fresh ginger, (about 1 oz/25 g) peeled and cut into very fine matchsticks
1 small butternut squash, peeled, seeded, and cut into 2 by ¼ by ¼-inch/ 5 cm by 5 mm by 5-mm batons (1¼ lb/600 g)
2½ tbsp peanut oil
5½ oz/160 g dried udon noodles
7 radishes, thinly sliced (⅔ cup/75 g)
1¾ oz/50 g snow peas (about 15), cut into very fine matchsticks
3 baby or Lebanese cucumbers, unpeeled and cut into very fine strips (10½ oz/300 g)
2 mild red chiles, cut into long, thin strips
⅔ oz/20 g baby shiso leaves, or 5 normal shiso leaves, chopped, or any baby cress
½ tsp sesame oil
1½ tsp black sesame seeds (or white, if unavailable)
⅔ cup/10 g cilantro leaves
salt

Somewhere between a pickle and a salad—there's a lot of vinegar and sugar here—this concoction is one of my all-time favorites. Thanks to the grilling, the butternut squash tastes both fresh and smoky at the same time and hence makes this dish feel like a complete and complex meal in a bowl. You can add crushed salted cashew nuts here, if you like, to enrich this even further.

Gently heat the vinegar, sugar, ginger, and ¾ teaspoon salt in a small saucepan, stirring so that the sugar dissolves. Remove from the heat and set aside.

Place a ridged grill pan over high heat and wait until it is red hot. Toss the butternut in the peanut oil and sear in batches for 3 minutes, turning once so that both sides get charred. You might need to do this in four batches, as you don't want to crowd the pan. Transfer the batons to a large bowl, pour over half the ginger dressing, and set aside to cool, stirring gently once or twice.

Bring a large pan of water to a boil. Add the noodles and cook for 6 to 7 minutes, or according to the package instructions, until al dente. Drain, refresh under cold water, and set aside to dry.

Add the noodles to the butternut, followed by the radishes, snow peas, cucumbers, chiles, shiso, sesame oil, sesame seeds, and cilantro. Stir gently, transfer to a serving plate, spoon the remaining dressing over the top, and serve.

See picture on preceding left-hand page

ZUCCHINI "BABA GHANOUSH"

SERVES FOUR
as a starter or as part of a mezze selection

5 large zucchini (about 2¾ lb / 1.2 kg)
⅓ cup / 80 g goat's milk yogurt
2 tbsp / 15 g coarsely grated Roquefort
1 egg, lightly beaten
1 tbsp / 15 g unsalted butter
2½ tbsp / 20 g pine nuts
½ tsp Urfa chile flakes, or a pinch of regular chile flakes
1 tsp lemon juice
1 clove garlic, crushed
½ tsp za'atar, to finish
salt and black pepper

This looks rather like a volcanic eruption, in the best possible sense. There is none of the tahini you'd associate with baba ghanoush: it's the garlic, smokiness, and texture of the mashed zucchini flesh that calls its purple friend to mind. I don't know why we don't broil zucchini more. Getting some smokiness into the naturally bland flesh is a real revelation. Served with bread, this is a delicate and delightful way to whet the appetite at the beginning of a meal.

Preheat the broiler. Place the zucchini on a baking sheet lined with parchment paper and broil for about 45 minutes, turning once or twice during the cooking, until the skin crisps and browns nicely. Remove from the oven and, once cool enough to handle, peel off the zucchini skin, discard it, and set the flesh aside in a colander to drain; you can also scoop out the flesh with a spoon. The zucchini can be served warm or at room temperature.

Put the yogurt in a small saucepan with the Roquefort and egg. Heat very gently for about 3 minutes, stirring often. You want the yogurt to heat through but not quite reach the simmering point. Set aside and keep warm.

Melt the butter in a small sauté pan with the pine nuts over low heat and cook, stirring often, for 3 to 4 minutes, until the nuts turn golden brown. Stir in the chile flakes and lemon juice and set aside.

To serve, put the zucchini in a bowl and add the garlic, a scant ½ teaspoon salt, and a good grind of black pepper. Gently mash everything together with a fork and then spread the mixture out on a large serving platter. Spoon the warm yogurt sauce on top, followed by a drizzle of the warm chile butter and the pine nuts. Finish with a sprinkle of za'atar and serve at once.

See picture on the following pages

SERVES FOUR

CORN ON THE COB WITH MISO MAYONNAISE

4 ears corn (1⅓ lb/600 g), husks removed and cut into 2-inch/5-cm segments
3 tbsp olive oil
2 tbsp finely chopped flat-leaf parsley
salt

Mayonnaise
1 egg yolk
1 tbsp Dijon mustard
3 cloves garlic, crushed
1½ tsp cider vinegar
2 tbsp tamarind paste
1 cup/250 ml sunflower oil
scant 5 tbsp/80 g white miso paste (not a sweet variety)
1 green chile, seeded and finely chopped

Fresh corn on the cob, or just shaved off the cob, is a delicacy that isn't celebrated enough—the awful sweet stuff that comes out of a can has a lot to answer for—but there isn't really anything like good fresh corn, lightly grilled or simmered, paired with butter, oil, or something else that's rich and savory. Here I smother it with sharp miso mayo, but a mixture of mayonnaise with feta or Parmesan will also taste great. The mayonnaise will make more than you need, but it will keep in the fridge for up to a week in a sealed container. Use it with grilled oily fish or to dress root vegetables such as celery root or potato.

First make the mayonnaise. Place the egg yolk, mustard, garlic, vinegar, and tamarind in the bowl of a small food processor. Turn it on and slowly start adding the sunflower oil, continually pouring in a light stream until half the oil is incorporated. With the machine still running, add the miso and continue with the last of the oil until the mayonnaise is thick. Add the chile and mix until combined.

Bring a large pan of water to a boil. Add the corn and blanch for 3 minutes. Drain, pat dry, and mix with the olive oil and ¼ teaspoon salt. Place a ridged grill pan over very high heat. When it starts to smoke, add the corn and grill, turning often so that all sides get colored, for about 8 minutes. As soon as the corn comes off the grill pan, brush a layer of the mayonnaise all over the ear, so that it gets a light glaze, about 2 tablespoons for all the corn. Sprinkle with the parsley and serve right away, dipping the corn into the remaining mayonnaise as you go, or spreading on more with a knife.

MARROW WITH TOMATO AND FETA

SERVES FOUR
generously

It's easy to dismiss marrow squashes (aka marrow vegetables) as the plain Jane cousins to sweeter, finer zucchini, but their mild flavor and meatiness make a great blank canvas on which to load other, more intense flavors. I like adding them to spicy curries or filling them with rich meat or cheese stuffings. When buying this summer squash, choose the smallest you can find: oversize marrows tend to taste bitter and have watery flesh; a small one should be firm and heavy for its size. Not everyone likes fennel seeds, so omit them if you prefer.

1 large marrow squash, skin on, cut crosswise into slices ⅔-inch/1.5-cm thick (1¾ lb/810 g)
5 cloves garlic
7 tbsp/100 ml olive oil, plus extra to finish
2 tsp fennel seeds
2¼ cups/400 g peeled and chopped tomatoes (canned are fine)
½ tsp superfine sugar
⅓ cup/50 g crumbled feta
⅓ cup/10 g basil leaves, coarsely shredded
salt and black pepper

Place each marrow disk flat on a chopping board and use a small serrated knife to cut out and discard the central seeds and fiber. Place the disks in a large bowl. Crush 2 of the garlic cloves and add them to the bowl along with 6 tablespoons/85 ml of the olive oil, ¼ teaspoon salt, and some black pepper. Mix well and set aside for 30 minutes.

Slice the remaining 3 garlic cloves and place them in a small sauté pan with the fennel seeds and 2 teaspoons of the oil. Place over medium heat and cook for 2 minutes. Add the tomatoes before the garlic starts to brown, along with the sugar, ¼ teaspoon salt, and some black pepper. Bring the sauce to a simmer and cook for about 7 minutes, until thick. Transfer to the bowl of a small food processor and blitz until silky smooth.

Put a large sauté pan over medium-high heat and add the remaining 1 teaspoon olive oil. Fry the marrow in batches for about 8 minutes each, turning once, until golden. While still warm, spread the slices out in a single layer on a large serving dish, pour the tomato sauce over the top, and leave to cool. Just before serving, sprinkle over the feta, followed by the basil and a final drizzle of olive oil. Serve at once.

ROASTED

SERVES FOUR

EGGPLANT WITH BLACK GARLIC

3 medium eggplants, sliced crosswise into rounds ⅔-inch/1.5-cm thick (2 lb/900 g)
scant 1 cup/200 ml olive oil
8 large or 16 small cloves black garlic (1¼ oz/35 g)
1 cup/200 g Greek yogurt
1½ tsp lemon juice
7 large cloves garlic, thinly sliced (1 oz/30 g)
3 red chiles, cut on the diagonal into slices ⅛-inch/3-mm thick
⅓ cup/5 g dill leaves
2½ tbsp/5 g basil leaves
2½ tbsp/5 g tarragon leaves
salt and black pepper

Slices of roasted eggplant have been through many incarnations and been a constant feature on the Ottolenghi menu since we first set up shop in 2002. Every now and then a new kid on the block will appear to shake up the old-timers, and our latest bright young thing is this black garlic sauce. I'd love black garlic to be more widely available: its taste is reminiscent of molasses and tamarind, and it gives an unexpected depth of flavor to dishes. You can simply slice a few thin slivers and add these to crunchy salads or creamy risottos—it's mellow enough not to dominate—or use it in sauces, dips, and purées, as here, to enliven (and challenge the rank of) old favorites.

Preheat the oven to 475°F/250°C.

Place the eggplant rounds in a large bowl with ¼ cup/60 ml of the olive oil, ½ teaspoon salt, and a good grind of black pepper. Mix well and spread out on 2 large baking sheets lined with parchment paper. Roast in the oven for about 30 minutes, until golden brown and completely soft. Remove from the oven and set aside to cool.

Place the black garlic cloves in the bowl of a small food processor with scant ½ teaspoon salt, 2 tablespoons of the oil, 2 tablespoons of the yogurt, and the lemon juice. Blitz for 1 minute to form a rough paste, and then transfer to a bowl. Stir in the remaining yogurt and keep in the fridge until needed.

Heat the remaining scant ½ cup/110 ml oil in a small saucepan over high heat. Add the garlic and chile slices, turn down the heat to medium, and fry for about 5 minutes, stirring from time to time, until the garlic is golden brown and the chile is crispy. Use a slotted spoon to transfer the garlic and chile to a paper towel–lined plate.

Arrange the eggplant slices, overlapping, on a platter. Take a large slotted spoon, spoon out some yogurt sauce, and, holding it over the eggplant, bash the handle onto the palm of your free hand to seriously shake the spoon and cause the sauce to escape through the holes and onto the eggplant. Sprinkle the chile and garlic over the top and finish with the herbs.

SQUASH WITH CARDAMOM AND NIGELLA SEEDS

SERVES FOUR

1½ tbsp/20 g unsalted butter
1 tbsp olive oil
1 large red onion, halved and thinly sliced (1½ cups/170 g)
1 large butternut squash, peeled, seeded, and cut into 1¼-inch/3-cm chunks (2¾ lb/1 kg)
3½ tbsp/30 g pumpkin seeds
1¼ tsp nigella seeds
½ tsp ground cumin
½ tsp ground coriander
¼ tsp ground turmeric
4 cardamom pods, lightly crushed
1 large cinnamon stick
1 green chile, halved lengthwise
1 tbsp superfine sugar
scant 1 cup/200 ml vegetable stock
¾ cup/150 g Greek yogurt
1 tbsp cilantro, chopped
salt

Getting the number of roasted squash recipes down to just two for this chapter involved much debate and much eating. The squash-off, judged in our test kitchen with discriminating web-store colleagues Maria and Saga, saw this uncommon pairing of the sweet squash with the clear and citrus note of the cardamom win out. Serve it with Lemon and Curry Leaf Rice (page 45) for a striking vegetarian main course.

Preheat the oven to 425°F/220°C.

Place the butter and oil in a large sauté pan over medium heat. Add the onion and fry for about 8 minutes, until soft. Add the squash, increase the heat to medium-high, and cook for a further 10 minutes, stirring occasionally, until it starts to color. Remove from the heat and add the pumpkin seeds, 1 teaspoon of the nigella seeds, the cumin, coriander, turmeric, cardamom, cinnamon, chile, sugar, and ¾ teaspoon salt. Mix well and transfer to a baking sheet large enough to hold the vegetables in a single but snug layer, about 10 by 12-inches/25 by 30-cm. Pour the stock over the squash and roast for 30 minutes, until the squash is tender. Set aside for about 10 minutes: the liquid in the pan will continue to be absorbed.

Serve warm, with the yogurt spooned on top or on the side, along with a sprinkling of the cilantro and the remaining ¼ teaspoon nigella seeds.

HONEY-ROASTED CARROTS WITH TAHINI YOGURT

SERVES FOUR

The inspiration for this was Sarah's "nan" (grandmother), Dulcie, in Tasmania, who always used to add some honey to the pan before roasting her carrots. I'm not sure what Dulcie would have thought about a tahini yogurt sauce served alongside, but the sweetness of the carrots certainly welcomes it. Make this extra vibrant by using different-colored carrots and serve alongside the Fava Bean Spread with Roasted Garlic Ricotta (page 222) and Eggplant Kuku (page 241).

Preheat the oven to 425°F/220°C.

Place all the ingredients for the tahini sauce in a bowl with a pinch of salt. Whisk together and set aside.

Place the honey, oil, coriander and cumin seeds, and thyme in a large bowl with 1 teaspoon salt and a good grind of black pepper. Add the carrots and mix well until coated, then spread them out on a large baking sheet and roast in the oven for 40 minutes, stirring gently once or twice, until cooked through and glazed.

Transfer the carrots to a large serving platter or individual plates. Serve warm or at room temperature, with a spoonful of sauce on top, scattered with the cilantro.

---

scant 3 tbsp/60 g honey
2 tbsp olive oil
1 tbsp coriander seeds, toasted and lightly crushed
1½ tsp cumin seeds, toasted and lightly crushed
3 thyme sprigs
12 large carrots, peeled and cut into ¾ by 2½-inch 2 by 6-cm batons (3 lb/1.3 kg)
1½ tbsp cilantro leaves, coarsely chopped
salt and black pepper

Tahini yogurt sauce
scant 3 tbsp/40 g tahini paste
⅔ cup/130 g Greek yogurt
2 tbsp lemon juice
1 clove garlic, crushed
salt

SERVES FOUR
as a starter

RED ONIONS WITH WALNUT SALSA

4 medium red onions
 (1⅓ lb/600 g)
1½ tbsp olive oil
1 cup/20 g arugula
½ cup/15 g small flat-leaf parsley leaves
2 oz/60 g soft goat cheese, broken into ¾-inch/2-cm chunks
salt and black pepper

Salsa
⅔ cup/65 g walnuts, coarsely chopped
1 red chile, seeded and finely chopped
1 clove garlic, crushed
3 tbsp red wine vinegar
1 tbsp olive oil
salt

When Tara moved to Clapham and was in the process of making friends, she had some moms over for lunch one day when their children were at school. The friendships endure to this day, and Tara's pretty sure that it was the secret handover of this roasted onion recipe that sealed the deal. The natural sweetness of red onions is accentuated when they are grilled or roasted and gives them enough individual character to take center stage. They also work well in a sandwich or alongside other dishes as a mezze. A few pomegranate seeds sprinkled on top of each portion would add special vibrancy and a nice sweet crunch.

Preheat the oven to 425°F/220°C.

Peel the onions and remove the tops and tails. Cut each crosswise into 3 slices, about ¾-inch/2-cm thick, and place on a baking sheet. Brush the slices with the olive oil, sprinkle with ¼ teaspoon salt and some black pepper, and roast in the oven for about 40 minutes, until the onions are cooked and golden brown on top. If they haven't taken on much color, place under a hot broiler for a few minutes. Set aside to cool slightly.

While the onions are cooking, put all of the salsa ingredients in a small bowl, add ¼ teaspoon salt, stir, and set aside.

To serve, put the arugula and parsley in a large bowl. Add the warm onions, the cheese, and half the salsa and toss carefully so the onions don't fall apart. Divide among shallow plates, spoon the remaining salsa over the top, and serve.

SERVES FOUR

CAULIFLOWER, GRAPE, AND CHEDDAR SALAD

1 large cauliflower, broken into bite-size florets (2 lb/900 g)
6 tbsp/90 ml canola oil
2 tbsp sherry vinegar
1 tsp Dijon mustard
½ tsp honey
scant ¼ cup/30 g raisins
scant ⅓ cup/40 g hazelnuts, toasted and roughly crushed
⅔ cup/100 g red grapes, halved and seeded
scant 3 oz/80 g creamy, mature Cheddar, coarsely crumbled
⅔ cup/20 g flat-leaf parsley leaves, coarsely chopped
salt and black pepper

This dish—a fantastic autumnal starter—was inspired by one I had at The NoMad, a great restaurant in New York run by the brilliant Daniel Humm of Eleven Madison Park. Sami, who has eaten a lot of good meals and is not a man prone to hyperbole, tweeted after a recent meal at The NoMad that he'd just had "one of the best meals of my life."

Preheat the oven to 425°F/220°C.

Toss the cauliflower florets with half the oil, ½ teaspoon salt, and some black pepper. Spread out on a baking sheet and roast for 20 to 25 minutes, stirring once or twice, until golden brown. Remove from the oven and set aside to cool.

To make the dressing, whisk together the remaining 3 tablespoons oil with the vinegar, mustard, honey, and ¼ teaspoon salt. Add the raisins and let them marinate for at least 10 minutes.

Just before serving, transfer the cauliflower to a large bowl and add the hazelnuts, grapes, Cheddar, and parsley. Pour the raisins and dressing over the top, toss together, transfer to a large platter, and serve.

EGGPLANTS WITH CRUSHED CHICKPEAS AND HERB YOGURT

SERVES FOUR
as a starter

Every single time I try an old recipe, I want to change it. I have no idea why that is; all I know is that what tasted perfect two years ago seems "slightly unbalanced" this year, or "too savory," "missing an oomph," "a little stodgy," or "a bit predictable." This is why recipes evolve. This recipe had a slow-cooked red pepper and tomato sauce with vinegar and smoky paprika, instead of herb yogurt, spooned over the eggplants and chickpeas. I felt I needed to freshen things up a little, but you could definitely reinstate the old red sauce for a vegan alternative: simply sauté some chopped onion, garlic, and red pepper in plenty of olive oil for a good 30 minutes; add canned tomatoes and cook slowly for another hour, adding some sherry vinegar and smoked paprika toward the end. Leave to cool before using.

The chickpeas should be very soft here. If cooking with dried chickpeas, you'll need to start with ½ cup/100 g to yield the 1½ cups/240 g of cooked, and make sure you boil them to the stage when they just start to fall apart. If using canned, cook them in their liquid, plus some extra water, for about 30 minutes.

When roasting eggplants (and not just for this recipe), I recommend placing a tray with water at the bottom of the oven to give out steam and prevent the eggplants from drying out.

---

3 large eggplants, cut crosswise into slices ¾-inch/2-cm thick (2¾ lb/1.2 kg)
½ cup/120 ml olive oil
1½ cups/240 g soft cooked chickpeas (see headnote), plus some of their cooking liquid
1½ tsp cumin seeds, toasted and lightly crushed
1 small lemon, rind, pith, and seeds removed, flesh coarsely chopped (1¼ oz/35 g)
½ cup/100 g Greek yogurt
⅓ cup/10 g mint, coarsely chopped
½ cup/15 g flat-leaf parsley, coarsely chopped
salt and black pepper

Preheat the oven to 475°F/250°C.

Place the eggplants in a large bowl with ¼ cup/60 ml of the oil, ¾ teaspoon salt, and a good grind of black pepper. Mix well, then spread out in a single layer on 1 or 2 baking sheets lined with parchment paper and roast in the oven for about 40 minutes, until golden brown and cooked through. Remove and set aside to cool.

Meanwhile, put the chickpeas in a bowl along with the cumin seeds, lemon flesh, 3 tablespoons of the oil, 2 tablespoons of the cooking liquid, ½ teaspoon salt, and a good grind of black pepper. Mash roughly using a fork or potato masher, adding a bit more of the cooking liquid if needed to get a thick, spreadable paste.

Place the yogurt in the bowl of a small food processor along with the remaining 1 tablespoon olive oil, 2 tablespoons water, the herbs, ¼ teaspoon salt, and some black pepper. Blitz until well combined. You need to be able to drizzle the yogurt, so add a tablespoon or two of water or oil if you need to.

To arrange, spread the eggplant slices out on a platter or individual plates. Spoon the crushed chickpeas on top, followed by a drizzle of the yogurt, and serve.

CARROT AND MUNG BEAN SALAD

SERVES FOUR

Mung beans are the ABBA of the food world: hearty and healthy but intrinsically bland and forever stuck in the 1970s. I'll leave ABBA fans to fight the band's corner, but the reputation of mung beans I can help to redress. Used right, mung beans soak up loads of flavor, pack a real punch, and just taste fantastic. To keep this dairy-free, omit the feta.

⅔ cup / 140 g dried green mung beans
4 tbsp / 60ml olive oil, plus extra to finish
1 tsp cumin seeds
1 tsp caraway seeds
1 tsp fennel seeds
2 cloves garlic, crushed
2 tbsp white wine vinegar
½ tsp chile flakes
3 large carrots, peeled and cut into 2 by ⅜-inch / 5 by 1-cm batons (11 oz / 320 g)
½ tsp superfine sugar
1⅓ cups / 20 g cilantro leaves, chopped
grated zest of 1 lemon
4½ oz / 140 g feta, broken into ¾-inch / 2-cm chunks
salt

Preheat the oven to 425°F/220°C.

Bring a saucepan of water to a boil, add the mung beans, and simmer for 20 to 25 minutes, until the beans are cooked but still retain a bite. Drain, shake well, and transfer to a large bowl. About 3 minutes before the beans are cooked, heat 2 tablespoons of the olive oil in a small sauté pan over medium heat and add the cumin, caraway, and fennel seeds. Cook, stirring often, for about 3 minutes, until the seeds start to pop. Pour the hot oil and seeds over the hot beans, along with the garlic, vinegar, chile flakes, and ½ teaspoon salt. Set aside to cool.

While the beans are cooking, mix the carrots in a bowl with about ⅔ cup / 150 ml water, the remaining 2 tablespoons oil, the sugar, and ½ teaspoon salt. Pour into an 8 by 12-inch / 20 by 30-cm baking dish and roast in the oven for 25 to 30 minutes untill all the water has evaporated and the carrots are nicely roasted and slightly caramelized. Remove from the oven and add the carrots to the mung beans along with the cilantro and stir gently. Transfer to a large platter, sprinkle the lemon zest over the top, dot with the feta, finish with a final drizzle of oil, and serve.

ROASTED BRUSSELS SPROUTS WITH POMELO AND STAR ANISE

SERVES FOUR

½ cup/100 g superfine sugar
2 cinnamon sticks
5 star anise pods
3 tbsp lemon juice
1 pomelo (2 lb/900 g in total; 2 cups/300 g after peeling and segmenting)
1⅓ lb/600 g brussels sprouts, trimmed
9 oz/250 g shallots, peeled
5 tbsp/75 ml olive oil
⅔ cup/10 g cilantro leaves
salt and black pepper

Why anyone ever thought that boiling brussels sprouts was a good idea when there is the option of roasting them is one of life's great mysteries. For those who have tried the oven version, there is no turning back. All sprout-doubters, I urge you to give them one more chance: like the brussels, you'll never be bitter again. If you can't get pomelo (see more in the Pomelo Salad headnote on page 19), use grapefruit segments but not as much lemon juice. Don't throw out the leftover sugar syrup: you can add it to fruit salads.

Place the sugar, 7 tbsp/100 ml water, the cinnamon, and star anise in a small saucepan and bring to a light simmer. Cook for 1 minute, stirring until the sugar dissolves, then remove from the heat, add 1 tablespoon of the lemon juice, and set aside to cool.

Peel the thick skin off the pomelo and discard. Divide into segments, release the flesh from the membrane, then break the flesh into bite-size pieces and put in a shallow bowl, taking care to remove all the bitter white membrane. Once the syrup has cooled a little, pour it over the pomelo. Leave to marinate for at least 1 hour, stirring occasionally.

Preheat the oven to 425°F/220°C.

Bring a large pan of salted water to a boil, add the sprouts and shallots, and blanch for 2 minutes. Drain, refresh under cold water, and pat dry. Cut the sprouts in two, lengthwise, and halve or quarter the shallots (so that they are similar in size to the sprouts). Place everything in a bowl with 3 tablespoons of the oil, ½ teaspoon salt, and some black pepper. Spread out on a baking sheet and roast in the oven for about 20 minutes, until the sprouts are golden brown but still retain a bite. Set aside to cool.

Before assembling the salad, remove and discard the cinnamon and star anise from the bowl. Drain the pomelo, reserving the juices. Just before serving, put the shallots, sprouts, pomelo, and cilantro in a large bowl. Add the remaining 2 tablespoons oil, the remaining 2 tablespoons lemon juice, 1 tablespoon of the pomelo marinade juices, and ¼ teaspoon salt. Gently mix, then check the seasoning—you might need to add another tablespoon of the marinade—and serve.

SMOKED BEETS WITH YOGURT AND CARAMELIZED MACADAMIAS

SERVES FOUR

With plain beets already divisive as an ingredient, a debating society will need to be set up to discuss the smoked version. Either way, constructing your own smoker requires no more than a big wok or pan for which you have a lid and a roll of aluminum foil. A timer is essential (as the flavor becomes too intense if smoked for too long); an exhaust fan is recommended. This is a stunner of a salad—both in flavor and looks—and a fantastic way to open a fancy meal.

1⅓ cups/250 g long-grain rice
shaved rind of 1 lemon
5 thyme sprigs
12 medium beets, skin on (2¾ lb/1.2 kg)
1 tsp maple syrup
2 tbsp olive oil, plus extra to finish
⅓ cup/50 g macadamia nuts
scant 3 tbsp/35 g superfine sugar
¾ cup/150 g Greek yogurt
½ tsp Aleppo chile flakes, or just a pinch if using other very hot chile flakes
⅓ cup/5 g cilantro leaves
salt and black pepper

Preheat the oven to 520°F/270°C.

Line a large sauté pan or wok with two large sheets of aluminum foil, with the edges generously overhanging the sides of the pan. Add the rice, lemon rind, and thyme and stir in 2 tablespoons water. Sit the beets on top of the rice and seal the pan with a large lid. Draw up the foil and fold it back over the lid to completely seal the lid in the foil; gaps will hamper the smoking process. Place over very high heat on the stove, and, once you see a little bit of smoke coming through, after 3 or 4 minutes, leave to smoke for exactly 8 minutes. Remove from the heat.

Discard the rice, lemon rind, and thyme, transfer the beets to a baking pan, and roast for a further 45 to 50 minutes in the oven, until a knife inserted into a beet goes in easily. Set aside to cool and then peel the charred skin off the beets. Cut the beets into slices ¹⁄₁₆-inch/2-mm thick and place in a large bowl with the maple syrup, 1 tablespoon of the olive oil, ½ teaspoon salt, and some black pepper. Mix together and set aside.

Lower the oven temperature to 325°F/160°C.

To caramelize the nuts, place them in a small roasting pan and roast for 15 minutes. Remove from the oven. Place the sugar in a small saucepan and cook over gentle heat. Don't stir as the sugar melts and starts to caramelize and turns golden. Carefully add the nuts, stir gently until they are coated, then pour them out onto a parchment-lined baking sheet to cool. Chop the nuts and set aside. Mix the yogurt with the remaining 1 tablespoon olive oil and set aside.

To serve, spread out the beet slices on a large platter, overlapping slightly. Drizzle the yogurt over the beets, then sprinkle with the nuts. Finish with the chile flakes, cilantro, and a final drizzle of olive oil.

SWEET POTATOES WITH ORANGE BITTERS

SERVES FOUR

1½ cups / 350 ml freshly squeezed orange juice (the juice of 4 to 5 oranges)
⅓ cup / 80 g brown sugar
¼ cup / 60 ml red wine vinegar
¼ cup / 60 ml Angostura bitters
1½ tbsp olive oil
4 to 5 sweet potatoes, unpeeled, halved crosswise, each half cut into 1-inch- / 2.5-cm wide wedges (3⅓ lb / 1.5 kg)
2 red chiles, slit open along the center
3 sage sprigs (½ oz / 15 g)
10 thyme sprigs (⅓ oz / 10 g)
2 heads garlic, unpeeled and halved horizontally
3 oz / 90 g chèvre (goat cheese) log, broken into pieces
salt

One of my greatest idols is Ruth Reichl, a clever writer who delightfully manages to approach food with just the right balance of weightiness and sense of humor, the latter often a rare commodity among "serious" authors. I love Reichl's recipes, I love her storytelling, and I always benefit from her vast knowledge. This recipe—a rhapsody for sweet, bitter, and salty—is based on one of hers, published in Gourmet Today, *a selection from the sadly defunct* Gourmet *magazine, which Reichl edited for many years.*

Preheat the oven to 425°F / 220°C.

Place the orange juice in a saucepan with the sugar and vinegar. Bring to a boil over high heat, then turn down the heat to medium-high and simmer fairly rapidly for about 20 minutes, until the liquid has thickened and reduced to a scant 1 cup / 200 ml (about the amount in a large glass of wine). Add the bitters, olive oil, and 1½ teaspoons salt.

Place the potatoes in a large bowl, add the chiles, sage, thyme, and garlic, and then pour in the reduced sauce. Toss well so that everything is coated and then spread the mixture out in a single layer on a baking sheet on which it fits snugly, about 12 by 16-inches / 30 by 40-cm.

Place in the oven and roast for 50 to 60 minutes, turning and basting the potatoes every 15 minutes or so. They need to remain coated in the liquid in order to caramelize, so add more orange juice if the pan is drying out. At the end, the potatoes should be dark and sticky. Remove from the oven and leave to cool slightly before arranging on a platter and dotting with the goat cheese. Serve warm or at room temperature.

CURRY-ROASTED ROOT VEGETABLES WITH LIME LEAVES AND JUICE

SERVES FOUR

Supermarkets are beginning to stock fresh curry leaves, which is very good news. The flavor they impart in a dish is worlds apart from the dried leaves. For the curry powder, I tend to use the Rajah or East End packages of mild Madras curry, but if you want an extra kick, the ante is there to be upped. Once you've stocked your freezer with plenty of lime and curry leaves—both freeze very well—this simple and quick dish can easily become a staple. All you need is some freshly steamed rice to serve alongside.

Preheat the oven to 475°F/240°C.

Place the carrots, parsnips, and rutabaga in a large roasting pan, about 12 by 16-inches/30 by 40-cm. Add the olive oil, half the lime juice, the curry powder, 1¼ teaspoons salt, and a good grind of black pepper. Mix well and place in the oven to roast for 30 minutes, turning the vegetables once or twice during the cooking. Add the lime leaves, curry leaves, and green onions and roast for a further 10 minutes. The vegetables should have taken on a nice golden brown color and the green onions should have softened. Remove the vegetables from the oven, pour the remaining lime juice over the top, sprinkle with the cilantro, and serve warm or at room temperature.

3 large carrots, peeled and cut into 2½ by ¾-inch/ 6 by 2-cm batons (12 oz/350 g)
2 large parsnips, peeled and cut into 2½ by ¾-inch/ 6 by 2-cm batons (14 oz/400 g)
1 small rutabaga, peeled and cut into 2½ by ¾-inch/6 by 2-cm batons (14 oz/400 g)
¼ cup/60 ml olive oil
3 tbsp lime juice
2 tsp curry powder
6 fresh or frozen Kaffir lime leaves, very finely shredded
2 stems fresh curry leaves (about 30 leaves), kept on the stem
6 green onions, white and green parts, cut crosswise into 2½-inch/6-cm segments (3 oz/85 g)
3 tbsp chopped cilantro
salt and black pepper

SERVES FOUR

BEET AND RHUBARB SALAD

9 medium beets of various kinds or, if you can't get them, one type is fine (1¾ lb/800 g) 10½ oz/ 300 g trimmed rhubarb (about 7 stalks), cut on the diagonal into 1-inch/ 2.5-cm pieces

scant 2½ tbsp/30 g superfine sugar

2 tsp sherry vinegar

2 tsp pomegranate molasses

2 tbsp maple syrup

2 tbsp olive oil

½ tsp ground allspice

1 small red onion, thinly sliced (about ¾ cup/75 g)

⅔ cup/20 g flat-leaf parsley leaves

3½ oz/100 g creamy Gorgonzola or similar blue cheese, torn into small chunks

salt and black pepper

For someone who didn't grow up with rhubarb, this vegetable (or stalk?) is a bit of an oddity. I guess the same could be said of the artichoke, a thistle, but for me, eating a thick, greenish, reddish branch will always seem much weirder than scoffing a thorny flower. Each to his or her own, I say.

One of my sweetest rhubarb memories dates from the early years of Ottolenghi, when one of our sales assistants, the lovely Alexandra from Mexico, used to come down to the kitchen on her breaks with a cappuccino cup full of superfine sugar and a raw rhubarb stalk to dip in the sugar as dessert. Slightly unusual but, as I said, each to his or her own.

During the beet season, the different varieties offer a great opportunity to play with colors and subtlety of flavor. If you can get some golden, red, white, and candy beets, you can mix them up; otherwise, one variety is absolutely fine.

Preheat the oven to 425°F/220°C.

Wrap the beets individually in aluminum foil, place on a baking sheet, and roast in the oven for 40 to 70 minutes, depending on their size, until cooked through. Set aside to cool before peeling and cutting roughly into ¾-inch/2-cm dice.

Toss the rhubarb with the sugar, spread the pieces out on a small roasting pan lined with aluminum foil, and bake for about 12 minutes, until the pieces have softened without becoming mushy. Set aside to cool.

Place the vinegar, molasses, maple syrup, oil, and allspice in a bowl with ½ teaspoon salt and a good grind of black pepper. Add the onion and set aside for a few minutes to soften. Add the parsley and beets and stir well. Just before serving, add the Gorgonzola and rhubarb, along with its juices. Give everything a very gentle mix and serve at once.

SQUASH WITH CHILE YOGURT AND CILANTRO SAUCE

SERVES FOUR

Sweet chile sauce has been making its way into dressings and dipping sauces for a while, but the rise in demand for the hot savory Sriracha sauce—originating in eastern Thailand and made from sun-ripened chile peppers and garlic, ground into a smooth paste—points to an increasing demand for the hot stuff. Recent threats of shortages have created a small panic among those addicted to the stuff. Mixing Sriracha with Greek yogurt and drizzling it over a dish like this is a fast-track way to reach a sweet-sharp depth of flavor. The fresh herb paste brings in another layer of freshness, along with a visual "wow." This is perhaps the simplest recipe in the book and, if I were a betting man, destined to become a favorite.

1 large butternut squash (3 lb/1.4 kg)
1 tsp ground cinnamon
6 tbsp/90 ml olive oil
1¾ oz/50 g cilantro, leaves and stems (about 22 sprigs), plus extra leaves for garnish
1 small clove garlic, crushed
scant 2½ tbsp/20 g pumpkin seeds
1 cup/200 g Greek yogurt
1½ tsp Sriracha or another savory chile sauce
salt and black pepper

Preheat the oven to 425°F/220°C.

Cut the squash in half lengthwise, remove and discard the seeds, and then cut into wedges ¾-inch/2-cm wide and about 2¾-inches/7-cm long, leaving the skin on. Place in a large bowl with the cinnamon, 2 tablespoons of the olive oil, ¾ teaspoon salt, and a good grind of pepper. Mix well so that the squash is evenly coated. Place the squash, skin side down, on 2 baking sheets and roast for 35 to 40 minutes, until soft and starting to color on top. Remove from the oven and set aside to cool.

To make the herb paste, place the cilantro, garlic, the remaining 4 tablespoons oil, and a generous pinch of salt in the bowl of a small food processer, blitz to form a fine paste, and set aside.

Turn down the oven temperature to 350°F/180°C. Lay the pumpkin seeds on a baking sheet and roast in the oven for 6 to 8 minutes. The outer skin will pop open and the seeds will become light and crispy. Remove from the oven and allow to cool.

When you are ready to serve, swirl together the yogurt and Sriracha sauce. Lay the squash wedges on a platter and drizzle the spicy yogurt sauce and then the herb paste over the top (you can also swirl the yogurt sauce and herb paste together, if you like). Scatter the pumpkin seeds on top, followed by the extra cilantro leaves, and serve.

FRIED

SERVES FOUR

as a main course; more as a starter or snack

3 tbsp olive oil
6 banana shallots, or 12 regular shallots, finely chopped (about 2 cups/300 g)
1 tbsp white wine vinegar
5¼ cups/700 g frozen shelled green peas, thawed
⅔ cup/20 g mint leaves, finely shredded
1 clove garlic, crushed
4 eggs
¾ cup plus 1 tbsp/100 g all-purpose flour
2½ cups/150 g panko bread crumbs
sunflower oil, for frying
salt and black pepper

Sauce
1 tsp dried mint
½ cup/120 g sour cream
1 tbsp olive oil
salt and black pepper

PEA AND MINT CROQUETTES

For a while, we had a pretty wicked trio running the evening service at Ottolenghi in Islington. Tom, Sam, and Myles were notorious for working hard and playing hard—in so many senses—but unfortunately the whiteness of this page prevents me from disclosing any details. All three had two things in common: a cheeky, irresistible grin and an unusual passion for what they cooked. These croquettes, which sound more complicated than they actually are, are their creation and worth a little effort. They can be made well in advance and taken up to the stage where they are covered in panko bread crumbs and frozen. You can then partially defrost and fry them as you need. The recipe makes 16 generously sized patties, ample for four people. To feed more, or to serve as a snack or starter, make them into smaller croquettes, weighing about 1½ oz/40 g each.

To make the sauce, place all the ingredients in a bowl with ¼ teaspoon salt and a grind of black pepper. Mix well and refrigerate until needed.

Place the olive oil in a sauté pan over medium heat. Add the shallots and sauté for 15 to 20 minutes, stirring often, until soft. Add the vinegar, cook for 2 minutes, and then remove from the heat.

Place the peas in a food processor and briefly blitz. They need to break down without turning into a mushy paste. Transfer to a bowl and stir in the shallots, mint, garlic, 1 egg, ½ teaspoon salt, and plenty of black pepper. Line a tray that will fit in your freezer with parchment paper and shape the pea mixture into 16 patties (around 2 oz/60 g each), about 2¾-inches/7-cm across and ¾-inch/2-cm thick. Freeze for a couple of hours to firm up.

Place the remaining 3 eggs in a bowl and gently beat. Place the flour in a separate bowl and the bread crumbs in a third. Remove the croquettes from the freezer and, one at a time, roll them in the flour, dip them in the egg, then coat in the crumbs. You can then either return them to the freezer at this point or leave them at room temperature for about 1 hour, until partly thawed. Whatever you do, it's important, when it comes to frying, that the patties are not entirely frozen: you want them to cook through without burning the crust.

Preheat the oven to 425°F/220°C.

Pour the oil to a depth of 1-inch/2.5-cm into a sauté pan. Place over medium-high heat and leave for 5 minutes for the oil to get hot. Turn down the heat to medium and fry the croquettes in batches for about 4 minutes, turning once, until both sides are golden brown. Transfer to a baking sheet and place in the oven for 5 minutes to warm through. Serve at once, with the sauce spooned on top or served alongside.

Pictured on previous pages

POLENTA CHIPS WITH AVOCADO AND YOGURT

SERVES SIX TO EIGHT
as a snack

For all of its versatility, polenta is one of those ingredients that spends too much of its time at the back of the kitchen cupboard, on the "no one knows quite what to do with me" shelf. Quick-cook polenta puts an end to tennis-elbow accusations, so there really isn't any reason to keep it abandoned and disused. These chips aren't quick 'n' easy like many polenta dishes, but they are fun and worth a little effort. Still, if you are after a quicker result, stop after you have boiled the polenta, before it's time to spread it on a board, spoon it into a big bowl, and top with a soft-boiled egg and some pesto.

3¼ cups/750 ml vegetable stock
1 cup/160 g quick-cook polenta
3½ tbsp/10 g chopped chives
5 tbsp/30 g finely grated Parmesan
scant ⅔ cup/100 g coarse semolina
about 1¼ cups/300 ml sunflower oil, for frying
salt and white pepper

Avocado dipping sauce
2 small avocados, halved, pitted, and flesh scooped out (about 1 cup/180 g)
½ cup/100 g Greek yogurt
1½ tbsp lime juice
1 tsp grated lime zest
1 tsp hazelnut (or olive) oil
salt and black pepper

Place all the ingredients for the dipping sauce in the bowl of a small food processor, along with a scant ½ teaspoon salt and some freshly ground pepper. Blitz to form a smooth paste and set aside.

Pour the stock into a saucepan and bring to a boil over high heat. Add the polenta and cook for about 5 minutes, stirring constantly, until all the liquid has been absorbed and the mixture is thick. Add the chives and Parmesan, stir for another 30 seconds, and then transfer the mixture to 2 large cutting boards or trays, each measuring about 10 by 16-inches/25 by 40-cm. Use an offset spatula to spread out the polenta very thinly. Don't worry about the surface being slightly uneven: ideally the thickness should be 1/32 to 1/8-inch/1 to 3-mm. Leave to set for about 20 minutes and then use the offset spatula to remove the polenta from the board in odd pieces of roughly 2 by 2¾-inches/5 by 7-cm. Dip each piece in the semolina—turning so that both sides are covered—and set aside. If they are fragile and tending to break, sprinkle the pieces on both sides while on the board.

Pour the oil to a depth of ⅜-inch/1-cm into a large sauté pan and heat over medium-high heat. Fry the chips in batches for about 5 minutes each, turning them once so that both sides become golden brown; ideally the edges will crisp up and brown while the center remains soft to the touch and golden in places. Transfer to a plate lined with paper towels to drain and sprinkle with a little salt. Serve hot, with the dipping sauce on the side.

SEARED CHANTERELLES WITH BLACK GLUTINOUS RICE

SERVES FOUR

2½ tbsp olive oil, plus extra to finish
6 shallots, chopped (⅔ cup/100 g)
2 lemons, rind shaved in long strips from one, ½ tsp finely grated zest from the other, plus extra to finish
4 thyme sprigs
1 bay leaf
1 cup/200 g black glutinous rice, soaked overnight
1⅓ lb/600 g chanterelle mushrooms
1½ tsp truffle oil
1 tsp unsalted butter
2 tsp lemon juice
2 tbsp chopped tarragon
4 oz/120 g soft and mild goat cheese (optional)
salt and black pepper

I love all rice but I really, really love this rice. Striking to look at, it is, like other short-grain rice, nutty and chewy, soft and starchy. Each grain retains its integrity when cooked, so it's slightly al dente too. You can use the Italian Nerone rice if that's what you find but, for the real deal, seek out ketan hitam *rice from Asian stores or online. Black glutinous rice is a hugely popular rice in Southeast Asia, where it's cooked in coconut milk for pudding and served with diced mango or banana, or in a range of savory dishes. Remember to soak the rice overnight, or it will take a very long time to cook. Chanterelles, which aren't always easy to find, can easily be substituted with oyster mushrooms.*

Pour 1 tablespoon of the olive oil into a saucepan. Add the shallots, lemon rind, thyme, bay leaf, ½ teaspoon salt, and some black pepper and place over medium-low heat. Cook for 5 to 6 minutes, until the shallots are soft. Drain the black rice and add to the pan. Pour in 1⅔ cups/400 ml water, bring to a boil, turn down the heat to a gentle simmer, cover the pan, and cook for 35 to 40 minutes, stirring from time to time, until the rice is well cooked and has a starchy consistency. Remove the lemon, thyme, and bay leaf and keep the rice somewhere warm until serving.

Place the remaining 1½ tablespoon olive oil in a large sauté pan and add the mushrooms, ¼ teaspoon salt, and some black pepper. Sauté for about 5 minutes, stirring so that all sides get a bit of color. Remove from the heat and add the truffle oil, butter, grated lemon zest, lemon juice, and tarragon.

Spoon the black rice onto individual plates. Top with the mushrooms, followed by the goat cheese. Drizzle with a little olive oil and more grated lemon zest and serve.

MIXED VEGETABLES AND YOGURT WITH GREEN CHILE OIL

SERVES FOUR

This is a dish I picked up on a visit to Istanbul. I had it in a kebab restaurant, but for me it was actually the vegetables that were the highlight. Try to overlook the fact the vegetables are fried; the dish is still extremely fresh tasting thanks to the yogurt and all the herbs. Serve it with Fava (page 221) and Crushed Carrots with Harissa and Pistachios (page 230) as a perfectly balanced mezze trio, with some fresh bread to pile the stuff on.

Preheat the oven to 325°F/170°C.

Place the zucchini and eggplant in a colander and sprinkle with 1 teaspoon salt. Set aside for 1 hour, allowing some of the water to release, then drain.

Spread out the tomatoes on a baking sheet, sprinkle with ¼ teaspoon salt, and place in the oven for 40 minutes to dry out a little. Remove and set aside to cool.

To make the herb oil, place all the ingredients in the bowl of a small food processor with a pinch of salt and process to a smooth, thick sauce.

Pour the sunflower oil to a depth of 2-inches/5-cm into a saucepan and heat over medium-high heat. Once the oil is hot, turn down the heat to medium. Pat the zucchini and eggplant dry and deep-fry them and the red pepper in batches for 12 to 15 minutes for each. The eggplant might take a little longer than the other vegetables: you want it to be golden brown. Drain in a colander, sprinkle with salt, and set aside to cool.

Finally, in a bowl, stir together the yogurt, garlic, fresh and dried mint, lemon juice, and plenty of black pepper. Add the vegetables and tomatoes and stir very gently. Spoon the herb oil on top and serve.

3 large plum tomatoes, each cut into 6 wedges (10½ oz/300 g)
sunflower oil, for frying
2 medium zucchini, cut into ¾-inch/2-cm chunks (about 3 cups/400 g)
1 large eggplant, cut into ¾-inch/2-cm chunks (about 5 cups/450 g)
2 large red peppers, stalks and seeds removed, cut into ¾-inch/2-cm chunks (about 3½ cups/420 g)
¾ cup/150 g Greek yogurt
1 large clove garlic, crushed
1 tbsp shredded fresh mint
1½ tsp dried mint
1½ tsp lemon juice
salt and black pepper

Chile and herb oil
1 green chile, coarsely chopped
⅔ oz/20 g flat-leaf parsley
1 tbsp chopped mint
1 tsp ground cumin
¼ cup/60 ml olive oil
salt

SMOKY POLENTA FRIES

SERVES FOUR

1⅔ cups/375 ml vegetable stock
scant ½ cup/60 g quick-cook polenta
4 tsp/20 g unsalted butter
2 oz/60 g scamorza affumicata, coarsely grated
3 large plum tomatoes (12 oz/320 g)
2 tbsp olive oil
½ medium onion, thinly sliced (1 cup/100 g)
2 cloves garlic, crushed
⅛ tsp chile flakes
1 tsp tomato paste
¾ tsp superfine sugar
vegetable oil, for frying
6½ tbsp/50 g all-purpose flour
salt and black pepper

Smoky, crisp, and cheesy with a rich tomato sauce, this is my version of fries with ketchup, though possibly even more addictive. I use a smoked Italian cheese, scamorza affumicata, *to give these fries a deep flavor and a gorgeous melting texture, but you can happily substitute another cheese with substantial flavor, such as Italian provolone or apple wood–smoked Cheddar.*

Bring the stock to a boil in a small saucepan. Slowly add the polenta while stirring with a wooden spoon. Cook over low heat for 5 to 7 minutes, stirring all the time. Remove the pan from the heat and mix in the butter, cheese, ½ teaspoon salt, and a good grind of black pepper. Once the cheese and butter have both melted into the mix, transfer to a small, shallow tray, 8½-inches/22-cm wide and 1¼-inches/3-cm deep, lined with plastic wrap. Use a wet offset spatula to smooth out and level the polenta to an even layer about ⅔-inch/1.5-cm thick. Cover the surface with more plastic wrap so that a skin does not form, and leave to cool completely, before chilling for at least 30 minutes.

Meanwhile, make a tomato sauce. Place a large nonstick sauté pan over high heat and turn on the exhaust fan, if you have one. Once hot, put the tomatoes inside and leave over high heat for about 15 minutes, stirring occasionally. The tomato skins need to blacken well; don't be tempted to remove them from the heat too early. Transfer the hot tomatoes to a bowl and break them up with a spoon. When cool enough to handle, pick out the skins and discard.

Heat the olive oil in a small pan over medium heat, add the onion, and cook for 5 to 6 minutes. Add the garlic and cook for another 4 minutes before transferring the mixture to the tomatoes, along with the chile flakes, tomato paste, sugar, and ½ teaspoon salt. Use a handheld blender or a small food processor to blitz to a rough paste. Set aside until the sauce comes to room temperature.

Once the polenta is chilled and properly set, remove it from the tray and cut into fries roughly ⅔-inch/1.5-cm thick and 2½-inches/6-cm long. Pour the vegetable oil to a depth of ¾-inch/2-cm into a saucepan and heat over medium-high heat.

Toss the fries in the flour until well coated, shake off the excess, and carefully place in the hot oil. Fry for about 6 minutes, until golden brown, and transfer to paper towels to drain. Don't fry too many at a time; if the pan is too crowded, the temperature of the oil will drop and the fries won't crisp.

Serve hot, with the tomato sauce spooned on top or in a bowl alongside.

BUTTERMILK-CRUSTED OKRA WITH TOMATO AND BREAD SAUCE

SERVES FOUR

One shouldn't really have favorites, but as with little people in the eyes of their doting parents, some just do shine a bit more brightly on particular days. This meal in a bowl was, for me, a revelation. I was inspired to make the batter after a trip to the iconic Californian restaurant Chez Panisse, where chef Cal Peternell used a similar batter with some young green onions. You'll get more basil oil than you need here: keep what remains in the fridge to drizzle over roasted vegetables or grilled white meat.

You can make the tomato sauce and the basil oil in advance. Heat the olive oil for the sauce in a large sauté pan over medium heat and add the garlic. Let it soften for 2 minutes before adding both types of tomato and 1¼ cups/300 ml water. Simmer gently for 30 minutes to thicken. Stir in the basil, a scant ½ teaspoon salt, some black pepper, and the bread; add a little water, if needed, to allow the bread to soak up the sauce and break up as you stir. The sauce should be thick and hearty yet runny enough to spoon.

Place all the ingredients for the basil oil and a pinch of salt in the bowl of a small food processor and blitz until smooth.

Just before serving, make the batter. Place the flour, polenta, sugar, ¼ teaspoon salt, and some pepper in a large bowl. Add the buttermilk and sparkling water and whisk until smooth. Pour the sunflower oil into a saucepan, making sure you have enough oil to deep-fry the okra. To hasten the process, double the quantity of oil and use 2 pans simultaneously. Heat the oil over medium-high heat, then turn down the heat to medium so the okra doesn't fry too quickly. Dip a few okra pods in the batter, shake off the excess, and fry for 2 minutes, turning once, until golden brown. Place on paper towels, sprinkle with salt, and keep warm, in a low oven, as you continue with the rest.

Warm the sauce and spoon it onto plates. Pile the okra on top and finish with the sour cream and the basil oil. Serve at once.

---

scant ⅔ cup/75 g all-purpose flour
3 tbsp/25 g fine polenta
¼ tsp superfine sugar
scant 1 cup/200 ml buttermilk
3 tbsp sparkling water
about 1½ cups/350 ml sunflower oil, for frying
9 oz/250 g okra, trimmed
4 tbsp sour cream
salt and black pepper

Tomato sauce
2 tbsp olive oil
1 clove garlic, sliced
7 oz/200 g fresh tomatoes, peeled and coarsely chopped
scant 1 cup/200 g canned Italian tomatoes
12 large basil leaves, coarsely shredded
1 small slice sourdough or another good white bread, crusts removed (about 1 oz/25 g)
salt and black pepper

Basil oil
scant 1 cup/25 g basil leaves
3 tbsp olive oil
1 large clove garlic, crushed
salt

SERVES FOUR

FRIED UPMA WITH POACHED EGG

½ cup / 100 g channa dal
1½ tbsp sunflower oil, plus extra for greasing the tray
1 small onion, chopped (about ⅔ cup / 90 g)
2 tsp cumin seeds
1½-inch / 4-cm piece fresh ginger (about 1 oz / 30 g), peeled and finely chopped
1 small green chile, seeded and finely chopped
20 fresh curry leaves (about 3 stems)
2 tsp black mustard seeds, toasted
scant ½ tsp curry powder
¼ tsp ground turmeric
3½ tbsp / 30 g unsalted peanuts, toasted and coarsely chopped
scant 1¼ cups / 200 g coarse semolina
about ¼ cup / 60 g ghee or clarified butter
1 tbsp white wine vinegar
4 eggs
3½ oz / 100 g Indian lime pickle (Patak's or another store-bought variety; optional)
scant ⅔ cup / 120 g Greek yogurt
salt

Upma, a thick semolina-based porridge, is a popular south Indian breakfast dish or tiffin-box staple. The spices are not as they might be if you were eating this later on in the day, but if your taste buds have woken up, you might want to increase the spices accordingly. The lime pickle is optional because it tends to slightly mask the wonderful flavor of the humble upma. *Still, I love it so much that I can't help but adding a little. I have a bit of reputation in the test kitchen for the nonreturn of Tupperware when leftovers have been taken home the night before. Entirely undeserved, of course, but the Indian way makes me think that designated tiffin boxes might be the way forward.*

Bring a small pan of water to a boil and add the dal. Cook for 30 minutes, until just cooked. Drain, refresh under cold water, and set aside.

Heat the oil in a large sauté pan over medium heat. Add the onion and cumin and cook for 4 minutes. Add the ginger, chile, curry leaves, black mustard seeds, curry powder, and turmeric and cook for 2 minutes more, stirring often. Add the peanuts, cooked dal, and 1 teaspoon salt and fry for another minute, stirring from time to time. Add the semolina and 1⅔ cups / 400 ml water and cook for a final 2 minutes, stirring continuously.

Lightly oil an 8-inch / 20-cm square tray and spread out the semolina mix. Use an offset spatula to flatten it down before setting aside for about 20 minutes, to cool and set. Wipe out the sauté pan, add the ghee, and place over high heat. Use a knife to cut the upma into 4 squares and then cut each square in half on the diagonal. Add the triangles to the pan and fry for about 6 minutes, turning once, so that both sides turn golden and crispy. You will need to do this in two batches, so keep them warm, in a low oven, while you continue with the second batch, adding more butter if needed.

Finally, poach the eggs. Fill a shallow saucepan with enough water for a whole egg to cook in. Add the vinegar and bring to a rapid boil. To poach each egg, carefully break it into a cup, then gently pour it into the boiling water. Immediately remove the pan from the heat and set it aside. After about 4 minutes the egg should be poached to perfection. Using a slotted spoon, carefully transfer the poached egg to a bowl of warm water to keep it from cooling down. Once all the eggs are done, dry them on paper towels.

Put 2 triangles on each plate, leaning one up against the other. Spoon a poached egg alongside, with some pickle and some yogurt. Serve at once.

FRIED CAULIFLOWER WITH MINT AND TAMARIND DIPPING SAUCE

SERVES FOUR

2 cups / 120 g panko bread crumbs
1 small clove garlic, crushed
1 tsp ground ginger
1¼ tsp ground cumin
2 tsp medium curry powder
1½ tsp coriander seeds
1½ tsp black mustard seeds
1 tsp chile flakes
1½ tsp superfine sugar
3 eggs, beaten
¾ cup / 90 g all-purpose flour
1 medium cauliflower, broken into 1¼-inch / 3-cm florets (about 6 cups / 600 g)
about 4½ cups / 1 liter sunflower oil, for frying
salt

Sauce
1⅓ cups / 40 g flat-leaf parsley leaves
1⅔ cups / 25 g cilantro leaves
⅓ cup / 10 g mint leaves
1 tbsp tamarind paste
1 tsp maple syrup
1 tbsp olive oil
2 tsp lime juice
salt

To me, fried cauliflower is up there as the best of all comfort foods. It possibly has to do with my childhood—when my dad simply dipped cauliflower in egg and bread crumbs, fried it, and served it to us with homemade mayonnaise—or, perhaps, it's just because fried cauliflower is so damn delicious.

The dipping sauce is not essential here—a squeeze of lime is perfectly fine—but it is fantastically fresh and delicious. Somehow I just know that you will find yourself making this sauce again and again and spooning it over everything, from grilled meat to various curries and stews.

To make the sauce, place the herbs, tamarind, maple syrup, olive oil, ½ teaspoon salt, and 2 tablespoons water in the bowl of a small food processor. Process until completely smooth and set aside.

Place the bread crumbs, garlic, ground spices, seeds, chile flakes, sugar, and ½ teaspoon salt in the bowl of a small food processor. Blitz a few times until the spices are mixed and the bread crumbs are slightly broken down; you don't want the texture to be completely fine. Transfer to a bowl.

Place the eggs in a separate bowl and the flour and ½ teaspoon salt in a third bowl. Dip a cauliflower floret into the flour so that it's completely covered. Next, dip it into the egg and then, finally, into the spicy bread crumbs, turning so that all sides get covered. Set aside on a large plate while you continue dipping the remaining cauliflower.

Pour the oil to a depth of 1¼ to 1½-inches / 3 to 4-cm into a saucepan and place over medium-high heat. When hot, carefully lower in about 8 pieces of cauliflower. Fry for 2 to 3 minutes, until golden brown. Use a slotted spoon to transfer them to a plate lined with paper towels and keep somewhere warm while you continue with the remaining cauliflower. (The oil can be strained and reused.) Stir the lime juice into the dipping sauce just before serving alongside the the fried cauliflower.

BRUSSELS SPROUTS WITH CARAMELIZED GARLIC AND LEMON PEEL

SERVES FOUR

There are about ten dishes in Plenty *that I keep hearing about from people who cook from the book. I call them the "Top Ten." One of them is my caramelized garlic tart, which seems to have been a revelation to many a garlic lover. A similar surprising transformation of the garlic cloves, from harsh and abrasive to mild and sweet, occurs here, allowing you to use tons of garlic without any risk of harming yourself or your loved ones.*

There are a couple of elements in this Christmassy affair that will come in handy elsewhere. The caramelized garlic makes a great condiment to lentils and roasted vegetables, and the candied lemon can be used to garnish creamy desserts or leafy salads. Panfrying sprouts is a great way to cook them: the flavor is enhanced and a healthy texture is retained.

7 oz/200 g garlic (5 heads or 3 large heads), cloves removed and peeled
about ½ cup/120 ml olive oil
2 tsp balsamic vinegar
3 tbsp superfine sugar
1 medium lemon
1⅓ lb/600 g brussels sprouts
1 red chile, seeded and finely chopped
⅔ cup/20 g basil leaves, coarsely shredded
salt and black pepper

Start with the garlic. Bring a saucepan of water to a boil, add the garlic, and blanch for 3 minutes. Drain, dry the pan, and pour in 2 tablespoons of the olive oil. Return the garlic to the pan and fry over high heat for 2 minutes, stirring all the time, until golden on all sides. Add the vinegar, 1 tablespoon of the sugar, 6 tbsp/90 ml water, and ¼ teaspoon salt. Bring to a boil and simmer gently over medium heat for 10 to 15 minutes, until hardly any liquid is left, the cloves have caramelized, and the syrup is thick. Set the pan aside.

To prepare the lemon peel, use a vegetable peeler to shave off wide strips of lemon skin; avoid the white pith. Cut the strips crosswise into paper-thin slices and place them in a small saucepan. Squeeze the lemon, measure the juice, and add water as needed to total 7 tablespoons/100 ml. Pour over the lemon rind, add the remaining 2 tablespoons sugar, and bring to a light simmer. Cook for 12 to 15 minutes, until the syrup is reduced to about one-third. Set aside to cool down and then drain the lemon, discarding the syrup.

Meanwhile, trim the sprouts and cut them in half lengthwise. Place about 3 tablespoons of the olive oil in a large, heavy pan and heat over high heat. Add half the sprouts, ⅛ teaspoon salt, and a good grind of black pepper and cook for about 5 minutes, stirring once or twice, so that they char well without breaking up; add oil if needed. The sprouts will have softened but still retain a bite. Transfer to a bowl and continue with the remaining oil and sprouts.

Once the sprouts are cooked, mix them with the chile and with the garlic and its syrup. Stir and leave aside for about 10 minutes. Stir in the basil and lemon peel and serve warm or at room temperature.

QUINOA AND WILD GARLIC CAKES WITH SALBITXADA SAUCE

SERVES FOUR
makes 16 cakes

As anyone who reads her 101 Cookbooks *blog will know, Heidi Swanson is the very lovely champion of all things vegetarian. She is also the source of inspiration for these quinoa patties, which are great with just a squeeze of lemon but work like a dream with the* salbitxada *sauce. Tara, who errs away from bread crumbs whenever she can, makes the cakes with ground flaxseeds instead, for those who want a gluten-free option. Make more than you need of the wonderfully versatile* salbitxada, *a Catalan sauce similar to romesco. Store it in the fridge for up to a week to have ready to serve alongside any rice-based dish or grilled vegetables, meat, or fish.*

Preheat the oven to 425°F/220°C.

First make the sauce. Place the red pepper, chiles, and garlic cloves on a baking sheet and roast for 10 minutes. Remove the chiles and garlic, turn the red pepper, and continue cooking for another 20 minutes. Once the skin is blistered and the pepper roasted, remove it and place in a bowl covered with plastic wrap. When cool, peel and seed the pepper. Do the same with the chiles and also peel the garlic.

Lower the oven temperature to 400°F/200°C.

Place the almonds in the bowl of a small food processor and grind to a coarse powder. Add the pepper, chile, garlic, and tomatoes and continue to process to a paste. Add the sherry vinegar and ¼ teaspoon salt and then slowly pour in the oil until you have a thick sauce.

Throw the quinoa into a saucepan with plenty of boiling water and simmer for 9 minutes, until tender but still with a bite. Drain in a fine sieve, refresh under cold water, and set aside until completely dry.

Place the garlic leaves, red onions, eggs, green chiles, cottage cheese, Cheddar, bread crumbs, cumin, 1 teaspoon salt, and a good grind of pepper in a large bowl. Add the quinoa, stir well, and form the mixture into 2 oz/60 g patties each about 2½-inches/6-cm wide and ¾-inch/2-cm thick.

Place a nonstick pan over medium heat and add half the oil. Fry the patties in batches for 3 minutes on each side, until golden, adding oil as needed. Transfer to a baking sheet and finish off in the oven for about 8 minutes. Serve hot with a squeeze of lemon juice, or with the sauce spooned on top or alongside.

1½ cups/250 g quinoa
16 wild garlic leaves, thinly sliced (1½ oz/40 g), or 6 green onions, white and green parts, thinly sliced (⅔ cup/60 g)
1 small red onion, finely diced (about 1 cup/100 g)
2 eggs, lightly whisked
2 green chiles, seeded and finely diced
½ cup/120 g cottage cheese
¼ cup/30 g coarsely grated aged Cheddar
½ cup plus 1 tbsp/60 g dried bread crumbs
2 tsp ground cumin
¼ cup/60 ml olive oil
1 large lemon, cut into wedges (optional)
salt and black pepper

Salbitxada sauce (optional)
1 medium red pepper (5 oz/150 g)
2 red chiles
5 cloves garlic, skin on
⅓ cup/40 g sliced almonds, toasted
4 tomatoes, peeled, seeded, and coarsely chopped (scant 1½ cups/250 g)
2 tsp sherry vinegar
7 tbsp/100 ml olive oil
salt

SERVES FOUR

as a main course; more as a starter or side

UDON NOODLES WITH FRIED EGGPLANT, WALNUT, AND MISO

3 green onions, white and green parts
1 1/3-inch/3.5-cm piece (about 1 oz/25 g), peeled fresh ginger, cut into very fine matchsticks
2 small eggplants (about 1 lb/500 g)
about 1 cup/250 ml sunflower oil, plus 1 tablespoon
6 shallots, thinly sliced (about 1 cup/100 g)
2 cloves garlic, crushed
1 1/4 cups/120 g walnuts, lightly toasted and coarsely chopped
3 tbsp/50 g sweet white miso paste
2/3 cup/150 ml vegetarian dashi or vegetable stock from cube
3 tbsp mirin
2 tbsp soy sauce
1 tbsp superfine sugar
1 tbsp sake (optional)
9 oz/250 g dried udon noodles
1/2 cucumber, unpeeled, cored and cut into very fine strips (5 oz/150 g)
salt

Miso has become a cupboard staple of mine since I wrote Plenty. *It's a fantastic way of getting tons of umami-rich flavor into vegetarian dishes, whether added to a marinade, sauce, soup, or dressing.*

A decent vegetarian dashi can be made by boiling kombu, an edible kelp often used in Asian cooking, for just 5 minutes. Kombu is available at health food shops and some Asian grocery stores.

Cut each green onion into 2-inch/5-cm lengths. Slice each length in two, from top to bottom, and then cut each half into long strips, as thinly as you can. Place the onions and two-fifths of the ginger in a bowl of iced water and put in the fridge.

Use a vegetable peeler to peel off 4 or 5 strips of skin from the eggplants, from top to bottom, so you are left with a striped pattern. Slice the eggplants into disks 1-inch/2.5 cm-thick and then cut each disk into quarters. Pour the 1 cup/250 ml sunflower oil into a saucepan and place over medium-high heat. Once hot, add the eggplant pieces in small batches and deep-fry for about 4 minutes, until they turn golden and cook through. Transfer to a colander to drain and sprinkle with a little salt.

Place the shallots and the remaining 1 tablespoon sunflower oil in a large sauté pan and sauté over medium heat for about 2 minutes, until they soften. Add the remaining ginger and the garlic and cook over low heat for 5 minutes. Add the walnuts and fried eggplant pieces and set aside.

Whisk together the miso, dashi, mirin, soy sauce, sugar, and sake in a small bowl. Add to the walnuts and eggplants.

Cook the noodles as instructed on the package. While you do this, heat up the eggplant and walnut sauce, allowing some evaporation so the sauce thickens a little but not much. Serve individual portions of hot noodles, topped in the center with the eggplant and walnut sauce. Drain and pat dry the green onion and ginger and sprinkle these on top, along with the cucumber.

CRISPY SAFFRON COUSCOUS CAKES

SERVES FOUR
makes 20 patties

This was inspired by Ana Sortun, a friend and the owner of the legendary Oleana restaurant in Cambridge, Massachusetts. Ana's original cakes are made to have the texture of tah-dig, *the crispy, lightly fried base of Iranian rice. My version—busier, of course—replaces the rice with couscous and has a sweet and salty edge, which makes them very popular with little people. It is the yogurt and the egg that make these so nice and crunchy. For an adult main, serve the patties with tomato chutney or relish and a green salad. If you want, add fresh herbs, such as dill, parsley, or mint, to the mix.*

Currants soaked for 20 minutes in lemon juice can be used instead of barberries, if you can't get hold of them.

½ tsp saffron threads
scant 1⅔ cups/275 g couscous
¼ cup/30 g barberries
¼ cup/50 g superfine sugar
⅔ cup/140 g Greek yogurt
2 eggs, lightly beaten
6½ tbsp/20 g chopped chives
3½ oz/100 g feta, broken into ¾-inch/1-cm chunks
about 4 tbsp/60 g clarified butter or ghee
salt and black pepper

Place the saffron in a large mixing bowl and pour in 2 cups/500 ml boiling water. Leave to infuse for a minute or two, then add the couscous. Stir with a fork, cover the bowl with plastic wrap, and let stand for 15 minutes.

Put the barberries and sugar in a small saucepan. Add ½ cup/120 ml water, bring to a light simmer, stir to dissolve the sugar, and remove from the heat. Once cool, drain the barberries and dry on paper towels.

Fluff up the couscous with a fork and then add the yogurt, eggs, chives, feta, barberries, 1¼ teaspoons salt, and some black pepper. Mix well and then use your hands to shape the couscous into firm round patties about ⅔-inch/1.5-cm thick and weighing 2 oz/55 g each; press and compact them well so they don't disintegrate during cooking.

Heat 2 tablespoons of the butter in a large sauté pan over medium-high heat. Turn down the heat to medium and fry the patties in batches, adding more butter if needed. Cook each batch for 5 minutes, turning once, until crisp and golden brown. Transfer to paper towels and keep somewhere warm while you continue cooking the remainder. Serve at once.

EGGPLANT, POTATO, TOMATO

SERVES FOUR TO SIX

I tried to think of a more inspired title for this recipe. It all got too long, with fried potatoes, spicy tomatoes, and poached eggs all trying to get a mention. Reverting back to basics, I tell it like it is.

For all you shakshuka *lovers, this is another dish to cherish for a late weekend breakfast, though it takes longer to make because the different components need to be prepared separately. You can prepare them in advance, though, and just put everything together at the last minute. This can be served straight out of the sauté pan. I recommend always stirring the tahini in the tub before using it.*

4 medium tomatoes, cut into ⅜-inch/1-cm dice (about 2¼ cups/400 g)
½ small red onion, finely chopped (⅓ cup/40 g)
2 tsp white wine vinegar
½ cup/15 g flat-leaf parsley leaves, chopped
1 tbsp Sriracha sauce or another hot savory chile sauce
2 medium eggplants, cut into 1¼-inch/3-cm chunks (1⅓ lb/600 g)
1 cup/250 ml olive oil
about 1¼ cups/300 ml sunflower oil
1⅓ lb/600 g Yukon gold potatoes or another waxy variety, peeled and cut into slices ⅛-inch/3-mm thick
scant ½ cup/80 g tahini paste
2½ tbsp lemon juice
1 small clove garlic, crushed
6 eggs, freshly poached (see page 198 for poaching instructions)
1 tsp sumac
1 tbsp cilantro leaves, chopped
salt and black pepper

Place the tomatoes in a colander for 30 minutes to drain. Transfer to a medium bowl and add the onion, vinegar, parsley, Sriracha, and ¼ teaspoon salt. Mix gently and set aside.

Mix the eggplants with 1½ teaspoons salt, place in a colander, and set aside over a bowl for half an hour, to remove any excess liquid. Transfer to a plate lined with paper towels and pat dry. Pour all but 2 tablespoons of the olive oil into a 10½-inch/26-cm sauté pan, along with all of the sunflower oil; the oil needs to reach ⅜-inch/1-cm up the sides of the pan, so add more if you need to. Place over high heat and, once hot, add the eggplant in batches. Fry for 3 to 4 minutes, until golden brown. Remove with a slotted spoon, transfer to a plate lined with paper towels, and set aside somewhere warm while you continue with the remaining batches. Leave the oil to cool, pour it into a jar—you'll be able to use it for future frying—and wipe out the pan.

Bring a saucepan of water to a boil, add the potatoes, and cook for 3 minutes. Drain, refresh under cold water, and set aside to dry. Add the remaining 2 tablespoons fresh olive oil to the sauté pan and place over medium-high heat. Add the potatoes, ¼ teaspoon salt, and a grind of black pepper and fry for 10 minutes, shaking the pan from time to time, until they are cooked through and golden brown. Remove the pan from the heat and set aside.

Place the tahini, ¼ cup/60 ml water, 1½ tablespoons of the lemon juice, the garlic, and a pinch of salt in a bowl and whisk until you have a thick, pourable consistency. Spoon half of this sauce over the potatoes and spread the eggplants on top. Follow this with the remaining tahini sauce and then spoon over the tomatoes. Poach the eggs just before you are ready to serve and then lay them on top of the tomatoes, along with a drizzle of the remaining olive oil, a sprinkle of the sumac and cilantro, and the last of the lemon juice. Bring to the table in the pan.

SERVES FOUR

COATED OLIVES WITH SPICY YOGURT

1 green chile, with seeds, coarsely chopped
¼ tsp ground cardamom
⅛ tsp ground cloves
¾ tsp superfine sugar
1⅓ cups / 20 g cilantro leaves, coarsely chopped
⅔ cup / 20 g flat-leaf parsley leaves, coarsely chopped
1 medium preserved lemon (1½ oz / 45 g), skin and flesh coarsely chopped
¼ cup / 60 ml olive oil
¾ cup / 80 g panko bread crumbs, processed to a very fine crumb
6½ tbsp / 50 g all-purpose flour
2 eggs, beaten
rounded 1 cup / 160 g pitted green olives
sunflower oil, for frying
1½ cups / 300 g Greek yogurt

This recipe is more or less stolen from the fantastic cookbook of the even more fantastic restaurant, Balaboosta, in New York's SoHo. The talented chef, Einat Admony, is the local face of the increasingly popular Israeli food scene. Coating and frying individual olives may seem, at first, a little painstaking, but they can be prepared in advance, at leisure; the resulting predinner nibble is, for those who can't face yet another platter of smoked salmon blini, really very special.

Place the chile, spices, sugar, cilantro, parsley, preserved lemon, and olive oil in a small blender and blitz to a rough paste. Pour into a small bowl and set aside until required.

Place the bread crumbs, flour, and eggs in 3 separate small bowls.

Drain the olives from their preserving juices and pat dry with paper towels. Once dry, take 1 olive and dip in the flour, then the egg, then finally coat well in the panko. Place on a plate to one side. Repeat with the rest of the olives.

Pour the sunflower oil to a depth of 1¼-inches / 3-cm into a small saucepan and place over medium-high heat. Once the oil is hot, add a couple of the olives. They should take 1 minute to go golden brown and need to be turned over during the process. If they brown too quickly, turn the heat down. Remove the olives from the oil and transfer to paper towels. Repeat with the rest of the olives until they are all cooked.

Spoon the yogurt into a shallow bowl, then swirl the green paste into it (don't mix them completely). Pile the olives, warm or at room temperature, into the center and serve.

FRIED

POT BARLEY AND LENTILS WITH MUSHROOMS AND SWEET SPICES

SERVES FOUR

I've always tended to cook with pearled barley, so pot barley was a real revelation after Diana Henry suggested I use it instead of rice for a take on lentil mejadra. *Unlike pearled barley, whose hulled, polished, and tender nature makes it very happy to take on more robust flavors, pot barley's inherent nuttiness and bite allows it to sing for its supper more independently in a dish. With more to get through before the grain is cooked, pot barley takes longer to cook than the pearled version, but soaking it in cold water the night before will speed things along. It's a robust and versatile grain that can be used instead of pasta, rice, couscous, or bulgur. I'm finding all sorts of excuses to eat it with every meal at the moment—savory and sweet (see Pot Barley, Orange, and Sesame Pudding, page 325).*

⅔ cup / 20 g dried porcini mushrooms
⅔ cup / 120 g pot barley, covered with cold water and soaked overnight
scant 1 cup / 170 g brown lentils
2 medium onions (8½ oz / 240 g), 1 halved and thinly sliced; the other halved and cut into wedges ¾-inch / 2-cm wide
2 tbsp all-purpose flour
about 2½ cups / 600 ml sunflower oil
2 tbsp olive oil
1½ tsp ground cumin
1 tsp ground allspice
1 tsp ground cinnamon
3 large portobello mushrooms (9 oz / 250 g), sliced into strips ⅜-inch / 1-cm wide
1 lemon, rind shaved into long strips
½ tsp superfine sugar
1 tbsp dried mint
1 tbsp lemon juice
⅔ cup / 10 g dill leaves, coarsely chopped
⅓ cup / 10 g flat-leaf parsley leaves, coarsely chopped
¼ cup / 60 g sour cream (optional)
salt and black pepper

Place the dried porcini in a heatproof bowl, cover with 1⅔ cups / 400 ml boiling water, and leave to stand for 1 hour. Once cool, lift out the mushrooms and strain the liquid through a fine sieve lined with cheesecloth, to remove any grit. Return the mushrooms to the liquid.

Drain the pot barley, rinse under cold water, and place in a large saucepan with the lentils. Pour in plenty of cold water—it should rise 2-inches / 5-cm above the barley and lentils—place over high heat, and bring to a boil. Turn down the heat to medium-high and cook for 15 to 20 minutes, until the lentils and barley are cooked but still hold their shape. Drain and transfer to a bowl to cool down.

Place the onion slices in a small bowl, add the flour, and shake gently. Pour the sunflower oil to a depth of ¾-inch / 2-cm into a saucepan and place over high heat. Once hot, add half of the onion and fry for 3 to 4 minutes, until golden brown. Use a slotted spoon to transfer the onion to a plate lined with paper towels. Repeat with the remaining slices and set aside to cool.

Place the onion wedges and olive oil in a large sauté pan over high heat and fry for 5 minutes, stirring frequently, until the onion is charred and soft. Add the ground spices and continue to cook for 30 seconds before adding the portobello mushrooms, lemon strips, sugar, and ½ teaspoon salt. Fry for 3 minutes, until the mushrooms are starting to soften and gain some color, stirring from time to time. Add the porcini and their soaking liquid and boil rapidly for 5 minutes, until you have about 6 tablespoons liquid left in the pan. Turn down the heat to low and return the lentils and barley to the pan along with the dried mint, ¾ teaspoon salt, and a generous grind of black pepper. Stir to combine and cook for a final minute. Remove from the heat and add the lemon juice, dill, parsley, and crispy onion slices. Transfer to a large serving platter or individual plates and serve warm, with a spoonful of sour cream on top.

See picture on the following pages

SERVES FOUR

EGGPLANT PAHI

about 1⅔ cups/400 ml grapeseed or sunflower oil
2 large eggplants, halved lengthwise, each half cut into 1 by 2-inch/2.5 by 5-cm wedges (1⅔ lb/750 g)
1 tsp ground turmeric
3 medium onions, each cut into 8 wedges (15 oz/420 g)
4 Romano or Ramiro peppers, halved lengthwise, seeded, and cut crosswise into strips ¾-inch/2-cm wide (about 4 cups/480 g)
1 mild red chile, seeded and quartered
1¼-inch/3-cm piece fresh ginger (about ⅓ oz/10 g), peeled and coarsely chopped

4 cloves garlic, coarsely chopped
1½ tsp curry powder
¼ tsp ground cloves
¼ tsp ground cardamom
1 tsp ground cinnamon
2 tsp mustard seeds
4-inch/10-cm pandan leaf, coarsely chopped (optional)
1¼-inch/3-cm piece lemongrass, soft white stem only, coarsely chopped
about 12 fresh curry leaves
¼ cup/60 ml cider vinegar
2½ tsp superfine sugar
salt

This Sri Lankan dry curry makes a thrilling condiment to rice, roasted vegetables, or plainly cooked chicken. It can be served warm but is even better the next day, at room temperature. Don't be afraid of it looking oily: any rice or bread will be grateful to soak it up. Jennifer Gomes, an Australian architect born in Sri Lanka who gave me the recipe, says she loves it best in a baguette with roasted beef. I couldn't agree more. It's also lovely with a drizzle of tahini or with Greek yogurt. Kept in a sealed jar, it will last in the fridge for two weeks.

Pour the oil into a very large sauté pan or Dutch oven and place over medium-high heat. Meanwhile, toss the eggplants with the turmeric in a bowl. Add to the oil in batches and fry for about 8 minutes, turning once, until lightly golden. Use a slotted spoon to transfer to a colander layered with paper towels, sprinkle with ¼ teaspoon salt, and leave to drain.

Add the onions to the oil and fry them for about 8 minutes, turning once, until golden brown, then add them to the eggplants, along with another ¼ teaspoon salt. Next, fry the peppers and chile for 5 minutes, until the edges begin to brown, and add to the rest, along with ¼ teaspoon salt. You should now have about 1 tablespoon oil in the pan. Add or remove some if you need.

Place the ginger, garlic, spices, pandan leaf, lemongrass, and curry leaves in the bowl of a small food processor or spice grinder and blitz to form a paste. Fry this paste in the pan with the oil over medium heat for 2 to 3 minutes, until it begins to color. Return all of the vegetables to the pan, along with the vinegar, ¼ cup/60 ml boiling water, and sugar. Stir gently and simmer for 8 minutes, until most of the liquid has boiled away, before serving warm or at room temperature.

MASHED

SERVES FOUR TO SIX

ROOT MASH WITH WINE-BRAISED SHALLOTS

scant ⅓ cup/80 g Puy lentils
½ large celery root, peeled and cut into chunks (about 2 cups/300 g)
2 large carrots, peeled and cut into chunks (about 2 cups/300 g)
½ kabocha squash or another type, peeled and cut into chunks (about 2 cups/300 g)
2 sweet potatoes, peeled and cut into chunks (about 4 cups/600 g)
scant 5 tbsp/70 g unsalted butter, diced
2 tbsp maple syrup
1½ tsp ground cumin
salt and black pepper

Braised shallots
2 tbsp olive oil
1⅓ lb/600 g shallots, peeled and left whole
1⅔ cups/400 ml red wine
scant 1 cup/200 ml vegetable stock
2 bay leaves
1 tsp black peppercorns
4 thyme sprigs
1 tbsp superfine sugar
2 tbsp/30 g unsalted butter
salt

It would be almost sacrilegious to serve this without a roasted bird alongside, but thanks to the hefty lentils and the slow-cooked shallots, it could easily be served as a vegetarian main course to feed a hungry crowd.

Start with the shallots. Place the oil in a saucepan and place over high heat. Add the shallots and fry for about 5 minutes, stirring occasionally, until colored all over. Add the wine, stock, bay leaves, peppercorns, thyme, sugar, and ¾ teaspoon salt. Cover, turn down the heat to low, and simmer gently for 1 hour. Remove the lid, increase the heat, and boil for about 8 minutes, until the remaining liquid is reduced by half. Use a slotted spoon to remove the shallots from the pan and keep them somewhere warm. Stir the butter into the sauce and set aside until ready to use.

Bring a saucepan of water to a boil over high heat, add the lentils, turn down the heat to medium, and simmer for about 25 minutes, until tender. Drain and set aside.

For the mash, half fill a saucepan with water and bring to a boil. Add the celery root and carrots and cook for about 10 minutes. Add the squash and sweet potatoes and cook for a further 10 to 15 minutes, until all the vegetables are cooked.

Drain the vegetables, shaking off as much liquid as possible, and mash well with a potato masher. Add the butter, maple syrup, cumin, cooked lentils, 1 teaspoon salt, and plenty of black pepper. Mix well and then divide the warm mash among the serving plates. Top with the shallots, spoon the sauce over the top, and serve at once.

FAVA

SERVES FOUR TO SIX

I thought I knew everything there was to know about pastes made of various legumes until a couple of summers ago, when I was holidaying on the charming Greek island of Kea (or Tzia) in the Cyclades and came across this variation, which is nothing like hummus or similar pastes. Fava is crushed split peas, eaten warm, topped with capers and caramelized onion, and served alongside meat or fish or as a starter dip. It is soothing yet exciting and got me licking many plates during this break. In Greece, fava *is made with yellow split peas. When it is made with dried fava beans, it is called* koukofava. *A minefield!*

3 large onions (1⅓ lb / 600 g)
1½ cups / 300 g yellow split peas
2 bay leaves
¼ tsp ground turmeric
7 tbsp / 100 ml olive oil, plus extra to finish
2 cloves garlic, crushed
2 tbsp lemon juice
3½ tbsp / 10 g finely chopped chives
¼ cup / 35 g capers, coarsely chopped
salt and white pepper

Peel and quarter 1 of the onions and place it in a saucepan. Add the split peas, bay leaves, and turmeric and cover generously with water. Bring to a boil, turn down the heat to a simmer, and cook for 50 minutes to 1 hour, until the peas are soft and just about holding their shape. Top up the water as they cook, if needed. Drain the peas, keeping the water, and discard the bay leaves, leaving the onion in. Leave to cool down just a little.

While the peas are cooking, peel and slice the 2 remaining onions ¼-inch / 5-mm thick. Place a large sauté pan over medium-high heat and add 1 tablespoon of the oil. Add the onions and cook for 15 to 20 minutes, until golden brown, sweet, and caramelized. Remove from the heat and set aside.

Remove ½ cup / 100 g of the cooked peas and set aside. Put the rest in a food processor bowl, adding the garlic, lemon juice, remaining 6 tablespoons olive oil, ¾ teaspoon salt, ⅛ teaspoon white pepper, and 3 tablespoons of the cooking water. Blitz until almost completely smooth, transfer to a large bowl, and fold in the reserved yellow peas, half the chives, and half the caramelized onion. Put in a shallow bowl and use an offset spatula to swirl the mixture. Top with the rest of the onions, the capers, and the chives and finish with a drizzle of olive oil.

SERVES FOUR TO SIX
as a starter

FAVA BEAN SPREAD WITH ROASTED GARLIC RICOTTA

1 head garlic (10 cloves), cloves separated, skin on
½ cup/125 ml olive oil
1 cup/240 g ricotta
3 tbsp sour cream
2 lemons, rind shaved in long strips from one, 2 tsp finely grated zest from the other
1⅓ lb/600 g fava beans (2⅔ cups/400 g if starting with shelled beans)
1½ tbsp lemon juice
½ cup/15 g mint leaves, chopped, plus 1 tbsp shredded mint leaves to garnish
salt and black pepper

An extra portion for all bean-sheller helpers here! Don't be put off by the need to start with shelled beans: buy them already shelled (I have seen them in a few Middle Eastern grocery stores) or else it's a fun and therapeutic task to delegate to helpers—little or big. This is a favorite with Tara's twins, Scarlett and Theo, who race to see who can catapult the beans out first and, crucially, fly them into the designated bowl. Serve with toasted sourdough as a starter.

Preheat the oven to 425°F/220°C.

Mix the garlic cloves with 1 teaspoon of the olive oil, place on a baking sheet, and cook for 15 minutes, until soft. Remove from the oven and when cool enough to handle, squash the garlic out of its skin using the back of a fork. Discard the skins, place the flesh in a small bowl, and add the ricotta, sour cream, ¼ teaspoon salt, and some black pepper. Use a whisk to mix everything together well and set aside.

Place the remaining olive oil in a small saucepan with the shaved lemon rind. Place over medium heat, bring to a gentle simmer, then remove from the heat to cool and infuse.

Bring a large pan of water to a boil. Add the fava beans, blanch for 1 minute, drain, and then remove them from their skins. Crush the beans with a fork, add all but 1 tablespoon of the lemon-infused oil (removing the rind first), the lemon juice, the chopped mint, ½ teaspoon salt, and some black pepper and mix together.

Spread the ricotta mix in a thin layer over the bottom of of each serving plate or one larger platter. Spoon the fava bean mixture on top, lightly spreading it out to cover most of the ricotta. Sprinkle the shredded mint and grated lemon zest over the fava mixture and finish with a drizzle of the lemon-infused oil.

See picture on the following pages

SERVES TWO
as a main course
or four as a starter

CRUSHED PUY LENTILS WITH TAHINI AND CUMIN

1 cup/200 g Puy lentils
2 tbsp/30 g unsalted butter
2 tbsp olive oil, plus extra to finish
3 cloves garlic, crushed
1 tsp ground cumin
4 medium tomatoes, peeled and cut into ⅜-inch/1-cm dice (scant 2 cups/330 g)
1⅔ cups/25 g cilantro leaves, chopped
¼ cup/60 g tahini paste
2 tbsp lemon juice
⅓ small red onion, thinly sliced (about ¼ cup/25 g)
2 hard-boiled eggs, quartered
½ tsp paprika, to garnish (optional)
salt and black pepper

This recipe has been through various incarnations before ending up uncannily similar to one of the typical Arabic hummus variations I am used to from my childhood: warm hummus topped with whole soft chickpeas and served with raw onion and hard-boiled egg. Here it is made with lentils and tomatoes, but essentially we are talking about a similar set of hearty flavors that can set you up nicely for a busy day, or be served as an early supper. For a dairy-free option, substitute more olive oil for the butter. Serve this with pita and nothing else.

Bring a saucepan of water to a boil. Add the lentils and cook for 20 to 30 minutes, until completely cooked. Drain and set aside.

Put the butter and oil in a large sauté pan and place over medium-high heat. Once the butter melts, add the garlic and cumin and cook for about 1 minute. Add the tomatoes, four-fifths of the cilantro, and the cooked lentils. Continue to cook and stir for a couple of minutes before adding the tahini, lemon juice, 4½ tablespoons/70 ml water, 1 teaspoon salt, and a good grind of black pepper. Lower the heat to medium and continue to stir and cook gently for about 5 minutes, until hot and thickened. Using a potato masher, roughly mash the lentils a little so that some are broken up and you get a thick porridge consistency.

Spread the lentils on a flat serving plate and sprinkle with the onion, the remaining cilantro, and a final drizzle of olive oil. Serve warm with the hard-boiled eggs alongside and a sprinkle of paprika.

CANNELLINI BEAN PURÉE WITH PICKLED MUSHROOMS AND PITA CROUTONS

SERVES FOUR
as a starter

This needs to be started a day in advance, both for the beans to soak and for the onions and mushrooms to pickle, but it is well worth the wait, as it is one of the most glorious mezze dishes, both in flavor and look. The pickle works just as well without the miso, so don't worry if you can't get hold of it; just add an extra tablespoon of sugar to the pickling liquid.

Prepare the pickle a day before serving. Place the sugar, vinegar, miso, and ¾ cup/180 ml water in a saucepan with 1 teaspoon salt. Bring to a boil and then pour into a heatproof, nonreactive bowl containing the mushrooms, onion, both peppercorns, allspice, and bay leaves. Leave to cool, then cover and refrigerate overnight. Take out of the fridge at least 1 hour before using.

The next day, drain and rinse the beans, put them in a large saucepan, and cover with plenty of water. Bring to a boil and then simmer gently for 30 to 60 minutes (beans vary greatly in cooking time), topping up the water if needed, until completely soft. You'll need to skim the surface a few times during cooking. Drain, keeping some of the cooking liquid, and transfer to a food processor, along with the tahini, 4 tablespoons of the olive oil, the garlic, lemon juice, ¾ teaspoon salt, and ½ teaspoon white pepper. Blitz well, until a very smooth paste has formed, and set aside. Once ready to serve, add a little cooking liquid if you need to get a soft and fluffy consistency (like runny mashed potatoes).

Pour the remaining 3 tablespoons olive oil and all of the sunflower oil into a sauté pan and place over high heat. When hot, add the pita and fry for about 3 minutes, shaking the pan from time to time, until golden and crisp all over. Transfer to a colander lined with paper towels and sprinkle with a pinch of salt.

When ready to serve, spread the puree out on a large platter. Spoon the mushrooms and onions, a few tablespoons of the pickling liquid, and a teaspoon or two of the aromatics over the puree. Dot with some of the pita croutons (serve the rest on the side), sprinkle with the parsley, and serve at once.

1⅓ cups/250 g cannellini beans, soaked in water overnight with 2 tsp baking soda
scant 3½ tbsp/50 g tahini paste
7 tbsp/100 ml olive oil
1 clove garlic, crushed
2 tbsp lemon juice
3 tbsp sunflower oil
2 pita breads (4 oz/120g), torn into 1¼-inch/3-cm pieces
1 tbsp chopped flat-leaf parsley, to garnish
salt and white pepper

Pickled mushrooms
2 tbsp superfine sugar
⅔ cup/160 ml cider vinegar
1 tbsp brown miso
scant 3 oz/80 g button mushrooms, cut into slices ¼-inch/5-mm thick
½ medium red onion, very thinly sliced into rounds (about ⅔ cup/60 g)
½ tsp black peppercorns
½ tsp red peppercorns
½ tsp allspice berries
3 bay leaves
salt

CRUSHED CARROTS WITH HARISSA AND PISTACHIOS

SERVES FOUR
as a starter

1 tbsp olive oil, plus extra to finish
1 tbsp/15 g unsalted butter
10 large carrots (2¼ lb/1 kg), peeled and cut into slices ¾-inch/2-cm thick
scant 1 cup/200 ml vegetable stock
grated zest of 1 orange
1 clove garlic, crushed
2 tsp harissa paste
grated zest of 1 lemon, plus 1 tbsp lemon juice
1 cup/200 g Greek yogurt
scant 3½ tbsp/25 g shelled unsalted pistachios, coarsely chopped
salt and black pepper

The sweetness of carrots makes them a best-selling vegetable in North Africa, where the combination of sweet, sour, and spicy is used to make some unusually harmonious creations: think a tagine blending hearty meats and dried fruit, a colorful salad spread to open a hefty meal, and a bunch of savory fillings encased in paper-thin pastry. Carrots are the ideal candidates for all these, as they are for various syrupy desserts. Here, cooked carrots are crushed to make a sharp and hot spread that you can bring to the table as a starter, on a large platter with a pile of warm pitas. You are welcome to increase the harissa, *if you like this very hot.*

Place the olive oil and butter in a large sauté pan over medium-high heat. Add the carrots and sauté for 6 minutes, stirring often; they need to soften and take on a bit of color. Add the stock, turn down the heat to medium-low, cover the pan, and cook for another 25 minutes, until the carrots are completely soft and there is hardly any liquid left. Transfer the carrots to a food processor, add ¾ teaspoon salt, and blitz briefly to form a coarse paste. Leave to cool and then add the orange zest, garlic, harissa, half the lemon zest, and some black pepper. Stir to combine.

Mix together the yogurt, lemon juice, the remaining lemon zest, and ¼ teaspoon salt.

Spread the yogurt out on a serving platter and spoon the carrot mixture on top. Sprinkle with the pistachios, drizzle with a little olive oil, and serve.

SPICE-STUFFED POTATO CAKES

SERVES FOUR
as a starter or snack

2¼ lb / 1 kg medium russet potatoes or another starchy variety, peeled and halved
1 tsp ground turmeric
1 tbsp black mustard seeds, toasted
3¾ cups / 60 g cilantro
1⅓ cups / 40 g mint leaves
2 green chiles, coarsely chopped
2 tbsp tamarind paste
2 cloves garlic
½ tsp superfine sugar
sunflower oil, for frying
1 lemon, cut into wedges, or a sweet chutney, to serve
salt

Fried patties of pretty much anything are generally a winner in my book, but smooth mashed potato running high on the spice and fresh herb front is both hard to beat and, delightfully, impossible to stop eating. Tamarind, like miso paste and Parmesan, has a strong and pungent taste that can impart a real depth of flavor to vegetarian dishes. Ready-made tamarind paste is widely available, if you can't get hold of the pulp to make your own. It can lack the fruity depth and sweet-sour-salty balance of the real deal, but it is a perfectly adequate substitute. Acidity levels vary widely from one brand to the next, so be sure to taste and assess these before adding the amount a recipe calls for, and adjust accordingly.

Bring a large pan of salted water to a boil. Add the potatoes and cook for 15 minutes, until soft. Drain well and transfer to a mixing bowl with the turmeric, mustard seeds, and ¼ teaspoon salt. Mash well and leave to cool.

Place the cilantro, mint, chiles, tamarind, garlic, sugar, and ¼ teaspoon salt in a food processor and blitz to form a smooth, dry paste.

Shape a small handful of the potato mixture—weighing about 1½ oz / 40 g—into a ball. Place the ball in the palm of one hand and use the thumb of the other to create a dent large enough to fill with 1 teaspoon of the spice mixture. Once the mixture is added, shape the potato back into a ball, with the stuffing sealed inside, and then flatten it between both hands so that the cakes are ⅔-inch / 1.5-cm thick. Continue with the rest of the potato and spice mixture until you have about 20 cakes, and then place them in the fridge for 20 minutes.

Smear the base of a large nonstick sauté pan with sunflower oil. Place over medium heat and fry the cakes for 5 to 8 minutes, turning once, until they are light, golden, and crisp on the outside. Serve at once, with a wedge of lemon or some sweet chutney on the side.

SERVES FOUR

YOGURT AND KAFFIR LIME LEAF SPREAD

1 small zucchini, grated (1⅓ cups/150 g)
½ cucumber, grated (5 oz/150 g)
4 large fresh Kaffir lime leaves, or 12 dried, coarsely chopped
1¼ cups/250 g Greek yogurt
4 tsp/20 g unsalted butter
1½ tsp lime juice
1 tbsp shredded mint leaves
1 clove garlic, crushed
salt

Were there to be an alternative word for dip *or* spread, *I would patent it as my own. In the meantime, we have to transcend the dodgy connotations and embrace this dish, which, along with a few slices of sourdough bread and some olive oil, is perhaps the perfect way to open a meal. Thanks to Gena Deligianni, one of our cooks in the early days of NOPI, for this dish. Nothing is literally mashed here but the grated cucumber and zucchini, with the addition of silky yogurt, gives a similar smooth effect that I love so much.*

Mix the zucchini and cucumber in a colander with ½ teaspoon salt. Leave to drain for about 20 minutes and then squeeze with your hands to remove as much liquid as you can. Transfer to a large bowl.

Process the lime leaves in a spice grinder to a fine powder (you can also chop them finely with a knife or crush with a pestle and mortar) and add most of it to the zucchini and cucumber, along with the yogurt.

Melt the butter in a small saucepan over medium heat and cook for 3 to 4 minutes, until it turns light brown and smells a little nutty. Add most of the butter to the dip along with all the remaining ingredients, mix well, and spread on a plate. Drizzle over the reserved butter, sprinkle with the reserved lime leaves, and serve.

CRACKED

SERVES SIX

CRESPÉOU

15 eggs, lightly beaten
7 oz/200 g feta, crumbled
⅓ cup/80 ml heavy cream
2 tsp olive oil

Red mix
¼ cup/60 ml olive oil
1 small red onion, thinly sliced (scant 1 cup/100 g)
2 tsp tomato paste
2 large red peppers, halved and cut lengthwise into strips ¼-inch/5-mm wide (about 3 cups/300 g)
¾ tsp ground coriander
¾ tsp superfine sugar
salt and black pepper

Yellow mix
¼ cup/60 ml olive oil
1 large onion, thinly sliced (about 1½ cups/180 g)
2 tsp ground turmeric
salt and black pepper

Green mix
4 green onions, white and green parts, trimmed and thinly sliced (⅔ cup/60 g)
scant 1 cup/25 g basil leaves, shredded
½ cup/15 g tarragon leaves, finely chopped
¾ tsp ground cumin
1 green chile, seeded and thinly sliced
salt

If I was going to sum up my cooking style in five words, 1970s-style retro-picnic bling *would not be them. And if there is one recipe that might make me cringe in the years to come, it will, for sure, be this one. Still, I'm keeping my head held high enough to peer over the top layer of this savory cake, which is, I will have you know, absolutely delicious and does make a perfect picnic dish.*

Mix together the eggs, feta, and cream and set aside. Start with the red mix. Place the oil in a nonstick sauté pan over medium heat. Add the onion and sauté for 10 minutes, until soft. Add the tomato paste, peppers, coriander, sugar, ¼ teaspoon salt, and some black pepper and continue to cook for another 5 to 7 minutes, stirring from time to time. Transfer to a bowl and leave to cool before stirring in one-third of the egg, cream, and feta mix.

For the yellow mix, clean the pan, pour in the oil, and place over high heat. Add the onion and sauté for 5 minutes, until parts of the onion are dark brown and crisp. Turn down the heat to low, add ¼ teaspoon salt, some black pepper, and the turmeric and continue to cook for about 5 minutes. Transfer to a bowl and leave to cool before stirring in half of the remaining egg, cream, and feta mix. Clean out the pan.

Place all the ingredients for the green mix in a bowl with ¼ teaspoon salt and the remaining egg, cream, and feta mix and stir to mix well.

Preheat the oven to 325°F/170°C.

Return the clean pan to medium heat. Add about ¼ teaspoon of the olive oil, then pour in half of the red mix to make a shallow omelet. Just before it sets completely on top—about 4 to 5 minutes—transfer it to a baking sheet lined with waxed paper. Repeat the process with the yellow mix and then the green mix—these need a slightly shorter cooking time, about 3 minutes—building the omelets one on top of the other, alternating in color. Repeat with the remaining half of each mix and stack the same way on top of the first 3 omelets. You should aim for a neat pile of 6 omelets. Place in the oven and cook for 12 minutes. Remove from the oven and leave to cool down a little.

Once warmish, place an inverted plate over the pile of omelets and flip the pan and plate together. Lift off the pan. Keep as is or use a sharp knife to trim the edge to get a nice round cake with distinct layers. Serve warm or at room temperature.

EGGPLANT KUKU

SERVES SIX

Looking back on the ingredients I relied on for Plenty, *there is a handful that has been resolutely pushed to the back of the cupboard in favor of the new. The dried sour cherries, for example, now mostly languish in the shadows of some new staples, barberries being one of them. These tiny sweet-and-sour Iranian berries have a dramatic sharpness that magically accentuates other flavors in a dish. There is a reason they look like little gems. Currants soaked in lemon juice or the old dried sour cherries, chopped up, can be used as alternatives, but barberries are worth seeking out in Middle Eastern groceries if you can. Don't be surprised by the slightly "wet" nature of my* kuku. *This is how it's meant to be, so serve it with a good hunk of bread.*

½ cup/120 ml sunflower oil, plus extra to brush the baking pan
4 small onions, thinly sliced (about 4 cups/400 g)
3 small eggplants, tops removed and peeled (1¼ lb/580 g)
5 eggs, lightly beaten
scant 3½ tbsp/25 g all-purpose flour
1½ tsp baking powder
¾ cup/35 g fresh bread crumbs
scant 1 cup/25 g flat-leaf parsley, finely chopped
½ tsp saffron threads, soaked in 1 tbsp hot water
3 cloves garlic, crushed
3 tbsp/20 g barberries
salt and black pepper

Preheat the oven to 400°F/210°C.

Pour the oil into a large, heavy pan and place over medium-high heat. Add the onions and sauté for 7 minutes, until they soften but don't brown.

While the onions are cooking, cut the eggplants in half crosswise and then cut each half lengthwise into slices ⅜-inch/1-cm thick. Cut the slices into strips ⅜-inch/1-cm thick, so that you end up with batons 2¾ to 3¼-inches/7 to 8-cm long and ⅜-inch/1-cm-wide and thick. Add the batons and ½ teaspoon salt to the cooking onions and continue to cook over medium-high heat, stirring occasionally and gently so that the eggplant does not break up, for 12 to 14 minutes, until the eggplant is completely soft. Leave aside to cool down.

In a large bowl, whisk together the eggs, flour, baking powder, bread crumbs, parsley, saffron water, garlic, ½ teaspoon salt, and a good grind of black pepper. Once smooth, fold in the barberries and the eggplant and onion mixture.

Line the base and the sides of an 8-inch/20-cm cake pan with waxed paper and brush the paper lightly with oil. Pour the egg mixture into the pan and bake for about 35 minutes, until golden brown and completely cooked. Insert a skewer into the middle of the cake to make sure the egg has set.

Remove from the oven and leave to cool down. Serve warm or at room temperature, sprinkled with parsley, if you like. The kuku will keep in the fridge for 2 days.

CRACKED

SERVES FOUR

EGGPLANT CHEESECAKE

¼ cup plus 1 tsp/65 ml olive oil, plus extra for brushing foil
2 medium eggplants, cut crosswise into slices ¾-inch/2-cm thick (1½ lb/700 g)
5 oz/150 g feta, crumbled into large chunks
5 oz/150 g cream cheese
3 eggs
¼ cup/60 ml heavy cream
1 cup/150 g baby plum tomatoes, halved lengthwise
⅓ cup/10 g oregano leaves, torn
1½ tsp za'atar
salt and black pepper

We weren't sure we'd have space to include this recipe and Eggplant Kuku (page 241). The process of elimination was totally unsuccessful, however, so we just had to find room for both. Heaven as a large square for lunch, it also works well cut down to smaller pieces for nibbles before supper.

Preheat the oven to 400°F/210°C. Line the base and sides of a deep 7½-inch/19-cm square baking pan (or a round baking pan 8-inches/20-cm in diameter) with aluminum foil and brush with a little olive oil.

Lay the eggplant slices on a baking sheet lined with parchment paper and brush with ¼ cup of the olive oil, making sure the eggplants absorb plenty of oil. Sprinkle with ¼ teaspoon salt and a generous grind of black pepper. Roast for 40 minutes, until the eggplant slices are soft and golden. Set aside to cool. Turn down the oven temperature to 325°F/170°C.

Place the feta, cream cheese, eggs, cream, and some black pepper in a bowl and beat with a handheld mixer until smooth and thick.

Arrange the eggplant slices in the prepared baking pan; they should fill up the pan as they lean against one another, almost standing on their sides. Fill the gaps between the pieces with tomatoes and sprinkle with half the oregano.

Pour the cream mixture into the pan, just enough to leave some eggplant pieces and tomatoes exposed, sprinkle with the remaining oregano, and bake in the oven for 35 to 40 minutes, until the custard sets and turns golden. Remove from the oven and let cool to room temperature.

Remove the cake from the pan and cut into 4 squares (or into wedges, if using a round dish). Mix the za'atar with the remaining 1 teaspoon olive oil, brush this gently over the top and sides of the cake, and serve.

FRITTER ROULETTE

SERVES FOUR

The stakes were considerably lowered once I changed the whole green chile—initially planned to be dropped in the center of each of these sweetish pancakes—to the altogether less fiery option of Padrón peppers. An air of excitement still lingers when a plate of these peppers is being devoured, as rumour has it that once in a while a really hot one will come along. But I've never seen anyone reach for the fire extinguisher yet. These are wonderful for a weekend brunch or a light supper, with just a simple salad alongside. Padrón peppers are not as widely available as they should be, but you'll often see them in packets on delicatessen counters, in some butcher shops and fish markets, in Spanish groceries, and at farmers' markets. If you can't get hold of any, don't worry: the fritters are still great without them.

3 eggs
½ cup/120 ml coconut milk
scant ⅔ cup/75 g self-rising flour
¼ cup/30 g cornstarch
¾ tsp ground cumin
1½ tsp ground coriander
½ tsp ground turmeric
3 tbsp coriander seeds, toasted and lightly crushed
½ butternut squash, peeled and coarsely grated (about 1⅔ cups/225 g)
about 2¼ cups/300 g fresh or frozen corn kernels (from 2 ears if using fresh)
3 green onions, white and green parts, thinly sliced (about ⅓ cup/30 g)
1 cup/15 g cilantro leaves, chopped
½ red chile, seeded and finely chopped
about 1 cup/250 ml sunflower oil, for frying
5 oz/150 g Padrón peppers
3 limes, cut into wedges
salt and black pepper

Place the first 8 ingredients (up to and including the coriander seeds) in a large bowl, along with 1½ teaspoons salt and a good grind of black pepper. Whisk to form a smooth batter. Add the butternut squash, corn, green onions, cilantro, and chile and stir well.

Pour the oil to a depth of ⅜-inch/1-cm into a sauté pan and place over high heat. Scoop 3 tablespoons of the batter into the oil and cook for about 2 minutes. Using your hands, carefully push 1 to 3 peppers (depending on size) into the surface of the fritter and fry for another minute. Flip the fritter over and fry for another 3 minutes, until golden brown. Transfer to a plate lined with paper towels and keep somewhere warm while you continue with the remaining batter. Serve warm, with a wedge of lime alongside.

CRACKED

SERVES FOUR TO SIX

CAULIFLOWER CAKE

1 small cauliflower, outer leaves removed, broken into 1¼-inch/3-cm florets (about 4 cups/450 g)
1 medium red onion (6 oz/170 g)
5 tbsp/75 ml olive oil
½ tsp finely chopped rosemary
7 eggs
½ cup/15 g basil leaves, chopped
1 cup/120 g all-purpose flour, sifted
1½ tsp baking powder
⅓ tsp ground turmeric
1½ cups/150 g coarsely grated Parmesan or another aged cheese
melted unsalted butter, for brushing
1 tbsp white sesame seeds
1 tsp nigella seeds
salt and black pepper

Having lived in Britain for more than sixteen years, there are certain names and phrases with which I am perfectly familiar: Doctor Who, Ring a Ring o' Roses, Curly Wurlies, Blue Peter, *and cauliflower cheese, to name just a few; but I have no clue as to their meaning. This is mostly a disadvantage because I miss out on all sorts of innuendos and references, but occasionally it works pretty well for me. When it comes to cauliflower cheese, for example, what to me sounds like the most indulgent and comforting of dishes has to an alumnus of the British school system a stomach-turning echo of drearily soft florets swimming in a puddle of greasy water. So when it comes to cauliflower and particularly when cheese is involved, I need to work extra hard to convince my readers that this is something they might want to eat. Well, I think I've got a winner here.*

Serve this cake as a light supper alongside a makeshift salad of sliced cucumber, dill, mint, a little sugar, cider vinegar, and canola oil. Wrapped well, this cake will taste even better the next day.

Preheat the oven to 400°F/200°C.

Place the cauliflower florets in a saucepan and add 1 teaspoon salt. Cover with water and simmer for 15 minutes, until the florets are quite soft. They should break when pressed with a spoon. Drain and set aside in a colander to dry.

Cut 4 round slices, each ¼-inch/5-mm thick, off one end of the onion and set aside. Coarsely chop the rest of the onion and place in a small pan with the oil and rosemary. Cook for 10 minutes over medium heat, stirring from time to time, until soft. Remove from the heat and set aside to cool. Transfer the onion to a large bowl, add the eggs and basil, whisk well, and then add the flour, baking powder, turmeric, Parmesan, 1 teaspoon salt, and plenty of pepper. Whisk until smooth before adding the cauliflower and stirring gently, trying not to break up the florets.

Line the base and sides of a 9½-inch/24-cm springform cake pan with parchment paper. Brush the sides with melted butter, then mix together the sesame and nigella seeds and toss them around the inside of the pan so that they stick to the sides. Pour the cauliflower mixture into the pan, spreading it evenly, and arrange the reserved onion rings on top. Place in the center of the oven and bake for 45 minutes, until golden brown and set; a knife inserted into the center of the cake should come out clean. Remove from the oven and leave for at least 20 minutes before serving. It needs to be served just warm, rather than hot, or at room temperature.

MEMBRILLO AND STILTON QUICHE

SERVES SIX

This quiche, in canapé form, was one of the most popular items on our catering menu at Ottolenghi a couple of years ago. The combination of a sharp blue cheese alongside the intense sweetness of membrillo (quince paste) creates a wonderfully satisfying drama in the mouth. It's the one-stop answer to Christmas meals for vegetarians. Membrillo can be bought in many cheese shops and well-stocked supermarkets.

1 medium butternut squash, peeled and cut into ¾-inch/2-cm cubes (5 cups/700 g)
1½ tbsp olive oil
9 oz/250 g best-quality shortcrust pastry
7 oz/200 g Stilton, crumbled
2½ oz/75 g membrillo (quince paste), cut into ⅜-inch/1-cm dice
3 eggs
⅔ cup/150 ml heavy cream
⅔ cup/150 ml crème fraîche
salt and black pepper

Preheat the oven to 425°F/220°C.

Toss the squash with the oil, ¼ teaspoon salt, and some black pepper and spread the cubes out on a baking sheet. Roast for 30 minutes, turning once, until golden brown. Set aside to cool and turn down the oven temperature to 375°F/190°C.

On a floured work surface, roll out the pastry roughly ⅛-inch/3-mm thick and transfer it to a 9½-inch/24-cm quiche pan or fluted tart pan with a removable bottom. When lining, leave some pastry hanging over the edge. Prick the base of the pastry with a fork and chill for 20 minutes in the fridge. Line the pastry shell with parchment paper, fill it with dried beans or pie weights, and bake for 30 minutes. Remove the beans and paper and continue to bake for 10 minutes, until the pastry is golden brown. Remove and leave to cool.

Spread the roasted squash in the cooled pastry shell, dot the Stilton between the pieces, and sprinkle the membrillo over the top. Place the eggs, cream, and crème fraîche in a bowl with ¼ teaspoon salt and some black pepper. Whisk together and then pour this mixture over the squash, leaving some of the filling exposed. Place in the oven for about 40 minutes, until the custard has set. Remove from the oven and allow to rest before removing from the pan and breaking off the hanging pastry. Serve warm or at room temperature.

CORN AND GREEN ONION PANCAKES

SERVES FOUR TO SIX
makes 15 pancakes

6 ears corn, husks removed (2¼ lb / 1 kg)
1½ tsp olive oil
5 green onions, white and green parts, finely chopped (about ¾ cup / 70 g)
1 green chile, coarsely chopped
1 tsp ground cumin
1½ tsp brown sugar
2 eggs
¾ cup plus 1 tbsp / 100 g all-purpose flour
½ cup / 120 g clarified butter
2 limes, cut into wedges
salt and white pepper

I'm not sure something that has been around for as long as corn fritters can claim to have a modern-day father, but credit is due to Bill Granger for getting these onto people's breakfast radar. Of all the corn pancakes I've tried over the years, these are certainly the most successful: fluffy and spongy but with nothing soft in terms of flavor.

Place a ridged grill pan over high heat until smoking. Brush 1 ear of corn with oil and grill for 5 minutes, turning regularly until charred all over. Set aside.

Remove the kernels from the remaining 5 ears by holding them upright on a work surface and running a sharp knife between the base of the kernels and the cob. Place the kernels in a food processor with half the green onions, the chile, cumin, sugar, 1 egg, ¾ teaspoon salt, and a good grind of black pepper. Blitz for 1 minute, until smooth, and then transfer to a bowl. Separate the remaining egg and add the yolk to the mix, along with the flour and the remaining green onions. Cut the smoky corn kernels off the grilled ear and gently stir them into the corn mixture. Whisk the egg white to soft peaks and then fold it into the mixture.

Heat a large sauté pan over medium-high heat and add half the butter. Add 2 heaped tablespoons of batter for each pancake and fry for about 2 minutes on each side, until golden brown. Cook the pancakes in batches of 3 or 4—you don't want to crowd the pan—and remove and keep them warm as you cook the rest, adding more butter as necessary. Serve warm, alongside the lime wedges.

SPICY SCRAMBLED EGGS

SERVES FOUR

Many of my brunch dishes were devised BC (before children), so food-meets-the-need-to-soothe was often in mind when cooking on a Sunday morning. A few dishes have remained part of the weekend breakfast repertoire since we started turning in early on a Saturday night. This is one of them.

....

Put a large, preferably nonstick sauté pan over medium heat and add the oil, cumin, caraway, onion, ginger, and chile. Cook for 8 minutes, stirring occasionally, until the onion is soft. Add the ground spices, tomato paste, and ¾ teaspoon salt and cook and stir for 2 minutes. Add the tomatoes and cook for a further 8 to 10 minutes, until most of the liquid has evaporated. Add the eggs, turn down the heat to medium-low, and continuously, but very gently, scrape the base of the pan with a wooden spatula. You want to end up with large, curd-like folds and you want the eggs to be soft and very moist. Cook the mixture for a total of about 3 minutes. Sprinkle with the green onions, cilantro, and chile flakes and serve at once.

2 tbsp sunflower oil
¾ tsp cumin seeds
½ tsp caraway seeds
1 small onion, finely diced (⅔ cup/100 g)
1¼-inch/3-cm piece fresh ginger (about ⅓ oz/10 g), peeled and finely chopped
1 medium red chile, seeded and finely chopped
¼ tsp ground turmeric
¼ tsp ground cardamom
½ tsp tomato paste
4 medium tomatoes, peeled and cut into ¾-inch/2-cm dice (1⅔ cups/300 g)
8 eggs, beaten
3 green onions, white and green parts, thinly sliced (about ½ cup/50 g)
⅔ cup/10 g cilantro leaves, chopped
½ tsp Urfa chile flakes, or ¼ tsp regular chile flakes
salt

SERVES FOUR

KALE AND CHEESE PIKELETS

1¾ oz / 50 g kale (2 to 4 medium leaves), tough stalks removed and thinly sliced
1⅓ cups / 170 g self-rising flour
1 tsp finely grated lemon zest
1 egg yolk
⅔ cup / 150 ml whole milk
5½ tbsp / 80 g unsalted butter, melted
⅔ cup / 150 g cottage cheese
1¾ oz / 50 g Stilton, broken into ⅜-inch / 1-cm chunks
1 cup / 15 g dill leaves, coarsely chopped
2 egg whites, whisked to soft peaks
salt

Sauce
1 tbsp olive oil
¼ tsp chile flakes
7 tbsp / 100 g sour cream
salt

Pancake Day (the day before Ash Wednesday) always takes me by surprise each year. I'm not one to abstain from food and definitely don't practice any sort of religious self-denial—but it's always a joy to have an excuse to fill batter with all sorts of things one is meant to give up for the month ahead. Pikelets, drop scones, Scotch pancakes—what these are called depends on who's cooking. In any case, they are soft and fluffy mini pancakes and reheat very well, whatever time of the year it happens to be.

Preheat the oven to 400°F / 200°C.

Bring a saucepan of water to a boil. Add the kale and blanch for 1 minute. Drain well, making sure all the water is squeezed out, and set aside.

For the sauce, place the olive oil in a small saucepan with the chile flakes. Cook over medium-high heat for just 1 minute before transferring to a small bowl. Leave to cool, then mix in the sour cream and ⅛ teaspoon salt. Keep in the fridge until needed.

In a large bowl, stir together the flour, lemon zest, and a scant ½ teaspoon salt. Make a well in the center and add the egg yolk and milk. Use a wooden spoon to combine the ingredients, starting from the center and working your way toward the edge, until you get a thick batter, almost like dough. Add the kale, half the butter, the cottage cheese, Stilton, and dill. Mix together before, finally, using a rubber spatula to gently fold in the whisked egg whites.

Heat a large nonstick sauté pan over medium heat with half of the remaining butter. When it starts to foam, use half the batter to make 4 round pikelets, each about 3½-inches / 9-cm wide and ⅔-inch / 1.5-cm thick. Fry for about 5 minutes over low heat, turning once, until both sides are golden brown. Transfer to a large baking sheet and repeat with the remaining butter and batter. Place in the oven for 10 minutes, until cooked through. Place 2 pikelets on each plate and serve warm, with a generous spoonful of the sauce on top or alongside.

BAKED

SERVES FOUR
as a main course

CORSICAN PIE WITH ZUCCHINI FLOWERS

2 tbsp olive oil, plus extra for brushing
½ small red onion, thinly sliced (about ¾ cup/85 g)
3 celery stalks and leaves, thinly sliced (8 oz/220 g)
8 large Swiss chard leaves, white stalks discarded, coarsely chopped (about 4 cups/175 g)
2 cloves garlic, thinly sliced
2 tbsp torn mint leaves
2 tbsp chopped flat-leaf parsley
2 tsp chopped sage
½ cup/75 g crumbled feta
½ cup/50 g finely grated pecorino
2 tbsp/15 g pine nuts, lightly toasted
grated zest of 1 lemon
12 oz/350 g all-butter puff pastry
6½ tbsp/100 g brocciu or ricotta
6 to 7 zucchini flowers, cut in half lengthwise if large, or 6 to 7 long, shaved strips of raw zucchini (optional)
1 egg, lightly beaten
salt and black pepper

Cooking on location is a very lengthy process. It often takes an hour or two, sometimes much more, to get the cooking station ready, the lighting right, the camera angles, and the sound. By the time we're ready to shoot, everybody is hungry and tired, so our generous hosts often spoil us with snacks and drinks. Setting up for the Swiss chard scene when shooting my Mediterranean Island Feast *program took even longer than usual because we had to wait for the restaurant's guests to finish their lunch and leave before we could even start getting ready. In the meantime, Monique, the chef and owner of the legendary Chez Sraphin, buttered us up with tremendous local charcuterie and lots and lots of red wine. By the time we were ready to start, everybody was pretty beat and completely unfocused. The result was utter lethargy and the shoot being dragged almost until sunset, when, of course . . . it was time to eat again.*

You can use a wide range of wild, cultivated, or supermarket greens in this recipe. Consider nettles, beet tops, turnip tops, spinach, or watercress in place of the chard. The combination is also up to you, so choose the ones you like most. The zucchini flowers look wonderful, but you can leave them out or substitute long shaved strips of zucchini for them, if you prefer. Brocciu, produced on the island of Corsica and considered a national food, is a fresh, young white cheese made with goat's or sheep's milk. I couldn't omit it from the ingredients—Monique would never forgive me!—but the easier-to-find Italian ricotta can be used just as well instead.

Place the olive oil in a large sauté pan over medium-high heat and sauté the onion, celery, chard, garlic, mint, parsley, and sage. Cook, stirring continuously, for 15 minutes, until the greens have wilted and the celery has softened completely. Remove from the heat and stir in the feta, pecorino, pine nuts, lemon zest, ¼ teaspoon salt, and a hearty grind of black pepper. Leave aside to cool.

Preheat the oven to 425°F/220°C.

Roll out the pastry ⅛-inch/3-mm thick, then cut it into a circle about 12-inches/30-cm in diameter. Place on a baking sheet lined with parchment paper. Spread the filling out on the pastry, leaving a 1¼-inch/3-cm border all the way around. Dot the filling with large chunks of brocciu and top with zucchini flowers. Bring the pastry up around the sides of the filling and pinch the edges together firmly to form a secure, decorative lip over the edge of the tart. Alternatively, press with the tines of a fork. Brush the pastry with the egg and refrigerate for 10 minutes.

Bake the tart for 30 minutes, until the pastry is golden and cooked on the base. Remove from the oven and brush with a little olive oil. Serve warm or at room temperature.

See pictures on the preceding pages

EGGPLANT KADAIFI NESTS

SERVES SIX
as a starter or light lunch

Kadaifi, which you can get online or in Greek, Arab, or Turkish grocery stores, is a type of shredded filo pastry, or you can think of it as a bit like shredded wheat, only ten times tastier.

The pepper salsa is not essential but tastes great. Use it sparingly, so as to not mask the flavor of the eggplant and cheese, and keep any extra in the fridge for up to five days to spoon over roasted vegetables. If you don't make the salsa, a lemon wedge is an essential condiment.

- 4 medium eggplants (2¾ lb/1.2 kg)
- ¾ cup plus 1 tbsp/200 g ricotta
- ¾ cup/65 g coarsely grated aged pecorino
- scant 1 cup/25 g flat-leaf parsley leaves, chopped
- 1 egg, lightly beaten
- scant ½ cup/110 g unsalted butter, melted, plus extra for greasing the baking sheet
- 5½ tbsp/80 ml sunflower oil
- 8 oz/240 g kadaifi pastry
- salt and black pepper

Red pepper and tomato salsa
- 1 medium red pepper (5½ oz/160 g)
- 1 red chile
- 3 cloves garlic
- 4 tomatoes, peeled (14 oz/400 g)
- 2 tsp sherry vinegar
- 3½ tbsp/50 ml olive oil
- ¼ medium red onion, very finely diced (3½ tbsp/30 g)
- salt

Preheat the oven to 500°F/250°C. Pierce the eggplants in a few places with a sharp knife. Place them on a baking sheet on the top rack of the oven (keeping space for the peppers underneath) for 1½ hours, turning them occasionally, to blacken all sides. Remove from the oven and, when cool enough to handle, scoop the flesh into a colander, discard the skin, and leave the flesh to drain for at least 30 minutes.

While the eggplants are roasting, prepare the salsa. Put the pepper, chile, and garlic on a baking sheet and place underneath the eggplants in the oven for 10 minutes. Remove the chile and garlic, turn the pepper, and roast for another 20 minutes. Once the skin is blistered, put the pepper in a bowl and cover with plastic wrap. When cool, peel and seed both the pepper and chile and peel the garlic.

Cut half of the tomatoes into ⅜-inch/1-cm dice and set aside. Seed the remaining tomatoes and place in the bowl of a small food processor along with the pepper, chile, and garlic. Whizz to a paste, add the vinegar and ¾ teaspoon salt, and then slowly add the oil to make a thick sauce. Transfer to a bowl, add the diced tomatoes and onion, stir gently, and set aside.

Mix the drained eggplant in a bowl with the ricotta, pecorino, parsley, egg, ¾ teaspoon salt, and a good grind of black pepper. Lower the oven temperature to 425°F/220°C.

Now make the kadaifi nests. Mix together the melted butter and sunflower oil. Remove a ⅔ oz/20 g bundle of pastry from the pack and place in a small bowl. Add 1 tablespoon of the melted butter and oil and toss together so the pastry soaks it up. Take the bundle and spread it flat on a work surface into a rectangle roughly 6 by 2-inches/15 by 5-cm. Spoon 1½ tablespoons of the eggplant mixture onto one end of the pastry and then roll the pastry very loosely around the filling into an airy ball, so all the filling is covered. Repeat with the remaining pastry and filling and arrange all 12 stuffed balls inside a buttered baking dish or baking sheet, 12½ by 9-inches/31 by 23-cm, so that they are touching one another snugly. Drizzle over all the remaining butter and oil. Bake for 25 to 30 minutes, until the top of the nests are golden and crunchy. Serve at once, with the salsa on the side.

See pictures on the following pages

SERVES SIX TO EIGHT

BREAD AND PUMPKIN "FONDUE"

12 oz/350 g sourdough bread, sliced into pieces ⅔-inch/1.5-cm thick
1 medium pumpkin, peeled and cut into ¾-inch/2-cm chunks (about 5¾ cups/ 800 g)
2 small turnips, peeled and cut into ¾-inch/2-cm chunks (1½ cups/200 g)
1½ cups/170 g coarsely grated Gruyère
1½ cups/170 g coarsely grated Emmentaler
2½ tsp dry mustard
1⅔ cups/400 ml heavy cream
1½ cups/350 ml dry white wine
1 large clove garlic, crushed
½ tsp grated nutmeg
⅓ cup/10 g sage leaves, coarsely chopped
salt and white pepper

This was inspired by Ruth Reichl's (learn more about her in the Sweet Potatoes with Orange Bitters headnote on page 174) brilliant, pot-saving trick, where she uses a whole pumpkin to house the pumpkin flesh, creamy cheese, and crusty bread that is layered inside. Although my version makes use of a dish, it shares with the original the advantage of being a kind of cheese fondue that will not provoke fishing about in a pool of melted cheese for lost chunks of bread.

Preheat the oven to 400°F/210°C. Lay the sourdough out on a baking sheet and bake for 10 minutes, until lightly toasted. Remove and set aside.

In a large bowl, mix together the vegetables with a rounded 1 cup/120 g of a mixture of both cheeses and 1 teaspoon of the dry mustard. Spread the mixture into a deep gratin dish, roughly 9 by 13-inches/23 by 33-cm.

Place the cream and wine in a saucepan over medium heat. Whisk gently as you add the remaining 1½ teaspoons dry mustard, the garlic, nutmeg, sage, ½ teaspoon salt, and ¼ teaspoon white pepper. Warm through before pouring over the gratin.

Cover the dish with aluminum foil, place in the oven, and bake for 45 minutes.

Remove the foil and layer the bread on top, each piece slightly overlapping with the next. Press the bread down and turn it over so that it soaks up some of the liquid. Sprinkle all the remaining cheese on top, cover with foil, and cook for a further 15 minutes. Remove the foil and cook for a final 15 minutes, until the top is golden and crispy. Remove from the oven and set aside for 10 minutes before serving.

SERVES SIX
generously

MUSHROOM AND TARRAGON PITHIVIER

1¼ cups/300 ml vegetable stock
1¾ cups/50 g dried porcini mushrooms
3 tbsp olive oil
3 tbsp/45 g unsalted butter
14 oz/400 g small shallots, peeled and left whole
7 oz/200 g cremini mushrooms, cleaned and quartered
5 oz/150 g shiitake mushrooms, cleaned and halved
5 oz/150 g oyster mushrooms, cleaned and quartered
5 oz/150 g buna-shimeji (brown beech) mushrooms, separated into clusters
¾ cup plus 2 tbsp/200 g crème fraîche
2 tbsp ouzo or Pernod
½ cup/15 g tarragon leaves, chopped
½ cup/15 g flat-leaf parsley leaves, chopped
2 lb/900 g all-butter puff pastry
1 egg, beaten
salt and black pepper

Many people refuse to believe that, of all places, I got my basic training at Le Cordon Bleu cookery school. There really is nothing French about my cooking. As a matter of fact, I often describe it as anti-French, or at least anticlassical French. This has probably to do with the fact that I am not too big on stocks, I don't do brunoise, *and I use less meat and more vegetables in my cooking and tend to be more concerned about cooking the latter to perfection than the former.*

Still, I don't want to undermine anything I learned at that legendary culinary institution. It gave me all the basic tools I needed to set out on a career in food. I particularly remember my thrill at making a pithivier—*a sweet version with almond cream—using my own puff pastry. It was the first professional-looking thing I had ever made and I beamed with pride. This savory version is wonderfully rich and aniseedy and needs only a sharp leafy salad alongside.*

Bring the stock to a simmer and add the porcini mushrooms. Remove from the heat and set aside to soften.

Place 1 tablespoon of the oil in a large, heavy sauté pan with 1 tablespoon of the butter. Add the shallots and cook over medium-high heat for 10 minutes, stirring from time to time, until the shallots have softened and colored all over. Transfer to a bowl and set aside.

Add another 1 tablespoon of the oil and 1 tablespoon of the remaining butter to the pan. Keeping the pan over medium-high heat, add the cremini and shiitake mushrooms, and leave them for a minute without stirring. Stir and then cook for another 2 minutes before adding them to the shallots.

Place the remaining each 1 tablespoon oil and butter in the pan and repeat the process with the oyster and buna-shimeji mushrooms. Return the shallots and cooked mushrooms to the pan, along with the stock, porcini, ¾ teaspoon salt, and a good grind of black pepper. Simmer vigorously for 8 minutes, until the stock has reduced to one-third. Turn down the heat to low, add the crème fraîche, and cook for another 8 minutes. When just 2 to 3 tablespoons of sauce are left, add the ouzo, tarragon, and parsley. Cook for a final minute before transferring the mixture to a bowl and setting aside to cool.

Preheat the oven to 425°F/220°C.

Divide the pastry into 2 equal blocks and roll out each block into a square about ⅛-inch/3-mm thick. Rest them in the fridge for 20 minutes and then cut into circles: one 11-inches/28-cm in diameter, the other 12-inches/30-cm. Leave them to rest in the fridge again for at least 10 minutes.

Place the smaller circle on a baking sheet lined with parchment paper. Spread the mushroom filling on top, leaving ¾-inch/2-cm clear around the edge.

Brush the edge with egg and place the other circle over the filling, sealing the two edges together. Use the tines of a fork to make decorative parallel lines around the edge. Brush the pie with egg and use the blunt side of a small knife to draw curved lines from the center of the pie to the edge. Make sure you just score the pastry without cutting through it.

Place the pithivier in the oven and bake for about 35 minutes, until golden on top and cooked on the bottom. Remove from the oven and leave to rest for at least 10 minutes. Serve warm or at room temperature.

STUFFED PEPPERS WITH FONDANT RUTABAGA AND GOAT CHEESE

SERVES SIX

This was inspired by a dish that Scully made when we were in the last and very stressful stages of opening NOPI in early 2011. All the decisions and madness surrounding which linen, tables, recipes, cocktails, suppliers, glasses, and food processors to choose from stopped just for a second while we all sat and devoured Scully's dish of fondant rutabaga with melted cheese and savory cabbage. Classic comfort food. Here I use the same method for cooking rutabagas for a rich, unctuous stuffing. You could serve the rutabaga on its own, without the pepper and cheese, as a side to roast beef or pork.

Melt the butter in a large sauté pan over medium heat. Add the rutabaga, thyme, 1½ teaspoons salt, and a good grind of black pepper. Turn down the heat to low and cook, uncovered, for about 50 minutes, spooning the butter over the rutabaga from time to time, until the rutabaga is completely soft and caramelized. Use a slotted spoon to remove the rutabaga from the butter and add it to a large bowl along with the Parmesan, garlic, and capers. Set aside until needed. (The leftover butter can be used for cooking carrots or zucchini, if you like.)

Preheat the oven to 500°F/250°C.

Cut the peppers in half lengthwise, keeping the stalks on. Remove the seeds and white flesh and place, cut side up, on a large baking sheet lined with parchment paper. Drizzle the oil over the top, sprinkle with a pinch of salt, and place in the oven for 30 to 35 minutes, until the peppers are slightly charred and the flesh is completely soft. Remove the peppers from the oven and turn down the oven temperature to 425°F/220°C.

Spoon the rutabaga mixture into each pepper and dot the goat cheese on top. Return to the oven for a further 10 to 15 minutes, so that the cheese gets some color. Remove from the oven and allow to cool for about 5 minutes before serving warm, or serve at room temperature. Top each stuffed pepper with a sprinkle of parsley.

- ⅔ cup/150 g unsalted butter
- 1 large rutabaga, peeled and cut into ⅜-inch/1-cm dice (7 cups/1 kg)
- ⅓ cup/10 g thyme leaves
- 1 cup/100 g finely grated Parmesan
- 2 cloves garlic, crushed
- scant 5 tbsp/40 g capers, coarsely chopped
- 3 small yellow bell peppers (10 oz/280 g)
- 3 small red bell peppers (10 oz/280 g)
- 2 tsp olive oil
- 6 oz/180 g chèvre (goat cheese) log, broken into ⅜-inch/1-cm pieces
- ⅓ cup/10 g flat-leaf parsley leaves, coarsely chopped
- salt and black pepper

BAKED ARTICHOKE AND PEARLED SPELT SALAD

SERVES FOUR

3 large globe artichokes (2¾ lb / 1.2 kg)
7 tbsp / 100 ml lemon juice (about 2 large lemons)
2 bay leaves
2 thyme sprigs
4 cloves garlic, thinly sliced
½ cup / 125 ml white wine
¼ cup / 60 ml olive oil
1 cup / 150 g fresh or frozen green peas
about ½ cup / 100 g pearled spelt or barley, rinsed
⅔ cup / 20 g flat-leaf parsley leaves, coarsely chopped
1 Little Gem lettuce, cut in half lengthwise, each half cut into 3 or 4 wedges (4½ oz / 140 g)
1½ tsp Urfa chile flakes, or ½ tsp regular chile flakes
salt and black pepper

The pearling that gives this spelt its name is the process of polishing off the outer bran layer of the nutty plump grains. You can buy spelt whole or semipearled, but for a clean and silky-smooth texture (and much quicker cooking time), pearled spelt works best. It is often confused with farro (see page 139), which is the Italian word for emmer wheat. The conflation is an easy one to make—both are ancient wheat varieties with a nutty al dente bite—but spelt has a higher protein content, which makes it a favorite of those who watch their intake of wheat. Either way, both are great—hugely versatile and very happy to be paired with robust flavors.

Urfa chile flakes are a Turkish variety that is mild on heat but big on aroma. They are sweet and smoky, have a fantastically dark, purplish-red color, and go well with almost anything. They are widely available online, but other types of chile flakes can be substituted for them.

Preheat the oven to 425°F / 220°C.

To clean the artichokes, cut off most of the stalk and remove the tough outer leaves by hand. Once you reach the softer leaves, cut off ¾ to 1¼-inches / 2 to 3-cm from the tops of the leaves with a sharp serrated knife. Cut the artichoke in half lengthwise so you can reach the heart and scrape it clean of all hairs with a small knife. Rub the clean heart with 1 teaspoon of the lemon juice to prevent discoloring. Cut each artichoke half into slices ¼-inch / 5-mm thick. Place in cold water and stir in 1 tablespoon of the lemon juice.

Drain the artichokes and spread them out on a baking sheet, about 8½ by 9-inches / 21 by 23-cm. Add the remaining lemon juice, the bay leaves, thyme, garlic, wine, and olive oil. Cover with aluminum foil and bake for 30 to 35 minutes, until tender. Remove the foil and set aside until cool.

Fill a saucepan with plenty of cold water and bring to a boil. Add the peas and blanch for 30 seconds. Use a slotted spoon to plunge them immediately into cold water—you want to reuse the boiling water—then drain and leave to dry. Add the spelt to the pan and simmer gently until al dente; spelt will take 20 minutes and the barley will take 30 minutes. Drain, refresh under cold water, and set aside.

Drain the artichokes, preserving the cooking juices in a small bowl. Place the artichokes, along with 4 tablespoons of their liquid, in a large bowl. Add the peas, spelt, parsley, lettuce, ¾ teaspoon salt, and a good grind of black pepper. Toss gently, adding a tablespoon or two more of the cooking juices if the salad needs it. Sprinkle with the chile flakes and serve.

WINTER SAFFRON GRATIN

SERVES FOUR
generously

Different combinations of seasonal vegetables can be used in this recipe. The blend I chose has a balance of textures and sweetness that I love, but feel free to add, omit, or substitute as you like using carrots, turnips, salsify, celery root, beets, or sweet potatoes. Just remember to keep the total weight of the vegetables the same.

Preheat the oven to 350°F/180°C.

Bring a large saucepan of water to a boil, add the sliced vegetables, and blanch for 1 minute. Drain into a colander and set aside.

Put the milk and 1¼ cups/300 ml water in a small saucepan, add the saffron and place over medium heat. Cook for about 4 minutes, until warmed through but not boiling. Set aside to infuse for 5 minutes.

Place the butter in a small saucepan over medium heat. Add the flour and stir to form a paste. Cook gently for 2 minutes, stirring the whole time. Pour in the infused milk and water and beat with a whisk as the liquid thickens. Continue cooking and stirring for another 2 minutes before removing from the heat.

Stir in the cream and then add the chopped herbs, two-thirds of the Parmesan, ¾ teaspoon salt, and ¼ teaspoon white pepper and stir until smooth. Transfer the drained vegetables to a bowl, pour the sauce over them, and mix well. Grease an 8-inch/20-cm square baking dish and pour the vegetables and sauce into it. Don't try to level out the mixture too much: it should look rustic. Cover the dish with aluminum foil and place in the oven for 40 minutes.

Remove the foil, mix the remaining cheese with the bread crumbs, and scatter over the top. Increase the oven temperature to 400°F/210°C and return to the oven for about 15 minutes, until the crust is golden brown. Remove from the oven and set aside for 10 minutes before serving.

- 4 small Jerusalem artichokes, peeled and thinly sliced (9 oz/250 g)
- ½ small rutabaga, peeled and thinly sliced (9 oz/250 g)
- 2 small kohlrabies, peeled and thinly sliced (9 oz/250 g)
- 2 small parsnips, peeled and thinly sliced (9 oz/250 g)
- 7 tbsp/100 ml whole milk
- ½ tsp saffron threads
- 2 tbsp/30 g unsalted butter, plus extra for greasing the dish
- 4½ tbsp/35 g all-purpose flour
- ⅔ cup/150 ml heavy cream
- 2 oz/60 g flat-leaf parsley, chopped
- 2 oz/60 g basil, chopped
- 2 tbsp chopped tarragon
- about 1 cup/90 g coarsely grated Parmesan
- about ¼ cup/15 g panko bread crumbs
- salt and white pepper

SERVES EIGHT

TOMATO AND ALMOND TART

scant ⅔ cup / 140 g unsalted butter, at room temperature
2 eggs, beaten
about 1⅓ cups / 65 g fresh bread crumbs
¾ cup plus 2 tbsp / 80 g ground almonds
2 cloves garlic, crushed
6½ tbsp / 100 g ricotta
scant 3½ tbsp / 20 g finely grated Parmesan
½ cup / 15 g thyme leaves
13 oz / 375 g all-butter puff pastry
sunflower oil, for greasing
2¼ lb / 1 kg medium tomatoes (about 10), cut crosswise into slices ⅜-inch / 1-cm thick
24 black wrinkly olives, pitted (1¾ oz / 50 g)
2 tbsp olive oil
salt and black pepper

This is a savory version of the ubiquitous French fruit and frangipane tart. Just as in the sweet variation, the almond paste soaks up the juices and flavors of the fruit to create the most luscious layer of rich, nutty sweetness. It's perfect for a lunch party, along with the Spring Salad (page 28) or another green leaf salad. Anchovies can be used instead of the olives.

Preheat the oven to 475°F / 240°C.

Using a stand mixer, beat the butter until light and aerated. With the machine running on medium speed, slowly add the eggs. If the mixture separates, add some bread crumbs to bring it back together and keep on adding the eggs. Stop the machine, add the bread crumbs, almonds, and garlic, and work until everything is just combined.

Remove the bowl from the mixer and add the ricotta, Parmesan, half the thyme leaves, and ¼ teaspoon salt. Fold gently, until just combined, then set aside.

Roll out the pastry into 2 rectangular sheets each about 8 by 12-inches / 20 by 30-cm and ¹⁄₁₆-inch / 2-mm thick. Grease 2 baking sheets with a little bit of sunflower oil and lay your pastry pieces on top. Use an offset spatula to spread the almond mixture evenly over the pastries, leaving a ¾-inch / 2-cm border around the edge. Lay the tomato slices on top of each rectangle in 3 long rows, with a fair amount of overlap in the rows and between them. Sprinkle the olives and the remaining thyme over the top. Drizzle the tomatoes with half the olive oil and season with ¼ teaspoon salt and a good grind of black pepper.

Place the tarts in the oven and bake for 15 minutes. Turn down the oven temperature to 400°F / 200°C and continue baking for another 8 to 10 minutes, until the base is golden brown. At the halfway point, switch the pans between the racks and rotate them back to front to ensure the tarts color evenly. Once cooked, remove from the oven and allow to cool slightly. Drizzle the remaining olive oil over the top and serve.

RICOTTA AND ROSEMARY BREAD PUDDING

SERVES FOUR

The straightforward list of ingredients here masks the number of times this was tried and tested before we were happy with the result. Just when we were quietly wondering whether it was all worth it, the dish came together and sang. Raise a Bloody Mary to the power of perseverance whenever this is served with Sunday lunch. It works well as a vegetarian main course but would not say no to being accompanied by a lemony roasted chicken. The turnips add a nice peppery touch, but you can leave them out, if you like.

14 oz/400 g white sourdough bread, cut into slices ¾-inch/2-cm thick
3⅓ cups/800 ml whole milk
1 cup/250 ml heavy cream
2 rosemary sprigs, plus 1½ tsp chopped rosemary
1 large onion, quartered (5½ oz/160 g)
¼ tsp grated nutmeg
8 eggs
2 medium turnips, peeled and cut into slices ⅜-inch/1-cm thick (about 2¼ cups/260 g)
generous ¾ cup/200 g ricotta
1 cup/90 g coarsely grated Parmesan
7 tbsp/20 g finely chopped chives
olive oil, to finish
salt and white pepper

Preheat the oven to 200°F/100°C.

Spread out the sourdough slices on a baking sheet and bake in the oven for 30 minutes, turning once, until dry.

Place the milk, cream, rosemary stalks, onion, and nutmeg in a saucepan and bring to a gentle simmer, then remove from the heat and set aside to cool. Once tepid, strain and discard the onion and rosemary. Put the eggs in a bowl and whisk as you pour the milk mixture over them, forming a smooth custard. Season the custard with ½ teaspoon salt and ¼ teaspoon white pepper.

Meanwhile, bring a saucepan of water to a boil and blanch the turnip slices for 2 minutes. Drain, refresh under cold water, drain again, and dry. Layer the slices in a rectangular baking dish about 8½ by 12-inches/22 by 30-cm, covering the bottom completely.

Mix together the ricotta, Parmesan, chopped rosemary, and chives and spread over one side of each bread slice. Place the slices, cheese side up, in the dish, slightly overlapping them. Spoon the custard over the bread and gently press down so that the bread is immersed and soaks up the custard well. Leave to sit for about 1½ hours, gently pressing down the bread from time to time.

Preheat the oven to 400°F/200°C.

Cover the pudding with aluminum foil and bake for 20 minutes. Remove the foil and continue baking for about 30 minutes, until golden brown and crusty. Poke a knife into the center and press down gently; if no cream surfaces, the pudding is ready. Allow to sit for 10 minutes before brushing the top with oil and serving.

BAKED ORZO WITH MOZZARELLA AND OREGANO

SERVES FOUR

7 tbsp / 100 ml olive oil
1 large eggplant, cut into ¾-inch / 2-cm dice (3⅔ cups / 300 g)
4 medium carrots, peeled and cut into ⅔-inch / 1.5-cm dice (2⅓ cups / 300 g)
4 celery stalks, cut into ⅔-inch / 1.5-cm dice (2 cups / 200 g)
1 large onion, finely diced (scant 1¼ cups / 170 g)
3 cloves garlic, crushed
9 oz / 250 g orzo pasta, rinsed
1 tsp tomato paste
1⅔ cups / 380 ml vegetable stock
3 tbsp fresh oregano, chopped, or 1½ tbsp thyme leaves
grated zest of 1 lemon
4 oz / 120 g firm mozzarella, cut into ⅜-inch / 1-cm dice
6½ tbsp / 40 g grated Parmesan
3 medium tomatoes, cut into slices ⅜-inch / 1-cm thick (2¼ cups / 400 g)
1 tsp dried oregano
salt and black pepper

Even the most standard baked polenta dishes will always hold a place in my heart, for they comfort me and remind me of my father's cooking. This is no sentimental journey, however. It's a proud, sophisticated, and rather luxurious take on the casserole. People can get a bit sniffy about the firm, low-moisture mozzarella sold in blocks. If eaten by itself, it's a very different beast from the buffalo, but it works brilliantly for grating or finely dicing in a dish like this.

Preheat oven to 400°F / 200°C.

Heat the olive oil in a large sauté pan over medium-high heat. Add the eggplant and cook for 8 minutes, stirring occasionally, until golden brown. Remove with a slotted spoon to paper towels and set aside. Add the carrots and celery to the pan and fry for 8 minutes. Transfer to paper towels. Turn down the heat to medium and add the onion and garlic. Cook for 5 minutes, stirring often. Add the orzo and tomato paste and cook for a further 2 minutes.

Remove the pan from the heat and add the stock, fresh oregano, and lemon zest. Add the cooked vegetables, mozzarella, Parmesan, 1 teaspoon salt, and ½ teaspoon pepper. Mix well and transfer to a rectangular baking dish, 8½ by 10½-inches (21 by 27-cm) or a round one, 10.5 inches (27 cm) in diameter. Arrange the tomatoes on top and sprinkle with the dried oregano, ¼ teaspoon salt, and a grind of black pepper.

Bake for 40 minutes, until all the liquid has been absorbed and the pasta is cooked through. Remove, leave to settle for 5 minutes, and serve.

SERVES SIX

TALEGGIO AND SPINACH ROULADE

Dough
2/3 cup / 160 ml whole milk
2 tsp active dried yeast
2¾ cups plus 1 tbsp / 350 g white bread flour
1 tsp superfine sugar
3½ tbsp / 50 ml sunflower oil plus extra for bowl
1 egg, plus 1 egg yolk
salt

Filling
1/3 cup / 80 g crème fraîche
3½ cups / 100 g baby spinach leaves
2/3 cup / 20 g basil leaves
1 cup / 100 g coarsely grated pecorino
9 oz / 250 g Taleggio, broken into ¾-inch / 2-cm chunks
5 oz / 150 g semidried tomatoes, drained (or 14 oz / 400 g fresh cherry tomatoes, baked in the oven—see headnote)
salt

To finish
1 egg, beaten
2 tsp poppy seeds

Not all cheeses are born equal, at least when it comes to melting. The queen of them all, in this department at least, is definitely Taleggio, an Italian cow's milk variety with a hefty aroma and the most soothing and creamy of textures, particularly when melted. This is a bread loaf with a built-in filling. Serve it warm and you've got a hearty cheese toastie, or at room temperature for a portable sandwich. You can make your own semidried tomatoes by halving some cherry tomatoes and spreading them out, cut side up, on a baking sheet. Drizzle them with olive oil, sprinkle with salt, and bake in a 375°F / 190°C oven for about 50 minutes. Alternatively, buy them marinated in oil labeled "sun-blushed" or "semidried" tomatoes.

To make the dough, place the milk in a saucepan and warm through very slightly, just to reach about 86°F / 30°C. Add the yeast, stir to dissolve, and set aside for 10 minutes.

Place the flour, sugar, oil, egg, egg yolk, and ½ teaspoon salt in a stand mixer. Add the milk and yeast and work with a dough hook on low speed for about 2 minutes. Increase the speed to high and knead for another 7 minutes, by which point the dough should turn into a smooth, shiny ball. You can also do this by hand; you'll just need to knead the dough for an extra 5 minutes.

Transfer the dough to a large bowl brushed with a little oil, cover the bowl with a wet tea towel, and set aside somewhere warm for about 45 minutes, until the dough has doubled in size. Line a 12 by 16-inch / 30 by 40-cm baking sheet with parchment paper. Transfer the dough to a lightly floured work surface and roll it out thinly to the size of the pan. Line the pan with the dough, pulling it right into the corners. Cover with the tea towel again and leave for 30 minutes, until the dough has risen slightly.

Using an offset spatula, spread the crème fraîche all over the surface of the risen dough. Sprinkle the surface with ½ teaspoon salt and then top evenly with the spinach, basil, pecorino, Taleggio, and semidried tomatoes. Carefully pick up one of the longer sides of the dough and roll it all up into a neat spiral log shape. Rest the log seam side down so it doesn't unravel when baked. Cover the pan with the tea towel again and leave for another 30 minutes.

Preheat the oven to 425°F / 220°C. Brush the surface of the roulade gently with the beaten egg and then scatter over the poppy seeds. Bake for 10 minutes, then turn down the oven temperature to 350°F / 180°C and continue baking for another 25 minutes. Don't worry if the roulade cracks a little. When ready, it should be a nice dark brown. Stick a sharp knife into it to check: it should come out with some melted cheese but not any dough. Let cool down a little before cutting into thick slices. Alternatively, allow to cool completely and slice as needed.

SERVES FOUR

BATATA HARRA

2¼ lb / 1 kg Yukon gold potatoes, peeled and cut into ¾-inch / 2-cm dice
2 tbsp olive oil
2 tbsp sunflower oil
6 large cloves garlic, crushed
1 tsp pul biber (Turkish chile flakes), or ½ tsp regular chile flakes
2 large red peppers, cut into ¾-inch / 2-cm dice (10 oz / 260 g)
2 cups / 30 g cilantro, chopped
grated zest of 1 lemon, plus 1 tbsp lemon juice
salt and black pepper

This Lebanese and Syrian dish is probably my favorite way with potatoes. It is simple, spicy, and soothing all at the same time. It is wonderful on its own or as a side dish, along with grilled fish or something yogurt based such as Mixed Vegetables and Yogurt with Green Chile Oil (page 193) or the Yogurt and Kaffir Lime Leaf Spread (page 234). You can adjust the degree of heat to suit your threshold; just remember, it is meant to be pretty spicy. Chile flakes vary widely, so you may want to assess how hot yours are before adding the full amount.

Preheat the oven to 500°F / 260°C.

Bring a large saucepan of salted water to a boil, add the potatoes, and cook for 3 minutes. Drain in a colander and set aside until completely dry.

Line a roasting pan with aluminum foil and spread out the potatoes in the pan. Pour both oils over the potatoes and sprinkle with 1½ teaspoons salt and some black pepper. Mix gently, then roast in the oven for 10 minutes. Add the garlic, chile flakes, red peppers, and half the cilantro and return to the oven for a further 25 minutes, stirring once halfway through, until the potatoes are nicely colored and completely tender.

Remove the potatoes from the oven and transfer to a large mixing bowl. Add the lemon zest and juice and give everything another gentle stir. Serve warm or at room temperature, stirring in the remaining cilantro at the last minute.

BAIGAN CHOKA

SERVES TWO TO FOUR

After all these years of cooking and writing recipes, I am still amazed every time I notice how even the minutest variation in technique can make a spectacular difference. This Trinidadian eggplant dip, served with roti or naan, was introduced to me by my ex-colleague Tricia Jadoonanan. In theory, it is not all that different from baba ghanoush or other Middle Eastern eggplant salads that I've cooked over the years. This recipe, however, uses hot oil flavored with onion and some vigorous whisking to achieve a wonderful creaminess and subtlety miles away from the intensity of those old favorites. To make it even milder, leave out the garlic and use less chile, if you like. Serve it as a dip, with bread, or as a condiment next to roasted lamb, chicken, or pumpkin.

3 medium eggplants (2 lb/900 g in total)
1 mild red chile
1½ tsp olive oil
1½ tsp sunflower oil
½ small onion, thinly sliced (about ½ cup/50 g)
1 clove garlic, crushed
1 tbsp chopped chives
salt

To cook the eggplants on a gas stove top, which is the best way to get a smoky flavor, line the area around the burner heads with aluminum foil and place the eggplants directly on 3 medium flames. Roast for about 15 minutes, turning frequently with metal tongs, until the skin is burnt all over. Burn the chile over a flame for just a minute or two, until it blisters and chars.

To broil the eggplants in the oven, preheat the broiler. Prick the eggplants in several places with a sharp knife. Put them on a baking sheet lined with aluminum foil and place under the broiler. Cook for about 1 hour and 10 minutes, turning them every 20 minutes, until they have deflated and their skin is charred and burnt all over. Add the chile to the pan for the last 10 minutes, so that it too gets charred.

Remove the eggplants from the stove top or broiler and leave to cool a little before scraping out the flesh and discarding the skin. Place the flesh in a colander to drain for at least 30 minutes. Peel the skin off the chile, remove the seeds, and finely chop the flesh.

Place the eggplant and chile flesh in a large bowl and whisk vigorously for 2 to 3 minutes until light and creamy. You can also use a handheld mixer.

Meanwhile, heat both oils in a small pan over high heat. Add the onion and fry for 2 minutes, stirring often, to cook the onion just a little. You want it to remain slightly crunchy. Pour the hot oil and onion into the bowl with the eggplant and keep whisking for another minute. Add the garlic, chives, and ½ teaspoon salt and whisk a little longer. Taste, add more salt if you like, and serve.

SERVES SIX

ROOT VEGETABLE PIES

scant 2 cups / 240 g all-purpose flour, plus extra for dusting
¾ cup plus 1½ tbsp / 190 g unsalted butter, fridge-cold, diced
¼ cup / 60 g sour cream
3 tbsp olive oil
1 tsp medium curry powder
2 tsp caraway seeds
2 tsp black mustard seeds
½ tsp ground cardamom
1 large onion, coarsely chopped (about 1⅓ cups / 180 g)
1 green chile, seeded and finely chopped
1 tbsp thyme leaves, chopped
2 cloves garlic, crushed
1 small russet potato, peeled and cut into ¾-inch / 2-cm dice (about 1 cup / 160 g)
1 medium carrot, peeled and cut into ¾-inch / 2-cm dice (about ¾ cup / 100 g)
1 medium parsnip, peeled and cut into ¾-inch / 2-cm dice (about ¾ cup / 100 g)
1 cup / 250 ml vegetable stock
½ small butternut squash, peeled and cut into ¾-inch / 2-cm dice (about 1¾ cups / 250 g)
¼ tsp superfine sugar
1 cup / 120 g coarsely grated aged Cheddar
1 cup / 15 g cilantro, chopped
1 egg, beaten
salt and black pepper

Serve these with a green salad for lunch or eat them as they are, as a snack. The filling is also delicious on its own, as a vegetarian rice topping. These are also great reheated and eaten the next day, so don't be afraid to make the whole batch if there aren't six of you to eat them the first time around. With thanks to Helen Goh.

Place the flour, butter, sour cream, and ½ teaspoon salt in a food processor and work until the mixture comes together. Transfer to a work surface and gently knead for 1 minute, adding a little flour if needed, until soft and malleable. Wrap in plastic wrap and let rest in the fridge for 30 minutes.

Place a large sauté pan for which you have a lid over medium-high heat. Add 2 tablespoons of the oil and, once hot, add the curry powder, caraway seeds, mustard seeds, and cardamom. Cook for just a few seconds, stirring and making sure the spices don't burn, before adding the onion, chile, and thyme. Cook for another 4 minutes, add the garlic, and cook for another minute, stirring. Add the potato, carrot, and parsnip, stir, and then pour in the stock. Turn down the heat to medium, cover, and cook for 5 minutes. Add the squash, sugar, ¾ teaspoon salt, a generous grind of black pepper and continue to simmer, covered, for 10 minutes, stirring from time to time, until the vegetables are cooked through and most of the liquid has evaporated. You should have about 3 tablespoons liquid left; add a little water if needed. Uncover, remove from the heat, and set aside to cool totally before stirring in the cheese and cilantro.

Preheat the oven to 400°F / 200°C.

Use the remaining 1 tablespoon oil to brush the sides and bases of a large 6-cup muffin tin (each cup should be 2½-inches / 6-cm wide and 1½-inches / 4-cm deep). Line the bases with circles of parchment paper and place the tin in the fridge. Roll out the pastry ⅟₁₆ to ⅛-inch / 2 to 3-mm thick, cut out 6 circles each 5½-inches / 14-cm in diameter, and press down into the tin. Trim the edges, reusing the spare pastry to roll out for a second time. Cut out 6 more circles, 3¼-inches / 8-cm in diameter—these will form lids.

Fill each pie with about ½ cup / 120 g of filling, brush the rims with egg, and place the lids on top. Pinch the edges together securely, brush the lids with the remaining egg, and prick each pie with a fork in a few places. Allow to rest in the fridge for 10 minutes. Place in the oven and bake for 30 to 35 minutes, until golden brown. Remove from the oven and set aside for 5 minutes before serving warm, or serve at room temperature.

SWEETENED

BLACK CURRANT FRIANDS

MAKES SIX

½ cup plus 1 tbsp/125 g unsalted butter, melted, plus an extra 4 tsp/20 g for brushing the tin
scant ½ cup/60 g all-purpose flour, plus extra for dusting
6½ tbsp/60 g blanched almonds
6½ tbsp/50 g pistachios, plus 1 tsp, chopped, to garnish
¼ tsp ground cinnamon
1 cup/200 g superfine sugar
grated zest of 1 lemon
1 tbsp mashed banana
3 egg whites (about 6 tbsp/100 g)
1 cup/120 g fresh or frozen black currants, tossed in 2 tsp all-purpose flour, plus extra for garnish (optional)
salt

Lemon glaze (optional)
3½ tbsp/50 ml lemon juice
1⅔ cups/200 g confectioners' sugar

The number of recipes I write means that I am incredibly systematic about the way they are filed. No sooner was this recipe perfected than it slipped, mysteriously, through the filing system net, only to be remembered years later. It's like when you find money in your jeans pocket that has been there for weeks: rediscovery feels like a gift, even though it was yours in the first place. Friands are small French cakes, popular in Australia and New Zealand as well as, of course, throughout France. The French word friand *means "dainty" or a "gourmet who delights in delicate tastes." I'd like to extend the definition, in this case, to anyone with a distinguished sweet tooth in need of the royal treatment.*

Preheat the oven to 400°F/200°C.

Place a large 6-cup muffin tin (each cup should be 2½-inches/6-cm wide and 1½-inches/4-cm deep) in the freezer for 10 minutes. Melt the 4 teaspoons/20 g butter, then brush it generously over the molds. Dust the molds with flour. Place a circle of parchment paper at the bottom of each mold, to prevent the cakes from sticking to the tin, and return to the freezer.

Put the nuts, flour, cinnamon, and all except 2 tablespoons of the superfine sugar into a food processor and work to a coarse, bread crumb–like texture. Tip the nut mix into a bowl and add the melted butter, lemon zest, and banana. Stir to combine.

Whisk the egg whites with ⅛ teaspoon salt and the remaining 2 tablespoons sugar until the whites form soft peaks (around 6 minutes with a handheld mixer). Gently fold one-third into the nut and banana mixture. Once incorporated, gently fold in another third, along with the currants. Finally, fold in the remaining egg whites.

Pour the batter into the muffin tin so that it rises two-thirds up the sides of each mold. Place in the oven and bake for 20 to 25 minutes, until a skewer inserted into the center of a cake comes out clean. Remove from the oven and leave to cool. To unmold, run a sharp knife along the edges of the friands and gently tip the tin over.

Once the friands have cooled, make the glaze. Whisk together the lemon juice and confectioners' sugar in a small bowl, adding more lemon juice or sugar if needed to make a thick yet easily pourable glaze. Spoon the icing liberally over the friands, letting it drip down the sides. Sprinkle with the chopped pistachios and put 3 or 4 black currants on top of each friand, if you have them to spare.

See pictures on the following pages

BAKED RHUBARB WITH SWEET LABNEH

SERVES FOUR

I am slightly obsessive about labneh. *I like it on its own, spread on a plate, drizzled with olive oil, sprinkled with* za'atar *and chile flakes, and served with warm pita. I also have it with grilled vegetables or dotted in a fresh tomato and cucumber salad. I serve it with roasted lamb chops or fried fish and even as a dessert, sweetened with confectioners' sugar and orange blossom syrup and accompanied with baked fruit.*

To those of you who haven't been following my pontificating about the merits of strained yogurt, which is essentially what labneh *is, I warmly invite you to join the fan club. Super popular around the whole of the eastern Mediterranean, you can buy it at many Middle Eastern grocery stores, either as small, white balls marinated in olive oil, to add to savory dishes, or as a thick and creamy yogurt sold at the cheese counter or in chilled tubs.*

The best, though, is to make your own by draining the yogurt overnight to reach a rich and creamy texture (although 4 to 6 hours will just about do). Squeeze the yogurt bundle a couple of times while it's draining to speed up the process. Plain Greek yogurt will work well if that's easier. The finished dish won't be as rich, but it will still be wonderfully fresh.

3¼ cups / 800 g natural yogurt
⅔ cup / 80 g confectioners' sugar
14 oz / 400 g trimmed rhubarb (about 9 stalks)
7 tbsp / 100 ml muscat or another dessert wine
5½ tbsp / 70 g superfine sugar
½ vanilla bean, halved lengthwise, seeds scraped
1 lemon, rind shaved in strips from half, zest grated from the other half
2½ tbsp / 20 g shelled pistachios, coarsely chopped
salt

Put the yogurt in a bowl with the confectioners' sugar and ¼ teaspoon salt and mix well. Assemble a large quadruple-layered square of cheesecloth on a layered work surface and transfer the yogurt mixture to the center of it. Bring up the sides of the cloth to form a bundle, tie the top with a rubber band or string, and hang it over a bowl in the fridge for up to 18 hours, squeezing the bundle from time to time.

Preheat the oven to 400°F / 200°C.

Cut the rhubarb into 2½-inch / 6-cm lengths and mix with the muscat, superfine sugar, vanilla bean and seeds, and lemon rind strips. Transfer to a baking dish just large enough to accommodate the rhubarb snugly. Roast, uncovered, for 20 minutes, until the rhubarb is tender but not mushy. Set aside to cool.

Just before serving, take the yogurt from the fridge and give it a good squeeze to release any extra water. Remove from the cloth and place in a bowl. Stir in the grated lemon zest and spoon into serving dishes. Spoon the rhubarb on top with some of the cooking juices and then sprinkle with the pistachios.

SERVES FOUR
generously

QUINCE POACHED IN POMEGRANATE JUICE

2 large quinces, peeled and quartered (scant 2 lb/ 850 g)
3⅓ cups/800 ml pomegranate juice
5½ tbsp/70 g superfine sugar
1 vanilla bean, halved lengthwise, seeds scraped
rind shaved in strips from 1 large orange, plus 3½ tbsp/50 ml juice (about ½ orange)
2 star anise pods
about ⅓ cup/65 g pomegranate seeds (seeds from about ½ pomegranate)
4 oz/120 g clotted cream
2 tsp freshly shredded mint leaves (optional)

This is a glorious and festive dessert and, if I may say so without enraging too many traditionalists, undeniably superior to the old Christmas pudding. It also has the further advantage that while Christmas pudding is incongruous 364 days of the year, quinces appear from October onward and stick around until after the last mince pie has been eaten.

Quinces take on a wonderful red color while poaching in the pomegranate juice. In the past, quince varieties sold in markets would take hours to cook and this would cause them to go red naturally due to the sugars slowly caramelizing. Today's quinces normally take less than half an hour to cook and stay pale; that is, unless they are cooked in pomegranate juice.

Remove the core from the quince quarters. Discard half of the cores and tie the remaining half in a bundle using a tea towel or double-layered cheesecloth. Place the quince quarters in a heavy saucepan and add the pomegranate juice, sugar, vanilla bean and seeds, orange rind and juice, and star anise. Add the wrapped-up cores and bring to a boil. Turn down the heat to a gentle simmer, cover the pan, and cook for about 20 minutes, until the quince quarters are soft.

Use a slotted spoon to remove the quince quarters and set aside. Keep the lid off the pan, increase the heat, and simmer the sauce for a further 20 minutes or so, until thick and syrupy. You should be left with about 5 tablespoons/75 ml.

Just before serving, squeeze all the thick juices out of the cheesecloth before discarding the core bundle, orange rind, star anise, and vanilla bean pods. Return the quince quarters to the syrup and gently warm through. Place 2 quince quarters on each plate, spoon some syrup over them, and then top with a sprinkle of pomegranate seeds, some clotted cream, and a sprinkle of mint.

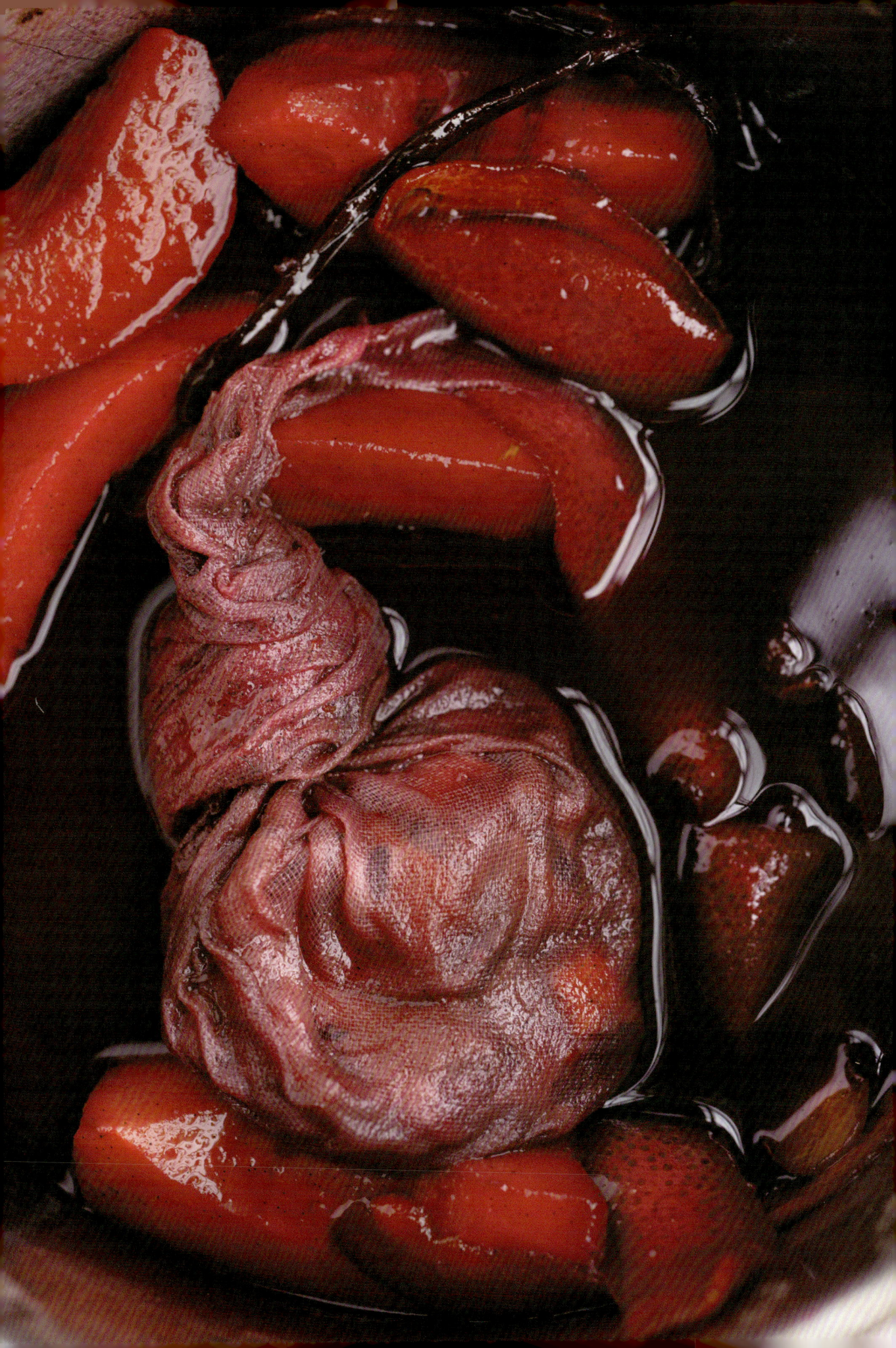

BITTER FROZEN BERRIES WITH WHITE CHOCOLATE CREAM

SERVES SIX

Years ago, when I was the pastry chef at Kensington Place restaurant in West London, one of my colleagues in the kitchen "leaked" the recipes from the pastry book of the legendary Ivy restaurant. This highly coveted document, of which I only caught an irritatingly short glimpse, included the recipe for the celebrated Scandinavian iced berries with white chocolate sauce. This was a myth of a dish among pastry chefs, and I couldn't forgive the man for depriving me a chance of copying the original recipe (obviously, this was well before the age of smartphones and digital cameras). This dish was inspired by the memory of that elusive recipe.

Use a mixture of berries here, either fresh or from a frozen package, and keep them all in the freezer until you prepare the dish. Make sure you have a sufficient amount of sharp berries—black currants and red currants—to balance the sweetness of the white chocolate. The white chocolate ganache needs to be kept cold in the fridge for at least 5 hours before you can whip it up.

3 oz/90 g white chocolate, chips or a block broken into very small pieces
1⅔ cups/400 ml heavy cream
13½ oz/380 g fresh (see headnote) or frozen berries (raspberries, blackberries, black currants, and red currants; about 3 cups)
generous 2½ tbsp/40 ml Angostura bitters, plus a few extra drops to finish
3 tbsp confectioners' sugar
6 biscotti or another hard cookie, to serve

First prepare a white chocolate ganache. Place the chocolate in a heatproof bowl. Pour ⅔ cup/160 ml of the cream into a small saucepan and bring to a boil, making sure it doesn't spill over. Pour the cream over the chocolate and stir until all the chips have melted. Leave to cool before covering the bowl with plastic wrap and chilling it in the fridge for at least 5 hours or overnight. When ready to serve, place the remaining 1 cup/240 ml cream in a bowl and add the ganache. Whisk together—by hand or with a handheld mixer—until very runny peaks form. Take care not to pass this stage, as the cream will separate if it's overwhipped.

Place the frozen berries in a plastic bag, place on a flat surface, and bash a few times with a rolling pin until the berries are roughly crushed. Pour them into a bowl, add the bitters and sugar, stir until the sugar dissolves, and leave to rest for 5 minutes, until the berries are semifrozen.

Divide the cream among glass bowls and spoon the berries on top. Alternatively, place the cream in a mixing bowl, add the berries, and swirl through before spooning into individual bowls. Finish with a few drops of the bitters and serve with a cookie alongside.

CARAMELIZED BRANDY PEARS WITH FENNEL SEED CRACKERS

SERVES FOUR

Cracker dough
1 cup / 125 g all-purpose flour, plus extra for dusting
½ tsp baking powder
1 tbsp olive oil
salt

Cracker topping
¼ cup / 60 ml olive oil
¼ cup / 35 g hazelnuts, chopped
2 tbsp fennel seeds, lightly crushed
2 tbsp superfine sugar

Caramelized pears
½ vanilla bean
scant 3½ tbsp / 40 g superfine sugar
3 Bartlett pears, peeled, cored, and each cut into 8 wedges (12 oz / 350 g)
1 tbsp / 15 g unsalted butter
3 tbsp brandy
⅓ cup / 80 g mascarpone

This wintry dessert is quite spectacular. The crackers are optional—good shortbread is a fine substitute—or, even better, commercial tortas de aceite *from Seville, which are the inspiration for these crackers. In case you do make them, I made sure the dough makes more crackers than you'll need, about 18. You can store them in an airtight container to snack on for a few days, though I doubt that they'll last that long. The pears can be cooked an hour or two in advance and then warmed through just before serving.*

Start by making the crackers. Put all the dough ingredients, 4½ tablespoons / 65 ml water, and ¼ teaspoon salt in a large bowl, use your hands to bring the mixture together, and then knead it on your work surface for a few minutes to form a soft dough. Cover with plastic wrap and leave to rest in the fridge for 1 hour.

Preheat the oven to 475°F / 240°C.

Dust some flour on a clean dry work surface. Pinch pieces of dough weighing roughly ½ oz / 12 g—you should make about 15—and roll out as thinly as possibly into long oval shapes, 8½ by 3¼-inches / 22 by 8-cm. Dust with flour as you go. Place the crackers on baking sheets lined with parchment paper. Brush with olive oil, then scatter the hazelnuts, fennel seeds, and superfine sugar over the top. Bake for roughly 6 to 8 minutes, until crisp and golden. Remove from the oven, leave to cool, and then put in an airtight container.

For the pears, place the vanilla bean in a spice grinder with 1 tablespoon of the sugar and blitz until the vanilla is finely ground (alternatively, chop the vanilla finely with a sharp knife and use a pestle and mortar to crush it with the sugar, or just use store-bought vanilla sugar). Transfer to a large bowl, add the remaining 2½ tablespoons sugar and the pears, and toss to coat evenly.

Put a large nonstick sauté pan over high heat and add the butter. Lay the pears, along with any excess sugar in the bowl, in the pan and cook for 3 minutes, turning once, so that the pears get nicely colored. Turn down the heat and continue to cook for another 3 to 5 minutes, stirring, until the pears soften and the sugar turns a golden caramel. Remove the pan from the heat and pour in 2 tablespoons water. Be careful, as it will spit a little.

Return the pan to the heat and, once boiling, add the brandy. Leave this to bubble away for 2 to 3 minutes. The caramel will thicken slightly to coat the pears. Place a cracker on each plate and serve the pears and their sauce alongside, with a spoonful of mascarpone on top.

SERVES SIX

FIG AND GOAT CHEESE TART

5 oz / 150 g soft goat cheese
⅔ cup / 85 g confectioners' sugar
½ tsp grated orange zest
1 tbsp chopped thyme leaves, plus extra leaves to garnish
2 eggs, beaten
1 cup / 100 g ground almonds
1⅓ lb / 600 g 12 ripe figs, cut in half lengthwise (about 18)
1 tbsp superfine sugar
1½ tbsp lemon juice

Yeasted pastry
2 cups plus 2 tbsp / 265 g all-purpose flour, plus extra for dusting
¼ cup / 50 g superfine sugar
1 tsp fast-acting yeast
grated zest of ½ lemon
2 eggs, beaten
5½ tbsp / 75 g unsalted butter, at room temperature, cut into ¾-inch / 2-cm cubes
sunflower oil, for brushing
salt

The last time I had to make this tart was in front of two television cameras and amid the most dreadful of hay fever attacks. It was part of my Mediterranean Feast *program and I was in a bakery in Tel Aviv. I soldiered on and managed to shoot the whole scene, with regular face- and nose-wiping intervals and not-so-charming snivels that were later masterfully edited out. More important, the pie looked and tasted fantastic. And if I could make it in that state, anyone can. If you don't have a stand mixer with a dough hook, or don't want to make the yeasted pastry, it can be replaced with a commercial all-butter puff pastry sheet of similar dimensions.*

First make the pastry. Place the flour, superfine sugar, yeast, and lemon zest in a stand mixer and, using the dough hook attachment, stir everything together on low speed for 1 minute. Add the eggs and ¼ cup / 60 ml water and work for a few seconds on low speed before increasing to medium and kneading for 3 minutes, until the dough comes together. Add ⅛ teaspoon salt and the butter, a few cubes at a time, until it all melts into the dough. Continue kneading on medium speed for about 10 minutes, until the dough is completely smooth, elastic, and shiny. You will need to scrape down the sides of the bowl a few times during kneading and throw a small amount of flour on the sides of the bowl to prevent the dough from sticking. Place the dough in a large bowl brushed with sunflower oil, cover with plastic wrap, and leave in the fridge for at least half a day, preferably overnight. It will increase in volume but only by about one-fourth.

Place the goat cheese in a bowl with 2 teaspoons / 10 g of the confectioners' sugar, the orange zest, thyme, and three-fourths of the beaten eggs. Whisk until smooth and then stir in the almonds. Mix until you get a smooth consistency. Lightly flour a clean work surface and roll out the pastry into an 11-inch / 28-cm square ¼-inch / 5-mm thick. Line a baking sheet with parchment paper. Roll the pastry around the rolling pin to help you transfer it to the baking sheet. Spread the goat cheese mixture on top, leaving a border of about ⅔-inch / 1.5-cm. Brush the remaining egg over the border.

Stand the figs on top of the mixture, placing them cut side up and slightly overlapping, as they will shrink when cooking. Sprinkle the superfine sugar over the figs, cover the tart with aluminum foil, and set aside in a warm place for 20 minutes. Preheat the oven to 375°F / 190°C. Remove the foil and place the tart in the oven. Bake for about 30 minutes, until the figs are caramelized and the base of the pastry is golden brown.

Whisk the remaining confectioners' sugar with the lemon juice. You want a thick, yet spreadable icing, so add a bit of juice or confectioners' sugar as needed. Remove the tart from the oven and use a spoon to drizzle the icing over the figs. Sprinkle with the thyme leaves and eat warm or at room temperature.

ROASTED FIGS WITH POMEGRANATE MOLASSES AND ORANGE ZEST

SERVES FOUR

I can't emphasize enough how crucial it is to choose good, sweet, squidgy figs, no matter what you do with them. It makes all the difference. These figs are extremely simple to prepare but have a magnificent deep, rich flavor that surprises me every time I make them.

3 tbsp pomegranate molasses
1 tbsp lemon juice
3 tbsp dark muscovado sugar
4 thyme sprigs, 2 whole and 2 with their leaves picked
1 orange, rind shaved in 1 long strip from half, zest grated from the other half
8 ripe figs, cut in half lengthwise (14 oz / 400 g)
½ cup / 100 g mascarpone
½ cup / 100 g Greek yogurt
1 tbsp confectioners' sugar
salt

Place the pomegranate molasses, lemon juice, 1 tablespoon of the sugar, 2 whole thyme sprigs, 1 tablespoon water, and the orange rind strip in a large bowl with a pinch of salt. Mix well to dissolve the sugar and then stir in the figs. Set aside to marinate for 30 minutes.

Place the mascarpone, yogurt, and confectioners' sugar in a small bowl and whisk until smooth. Set aside in the fridge until ready to use.

Preheat the boiler. Remove the figs from the bowl (keeping the marinade) and arrange them snugly, cut side up, in a shallow baking dish 8 inches / 20 cm in diameter. Sprinkle the figs with the remaining 2 tablespoons sugar and place under the hot broiler. Don't put them too close to the heat source or they will burn. Broil for 10 minutes, until the sugar has caramelized and the figs have softened.

Meanwhile, pour the marinade into a small saucepan, bring to a boil, and simmer for 2 to 4 minutes, until the sauce is reduced by half and has a consistency of runny honey.

Transfer the hot figs to serving plates and spoon any syrup left over in the baking sheet over the top. Drizzle the sauce reduction over the figs, then sprinkle with the picked thyme leaves. Place a spoonful of the yogurt cream on top or alongside the figs, sprinkle with the orange zest, and serve.

GRILLED STONE FRUIT WITH LEMON GERANIUM WATER

SERVES FOUR

4 peaches and/or nectarines, each pitted and cut into 6 wedges (about 1 lb/500 g)
6 apricots, halved and pitted (7 oz/200 g)
1 tbsp olive oil
3 large ripe figs, each torn into 2 or 3 pieces (6½ oz/180 g)
2 tsp aniseeds or fennel seeds, toasted and finely crushed
⅓ cup/10 g small basil leaves
1 tsp fresh lavender

Scented yogurt
scant ⅔ cup/150 g full-fat yogurt
1½ tbsp thyme flower honey or another floral honey
1 tbsp lemon geranium water or orange blossom water
1½ tsp lemon juice

The strength of opinion of online Guardian *readers of my weekly column never fails to surprise (and delight) me. What readers comment most about is my tendency to use obscure ingredients "just for the heck of it." "I'll just nip out to the corner shop for some Iranian limes and barberries," wrote one commentator recently. Others stick up for me with their own brand of parody: "For god's sake, where am I supposed to buy potatoes? Or tomato paste? Bloody elitist London-centric recipes." I find this banter amusing, but I also see it as eye-opening feedback.*

So before I am accused of introducing yet another impossible-to-find ingredient, I would like to say that lemon geranium water is a wonderfully exotic scented liquid that is extremely difficult to find anywhere but in Tunisia, where I first came across it. However, other flower distillations, like orange blossom water or rose water, are perfectly adequate substitutes.

The peaches, apricots, and figs were at their height of perfection when I made this dish in Tunisia, but you can use any seasonal stone fruit. If the fruits are really soft and juicy, leave them as they are and just grill the harder fruits. Bring this to the table on a large platter at the end of a healthy meal.

Put a large ridged grill pan over high heat and leave until it is very hot. In a bowl, mix the peaches and/or nectarines and the apricots that you are grilling with the oil. Place them on the grill pan and cook for 1 to 2 minutes on each side, until they are charred and slightly softened. Remove and set aside to cool.

To make the scented yogurt, in a small bowl, stir together the yogurt, honey, and lemon geranium water. Stir in the lemon juice and refrigerate until needed.

Before serving, arrange the peaches and/or nectarines and the apricots on a large platter and dot the torn figs on top. Drizzle the yogurt sauce over the fruit, leaving parts of the fruit exposed. Scatter the crushed seeds over the top, followed by the basil leaves. Finish with the fresh lavender and serve.

STEWED BLACKBERRIES WITH BAY CUSTARD AND GIN

SERVES FOUR

Some puddings have got to be just for the adults, right? I figure that once you are too old to fit the number of candles your age requires on top of a dessert, it's time to ditch them entirely and douse the whole thing with booze (though I wouldn't go for the lighting-up stage). As well as giving a sense of occasion, a proper boozy soak also introduces an incredible depth of flavor.

about 1 lb/480 g blackberries
scant 3½ tbsp/40 g superfine sugar
1½ tsp rose water
2½ tbsp gin
16 ladyfingers, broken into ¾-inch/2-cm pieces (about 3 oz/90 g)
about 1½ pints/360 g vanilla ice cream

Custard
6 tbsp/90 ml heavy cream
scant 5 tbsp/70 ml whole milk
3 bay leaves
1 egg yolk
3½ tsp/15 g superfine sugar

First make the custard. Place the cream, milk, and bay leaves in a small saucepan and bring to a boil. Remove from the heat immediately. In a small bowl, whisk the egg yolk and sugar until well combined. While whisking, add a little of the milk mixture. Slowly add the remaining milk mixture, continuously whisking until combined. Return the liquid to the saucepan and place over medium-low heat. Stir continuously for about 10 minutes, until the sauce thickens to a custard. Remove from the heat and set aside to cool. Keep in the fridge until ready to use.

Place 2 cups/300 g of the blackberries in a small saucepan along with the sugar and simmer over medium-low heat for 10 minutes, stirring occasionally, until the berries are soft but still hold their shape and lots of liquid has come out. Remove from the heat and leave to cool.

Drain the juices from the blackberries and stir the rose water and gin into the juices. Soak the ladyfingers in the juices until they have absorbed all the juice.

To serve, scoop a large portion of ice cream into each of 4 glasses or tumblers. Top with the soaked ladyfingers and then pour the custard over the top. Add the stewed blackberries and the remaining fresh blackberries and serve.

SET "CHEESECAKE" WITH PLUM COMPOTE

SERVES EIGHT

14 oz/400 g cream cheese
1 cup/200 g mascarpone
½ cup plus 2 tbsp/125 g superfine sugar
¾ cup plus 1½ tbsp/200 ml heavy cream
grated zest of 1 lemon
2 tbsp olive oil
½ orange, rind shaved in long strips
8 plums (about 1 lb/500 g), pitted and cut into small cubes
1 tbsp lemon juice

Crumble
½ cup/60 g whole wheat flour
about 3 tbsp/30 g light brown sugar
3½ tbsp/50 g unsalted butter, cut into small dice
⅓ cup/50 g blanched hazelnuts, lightly crushed
2 tbsp/20 g black sesame seeds
coarse sea salt

For all of Ottolenghi's manager Cornelia's powers of persuasion, she has not yet managed to elicit the highly coveted deconstructed cheesecake recipe from our good friends at Honey & Co. I am still working on Itamar and Sarit to gain details of their kadaifi*-based version but, in the meantime, offer my own, which I used to make in my old days as a pastry chef at Launceston Place and serve with greengages or gooseberries.*

Tara's mum has made this so many times that she has, regardless of where the recipe might have come from, begun to feel very territorial about it indeed. The cheese mixture needs to set for 24 hours before serving, so it makes sense to make the compote and crumble a day or two in advance as well, so that you simply put it together when you're ready to serve. Use gooseberries instead of plums when they are in season, for a divine alternative compote.

The day before serving, place the cream cheese, mascarpone, and ½ cup/100 g of the sugar in a stand mixer and beat on medium speed until soft and smooth. Separately whisk the cream until soft peaks form. Fold the cream into the cream cheese mixture, followed by the lemon zest, stirring until just combined. Transfer to a glass bowl, or even leave in the mixer bowl, cover with plastic wrap, and refrigerate for 24 hours.

Put the oil and orange rind in a small saucepan and place over medium heat. When the orange starts to sizzle, remove it from the heat and leave the oil to cool with the orange rind immersed.

Put the plums, the remaining 2 tablespoons/25 g sugar, and the lemon juice in a saucepan and cook over medium-low heat for about 30 minutes, until it has a compote consistency, a bit runnier than jam. Set aside to cool.

Preheat the oven to 375°F/190°C.

To make the crumble, place the flour, sugar, butter, and ½ teaspoon coarse sea salt in a small bowl and, using your fingers, rub in the butter to form the consistency of bread crumbs. Mix in the hazelnuts and sesame seeds and spread out in a thin layer on a baking sheet. Bake for 15 minutes, until golden brown. Remove from the oven and set aside to cool before breaking the crumble up again with your fingers.

To assemble, spoon the cream mixture onto individual plates. Add a dollop of fruit on the side of the cream, followed by a scatter of the crumble. Drizzle ½ teaspoon of the orange-infused oil over each cheesecake and serve at once.

SERVES EIGHT

APRICOT, WALNUT, AND LAVENDER CAKE

¾ cup plus 1 tbsp/185 g unsalted butter, at room temperature, diced
2 tbsp walnut oil
1 cup plus 1½ tbsp/220 g superfine sugar
1¼ cups/120 g ground almonds
4 eggs, beaten
1 cup/120 g walnuts, freshly blitzed in a food processor to a coarse powder
scant ¾ cup/90 g all-purpose flour
½ tsp vanilla extract
grated zest of 1 lemon
1½ tsp picked lavender flowers, fresh or dry
15 apricots (about 1⅓ lb/600 g), halved and pitted
salt

Icing
about 6 tbsp/50 g confectioners' sugar
1 tbsp lemon juice

The combination of walnuts, apricots, and lavender is as French as a good baguette with butter and ripe Brie, and it is every bit as invincible. I seriously urge you to try this cake, and not just as a French classic. It has a moist and soft crumb and a delicate fruity topping, and it will keep well, covered, for a few days.

Preheat the oven to 375°F/190°C.

Place the butter, oil, superfine sugar, and almonds in a stand mixer and beat on medium-high speed until light and fluffy. Add the eggs in small additions and continue to beat until well incorporated. Fold in the walnuts, flour, vanilla, lemon zest, 1 teaspoon of the lavender, and ⅛ teaspoon salt.

Line the base and sides of a 9-inch/23-cm cake pan with parchment paper. Pour in the cake batter and level the top. Arrange the apricot halves, skin side down and slightly overlapping, over the top, right to the edge. Bake in the oven for 70 to 80 minutes, covering with aluminum foil if the top starts to brown too much.

While the cake is baking, make the icing. Whisk together the confectioners' sugar and lemon juice to get a light, pourable icing, adjusting the amount of sugar or juice if needed. As soon as the cake comes out of the oven, brush the icing on top. Sprinkle the remaining ½ teaspoon lavender over the top and leave the cake to cool before serving.

ESME'S OLD-FASHIONED APPLE AND RHUBARB PUDDING

SERVES FOUR TO SIX

7 tbsp / 100 g unsalted butter, softened

¾ cup / 160 g packed dark muscovado sugar

1 cup / 100 g ground almonds

1 egg

1½ lb / 700 g cooking apples, peeled, cored, and coarsely grated (about 3½ cups / 550 g)

2 cups / 250 g trimmed and sliced rhubarb, in ¾-inch / 2-cm pieces

¼ cup / 50 g Demerara sugar

scant 1 cup / 40 g fresh bread crumbs

⅓ cup / 10 g sage leaves, coarsely chopped

1¼ cups / 250 g Greek yogurt

This hot and sweet pudding, with its super-crusty almond topping, is normally cooked for hours in an AGA (traditional radiant-heat cast-iron oven) using windfall apples. Savor this romantic image even with my real-world adjustments. With thanks to Esme Robinson for remembering this from her childhood, and for letting me shake up the old school with the addition of rhubarb and sage.

Preheat the oven to 325°F / 170°C.

Place the butter and muscovado sugar in the bowl of a small food processor and process for about 2 minutes, until smooth. You will need to scrape down the sides of the bowl once or twice. Add the almonds and egg—these will almost fill up the bowl but should just fit—and continue to process for 4 to 5 minutes, until the batter is completely smooth.

Place the apples, rhubarb, Demerara sugar, bread crumbs, and sage in a large bowl and stir to mix. Transfer to a round, deep baking dish about 7-inches / 18-cm in diameter. Press down firmly with your hands and pour the batter over the fruit. Use an offset spatula to spread it evenly, forming a layer about ⅔-inch / 1.5-cm thick.

Place the pudding in the oven, uncovered, for 2 hours, until the batter has formed a thick crust. Remove from the oven and leave to cool down a bit, 10 to 15 minutes, before serving with the yogurt alongside.

RICOTTA PANCAKES WITH GOOSEBERRY RELISH

SERVES FOUR
makes 10 to 12 pancakes

You need to adjust your expectations slightly before making these. They are not your ordinary fluffy-cakey pancakes, but rather more eggy and cheesy (and comforting, I think) like a cross between cheesecake and French clafoutis. The relish recipe yields more than you'll need here, but because gooseberry season is short and they are so wonderful, I've left some for the fridge. You can spoon this over granola or your breakfast toast. Plums are a good substitute for gooseberries.

Place the gooseberries, ¾ cup plus 2½ tablespoons/180 g of the sugar, the orange rind, ginger, and cinnamon in a saucepan and cook over medium-low heat for roughly 30 minutes, until a semithick compote consistency has formed. Set aside to cool.

In a large bowl, whisk together the eggs and ricotta until smooth. Add the flours, the remaining 4½ tablespoons sugar, the vanilla, and ⅛ teaspoon salt and mix well. Cover and refrigerate for 1 hour.

To cook, put a large sauté pan over medium heat, add 1 teaspoon of the oil and, once hot, turn down the heat to low. Make pancakes 4-inches/10-cm in diameter by ⅜-inch/1-cm thick and cook for 3 to 4 minutes on one side before flipping and cooking for a final minute, until golden brown on both sides. It is important the pancakes are cooked over low heat so they start to set on top before being flipped over, or you will end up with splashes of batter all over the pan. Transfer to a plate lined with paper towels and keep somewhere warm while you repeat with the remaining batter, adding oil as you go.

Serve 2 warm pancakes on each plate, with the relish and crème fraîche spooned alongside.

Ingredients

- 1¾ lb/750 g gooseberries or pitted plums, fresh or frozen
- 1 cup plus 3 tbsp/240 g superfine sugar
- ½ orange, rind shaved in long strips
- 1¼-inch/3-cm piece fresh ginger (about ⅓ oz/10 g), peeled and cut into thin matchsticks
- 1 cinnamon stick
- 4 eggs, lightly whisked
- 2 cups/500 g ricotta
- 2½ tbsp/25 g potato flour
- 4½ tbsp/35 g all-purpose flour
- ¼ tsp vanilla extract
- 2 tbsp sunflower oil
- scant ½ cup/100 g crème fraîche
- salt

WALNUT AND HALVAH CAKE

MAKES 1 LARGE LOAF

I wondered, for a second, whether it was too much to have two sweet recipes using halvah in one book. I then realized that you could have an entire baking book in celebration of the Arab-style sesame halvah, so I didn't worry about it again. It's one of the ingredients I'd sneak into my treasure box if I were packed off to a desert island, to nibble on with black coffee or to use in my cooking. This cake is a treat for all ages, for teatime fun or served as a dessert, with thick whipped cream.

Preheat the oven to 350°F/180°C. Grease a 9 by 5-inch/23 by 12-cm loaf pan with a little butter and line the base and sides with waxed paper.

Start with the topping. Put the butter in a small saucepan and place over medium-low heat. Melt and then allow it to sizzle for about 3 minutes, until light brown and smelling slightly nutty. Remove from the heat and set aside to cool. Once cool, mix the butter, walnuts, and cinnamon together. Divide the mixture in half and stir the muscovado sugar into one of the portions; you may need to use your hands to ensure that the sugar breaks up and spreads evenly throughout the nuts.

Now for the cake batter. In a stand mixer, cream the butter and superfine sugar on medium speed until the mixture becomes light in color and the texture is fluffy. Add the eggs, a little at a time, until they are incorporated.

Sift together the flour, baking powder, baking soda, and a pinch of salt. Add this to the batter, alternating with the sour cream, in a couple of additions: Be sure not to overmix.

Spread half the batter onto the bottom of the prepared loaf pan and scatter the sugarless nut mixture evenly over the batter. Dot the halvah on top. Spread the remaining batter on top; this may be slightly challenging, as the halvah drags into the batter, but you shouldn't worry about it too much. Finish by sprinkling the sugary nuts on top.

Bake in the oven for 40 to 45 minutes, until a skewer inserted into the center comes out clean. Leave to cool for 20 minutes, then gently remove from the pan by lifting the waxed paper. Remove the paper and leave the cake to cool completely on a wire rack (otherwise it might crumble). Wrapped in aluminum foil, the cake will keep for a day or two.

---

6 tbsp/85 g unsalted butter, at room temperature, plus extra for greasing the pan
½ cup/100 g superfine sugar
2 eggs, lightly whisked
1⅔ cups/200 g all-purpose flour
¾ tsp baking powder
¾ tsp baking soda
½ cup plus 1 tbsp/130 g sour cream
salt

Topping
¼ cup/60 g unsalted butter
scant 1¼ cups/120 g walnuts, coarsely chopped
1 tsp ground cinnamon
scant 3 tbsp/25 g dark muscovado sugar
6 oz/170 g plain sesame halvah, broken into 1¼-inch/3-cm pieces

HALVAH ICE CREAM WITH CHOCOLATE SAUCE AND ROASTED PEANUTS

SERVES FOUR TO SIX

1 cup / 250 ml heavy cream
1½ cups / 350 ml whole milk
1 vanilla bean, split lengthwise, seeds scraped
2 egg yolks
scant 3½ tbsp / 40 g superfine sugar
2 tbsp / 30 g tahini paste
3½ oz / 100 g halvah, cut into ¼-inch / 5-mm dice
scant ½ cup / 60 g salted roasted peanuts, coarsely chopped (store-bought are best)
1 tsp black sesame seeds (or white, if unavailable)

Chocolate sauce
⅔ cup / 150 ml heavy cream
scant 3 oz / 80 g dark chocolate (70 percent cacao), finely chopped
½ tsp brandy

The flavor of halvah works brilliantly in an ice cream. Make it once and you'll go back to it over and over again, even without the chocolate sauce and peanuts. With the two condiments, it tastes a bit like a luxurious Snickers ice cream: sweet, nutty, and comforting. The chocolate can mask the halvah flavor a little, so better not drench it with sauce; just drizzle lightly. With an ice cream machine, you would need to churn the ice cream for at least a few hours ahead of time, preferably a day in advance. If you don't have an ice cream machine, make this the old-fashioned way: make the custard, pour it into a shallow container, and put the container in the freezer for 4 to 5 hours, removing it every 30 to 45 minutes and beating it vigorously with a spatula or whisk to break up the frozen areas. Add the halvah halfway through. Using this method works well for serving immediately, but the next day the ice cream tends to go hard.

Heat the cream, milk, and vanilla bean and seeds in a saucepan over medium heat until the mixture just comes to a boil. Remove from the heat.

In a bowl, whisk the egg yolks and sugar until combined. Use a ladle to spoon a little of the hot cream mixture into the egg mixture, whisking the whole time. Continue with more cream mixture until it is all incorporated. Return to the saucepan and place over medium heat. Stir with a wooden spoon continuously for 10 minutes, until the sauce thickens to a light custard consistency. Remove from the heat and whisk in the tahini. Leave to cool for 20 minutes, then remove the vanilla bean pods.

Pour the custard into an ice cream machine and churn for about 35 minutes, or according to the manufacturer's instructions, until semifrozen but creamy. (Alternatively, transfer it to a freezer-proof container and place in the freezer for 4 to 5 hours, stirring in the halvah halfway through freezing; see headnote.) Remove from the machine and stir in the halvah pieces. Place in a prefrozen container and freeze. Remove from the freezer 10 minutes before serving to let it soften.

Make the chocolate sauce just before serving. Place the cream in a small saucepan over medium heat and bring to a gentle boil. Immediately pour this over the chocolate and stir until soft and uniform. Stir in the brandy. Divide the ice cream among bowls and drizzle some warm sauce over the top. Sprinkle with the peanuts and sesame seeds and serve immediately.

GRILLED BANANA BREAD WITH TAHINI AND HONEYCOMB

MAKES 1 LARGE LOAF

Telephone calls were put through to the next-door arches when this came together in the test kitchen: "Stop what you are doing, you must come for tea." This is all about three things: an incredibly perfect banana bread (thank you, Helen); tahini, which is so smooth and nutty you could eat it with a spoon; and arriving at the table with a big cup of tea and a rumbling tummy. I pitched this to the team as my offering for Christmas breakfast. Raised eyebrows relaxed back down once the trilogy was tried.

For me, tahini is the new peanut butter. It is runnier and earthier but has a similarly rich flavor and is completely impossible to resist. In many Middle Eastern cultures, it is served not only as a base for hummus and other savory sauces and dips but also as a spread served at breakfast with sweet condiments, such as grape or date syrup.

The banana bread can be baked in advance—a day or two, or even more—and then just sliced and broiled when you need it. Drizzle it with tahini as I do here, or leave out the tahini and make do with the butter, honeycomb, and salt.

scant 2 cups / 180 g pecans
3 large ripe bananas, mashed (1⅓ cups / 300 g)
1¼ cups / 275 g packed light brown sugar
3 eggs, lightly beaten
½ cup plus 1½ tbsp / 140 ml whole milk
scant 5 tbsp / 70 ml sunflower oil
2 cups plus 3½ tbsp / 275 g all-purpose flour
1 tsp baking soda
1½ tsp baking powder
salt

To finish
5½ tbsp / 80 g unsalted butter, softened
¼ cup / 60 g tahini paste
7 oz / 200 g honeycomb in honey
¾ tsp coarse sea salt

Preheat the oven to 325°F / 170°C. Line a 9 by 5-inch / 23 by 12-cm loaf pan with waxed paper.

Start with the banana bread. Place the pecans on a baking sheet and toast for 10 minutes, then chop coarsely and set aside.

Place the bananas, sugar, and eggs in a stand mixer and beat on medium speed until combined. On low speed, add ½ teaspoon salt, the milk, and then the oil. Sift together the flour, baking soda, and baking powder and, with the mixer still running, add this to the banana mixture. Continue to mix on medium speed for about 5 minutes, until thoroughly combined. Stir in the pecans and then pour the batter into the prepared loaf pan.

Place in the oven and bake for about 1 hour and 10 minutes, until a skewer or knife inserted into the center comes out clean. Leave to cool for 10 minutes, then remove the cake from the pan and set aside on a cooling rack until completely cool. You can now wrap the bread in aluminum foil and keep it for up to 5 days, or freeze it for a few weeks.

Preheat the broiler. Cut the banana bread into slices ¾-inch / 2-cm thick and brush with butter. Place under the broiler for up to 2 minutes, until lightly toasted on one side, and remove. Lean one against the other on each plate. Drizzle with the tahini, place a chunk of honeycomb on each slice, and sprinkle with the sea salt. Serve at once.

SUPER FRENCH TOAST

SERVES EIGHT

2½ cups/600 ml whole milk
¾ cup plus 1 tbsp/200 ml heavy cream
1 orange, rind shaved into long strips
3 long cinnamon sticks, broken in half
1 vanilla bean, sliced lengthwise, seeds scraped
14 oz/400 g brioche loaf, crusts removed, cut into 8 slices each 1 inch/2.5 cm thick
6 eggs
8 tsp/40 g superfine sugar
4 tbsp/60 g unsalted butter
⅓ cup/40 g confectioners' sugar
1 cup/240 g sour cream
maple syrup, to serve

Last year, Sami and I were on a book tour in Toronto and were taken by our "Canadian mother," Bonnie Stern, to the fantastic Rose and Sons, a restaurant-diner serving rich food in every sense of the word: rich in flavor, rich in tradition, rich in love, and rich in calories. It was definitely one of the most memorable meals we have ever had. One of Rose and Sons's most outstanding creations is a cross between bread pudding and French toast. I reckon their secret involves double dipping: the bread being soaked in custard once, before it is cooked like a pudding, and then dipped one more time, before it is fried like French toast. I don't have confirmation of this, but this is my hunch and that's what I do here.

To say that this "needs" anything extra would, frankly, be decadent, but to elevate it to the realm of the serious brunch, some stewed seasonal fruit or fresh berries would not be amiss. Brioche loaf is available from most supermarkets.

Preheat the oven to 375°F/190°C.

Place the milk, cream, orange rind, cinnamon, and vanilla bean and seeds in a saucepan. Heat gently over medium-low heat and remove just before it comes to a boil, about 5 minutes. Set aside for about 20 minutes, for the cream to cool a little and for the flavors to infuse.

Meanwhile, line a 12½ by 8½-inch/32 by 22-cm baking dish with parchment paper and lay the brioche slices flat on the base.

Place the eggs and superfine sugar in a bowl and whisk well. Gradually pour the warm milk into the eggs, continuing to whisk the whole time. Strain the custard and then pour two-thirds of it over the brioche, so that it's fully covered. Place the remaining custard in a wide, shallow bowl and set aside.

Bake the brioche for 20 minutes, until the custard is cooked through and golden brown. Set aside to cool and then cut into 8 square pieces.

Put half the butter in a large nonstick sauté pan and place over medium-high heat. Dip half the bread squares into the remaining custard, transfer to a plate, and sprinkle ½ teaspoon of the confectioners' sugar over each square. Immediately put them, sugar side down, in the pan and fry for 30 seconds to 1 minute, to caramelize the sugar. While they are frying, sprinkle ½ teaspoon of the confectioners' sugar over each slice. Flip over and cook for the same amount of time, until the sugar is dark brown and crispy. Remove from the pan, let rest on a wire rack, and repeat with the remaining brioche slices and butter.

To serve, place 1 slice of toast on each plate with 2 tablespoons of the sour cream and as much maple syrup as you like.

SERVES SIX

RICOTTA FRITTERS WITH ORANGE AND HONEY

scant 2 cups/470 g ricotta
2 oz/60 g fresh caprino goat cheese or another soft goat cheese
3 eggs
4 tbsp/60ml whole milk
1½ tbsp mint leaves, finely chopped
grated zest of 1 orange
1¼ cups/160 g all-purpose flour, possibly more
1½ tsp baking powder
¼ cup/50 g superfine sugar
about 3 cups/700 ml sunflower oil, for frying
4 tbsp honey, warmed slightly for drizzling
confectioners' sugar, for dusting
salt

Orange syrup
½ cup/100 g superfine sugar
1 orange, rind shaved in a single piece, then cut into very thin strips

You know how slightly terrifying certain grandmother figures can be? Well, I had to cook these fritters for that type. Signora Assunta proved completely harmless in the end (of course), but I was sure she was going to eat me alive if I didn't produce something extra-special for her on a recent visit to Sardinia. Luckily, I did her proud and she even gave me a kiss (I had to promise her husband would never know).

Start by making the orange syrup. Place the superfine sugar and 7 tablespoons/100 ml water in a small saucepan over medium heat and stir until the sugar has dissolved. Gently simmer for 3 to 4 minutes. Add the orange strips and continue cooking for another 2 minutes. Remove from the heat and leave the orange strips to cool down in the syrup.

Place a scant 1½ cups/350 g of the ricotta in a bowl with the goat cheese and eggs. Beat until fairly smooth, then whisk in the milk, mint, and orange zest. Set aside.

In a separate bowl, mix together the flour, baking powder, sugar, and ¼ teaspoon salt. Stir the ricotta mixture into the dry ingredients to form a batter, adding more flour if necessary to reach a dropping consistency. Set aside for 10 minutes to rest.

Pour the oil to a depth of 1½-inches/4-cm into a small, heavy saucepan and heat to 350°F/180°C. Gently drop heaped teaspoonfuls of the batter into the oil and cook for 3 to 4 minutes, turning occasionally, until golden brown; turn down the heat if the fritters are browning too quickly. Remove with a slotted spoon and drain on paper towels. Continue with the remaining batter.

Pile the fritters onto individual plates and drizzle with the warmed honey. Top with a dollop of the remaining ricotta and dust with confectioners' sugar. To finish, spoon orange strips and some of the syrup on top of the ricotta and serve immediately.

POT BARLEY, ORANGE, AND SESAME PUDDING

SERVES TWO TO FOUR

This is like rice pudding with texture for people who don't mind using their teeth for a dessert. It is also fantastically delicious. It works just as well with pearled barley, if that's what you have. Pearled barley won't need the overnight soaking, but it will require a little bit more milk—about 7 tablespoons/100 ml—and a little bit more cooking (about 20 minutes).

Start with the orange syrup. Place the shaved strip of orange rind in a small saucepan. Add the superfine sugar and 5 tablespoons/75 ml water. Place over high heat, bring to a boil, and cook for less than 1 minute, stirring, until the sugar dissolves. Set aside to cool.

Using a small, sharp serrated knife, slice off the top and tail of the orange. Cut down the sides of the orange, following its natural line, to remove the skin and white pith. Over a small bowl, to capture the juice, remove the segments by slicing between the membranes. Add the segments and juice to the orange syrup in the pan along with the orange blossom water and set aside.

Put the sesame seeds in a mortar with 1 teaspoon of the muscovado sugar. Roughly crush with a pestle and set aside.

Drain and rinse the barley. Place in a saucepan with the remaining 1 tablespoon plus ½ teaspoon muscovado sugar, the milk, vanilla bean and seeds, citrus zests, and ⅛ teaspoon salt. Place over high heat, bring to a boil, and then turn down the heat to medium-low. Simmer for 1 hour, stirring occasionally, until the barley is cooked but still has a bite. You might need to add a little bit of milk toward the end if the barley becomes very thick. Allow to cool for 5 minutes before removing the vanilla bean, spooning the pudding into bowls, and drizzling 1 teaspoon tahini over each portion. Spoon the orange segments and syrup, avoiding the rind, over the top, sprinkle with the crushed sesame seeds, and serve.

1 tbsp sesame seeds, a mixture of white and black or just white, toasted

1½ tbsp dark muscovado sugar

⅔ cup/125 g pot barley, covered with cold water and soaked overnight

scant 3¼ cups/750 ml whole milk

½ vanilla bean, halved lengthwise, seeds scraped

finely grated zest of ½ lemon

finely grated zest of 1 orange

2 to 4 tsp/10 to 20 g tahini paste

salt

Orange syrup
1 medium orange, rind shaved in a single strip

3½ tbsp/40 g superfine sugar

¼ tsp orange blossom water

SERVES SIX

TAU FU FA

10 pandan leaves (see headnote) (1 oz/30 g)
4½ cups/1 liter unsweetened soy milk
3½ tbsp/40 g superfine sugar
3½ oz/100 g palm sugar, crushed into ⅜-inch/1-cm chunks
⅔-inch/1.5-cm piece fresh ginger, peeled and cut into thin strips
½ small pineapple, peeled, quartered lengthwise, core removed, then cut crosswise into paper-thin slices
¾ tsp/2 g powdered agar agar
2 tbsp coconut cream
salt

I first came across this tofu dish—popular all over East Asia, where it has many variations, sweet or savory, hot or cold—in a Malaysian food market. It is a bit like crème caramel but even more silky smooth. I've used agar agar here, rather than gelatin, to make it vegetarian. This can be found in supermarkets (next to the gelatin) or online and is very easy to use. Pandan leaves are widely used in Southeast Asian cooking to infuse a range of sweet and savory dishes with their almost grassy fragrance. You'll need to pay a visit to an Asian market to find them. You can, however, substitute the seeds from a vanilla bean halved lengthwise, adding half to the milk and the rest to the pineapple.

Tie half the pandan leaves in a knot and place them in a saucepan with the soy milk and superfine sugar. Place over medium-high heat and cook for about 5 minutes, just until the mixture starts to simmer. Remove from the heat and set aside to cool. Transfer to a bowl, cover, and rest in the fridge to infuse overnight.

Put the palm sugar, ¼ teaspoon salt, the ginger, and 3½ tablespoons/50 ml water in a saucepan. Place over medium-high heat and cook, stirring from time to time, until the sugar dissolves. Increase the heat and boil for 2 minutes before adding the pineapple and the remaining pandan leaves, also tied in a knot. Turn down the heat a little and simmer for 8 minutes, stirring once or twice, until the liquid starts to thicken. Remove from the heat and set aside. It will continue to thicken as it cools. Pour into a bowl, cover, and leave in the fridge to infuse overnight.

Line a sieve with a quadruple layer of cheesecloth and strain the soy milk infusion straight into a saucepan. Place over medium-high heat and cook until the mixture is hot, about 5 minutes. Remove from the heat and transfer 3 tablespoons of the hot mixture to a small bowl. Whisk in the agar agar and set aside until dissolved, about 5 minutes. Add this to the hot pan and whisk everything well. Place over medium-high heat, bring to a gentle boil, and stir constantly for 5 minutes. Remove from the heat, strain the soy milk infusion into a bowl, then ladle into 6 individual glasses. Set aside to cool, then place in the fridge to firm up for at least 2 hours. You want the mixture to set but still have a good wobble.

Place the coconut cream in a small bowl, add 1 tablespoon water, and stir until the cream is just runny enough to pour; add more water if needed. Keep in the fridge until serving.

Half an hour before serving, remove the pineapple from the fridge so it's not cold. When ready to serve, spoon 2 tablespoons of the pineapple and sauce on top of the set milk, followed by a drizzle of the coconut cream.

See pictures on the following pages

COLD RICE AND PANDAN PUDDING WITH ALPHONSO MANGO AND LIME SYRUP

SERVES SIX

Pandan, the Asian vanilla, gives a mellow, slightly coconutty aroma to savory and sweet dishes. If you don't like it or can't get it, half a vanilla bean with the seeds scraped would be a good alternative.

My obsessive adoration for Alphonso mangoes has been established elsewhere (see page 93), but, if need be, other varieties can be used, as long as they are sweet and ripe.

For the meringues, you can easily use store-bought. If you want to make your own, beat the 2 egg whites remaining from making the pudding in a stand mixer, adding ½ cup plus 1½ tablespoons / 120 g superfine sugar gradually once the whites froth. Continue to beat until glossy and firm, about 10 minutes. Make as many small disks as you like on a baking sheet lined with parchment paper and bake for about 40 minutes at 250°F / 120°C, until completely dry. Use the amount the recipe calls for and keep the rest in a jar for up to a month.

7 tbsp / 100 ml heavy cream
3 cups / 700 ml whole milk
1 pandan leaf
½ cup / 100 g short-grain white rice
¼ cup / 50 g superfine sugar
2 egg yolks
1 oz / 30 g meringue, broken into pieces
2 passion fruits, pulp spooned out
salt

Lime syrup
scant 5 tbsp / 70 ml lime juice
1 tsp grated lime zest
2 tsp superfine sugar
4 Alphonso mangoes or other sweet mangoes, peeled and cut into ⅜-inch / 1-cm dice (about 2½ cups / 400 g)

Preheat the oven to 300°F / 150°C.

Put the cream, milk, pandan leaf, and ⅛ teaspoon salt in a saucepan. Place over medium-low heat and, once it begins to simmer, add the rice. Simmer very gently for 15 minutes, stirring occasionally, until semicooked. Remove from the heat.

Place the sugar and egg yolks in a large bowl and whisk well. Gradually pour in the rice and liquid as you continue to whisk. Transfer to a 6½ by 10½-inch / 16 by 26-cm baking dish and place the dish in a bain-marie (a baking pan with enough boiling water to reach halfway up the sides of the dish). Transfer carefully to the oven and cook for 55 minutes to 1 hour, until just beginning to set but still a little runny. It will continue to thicken as it cools down. Take everything out of the oven, remove the dish from the pan, and leave to cool, then chill for a few hours or overnight.

Meanwhile, make the lime syrup. Put the lime juice and zest and the sugar in a small saucepan and place over medium heat. Stir until the sugar dissolves and then set aside to cool. Transfer to a bowl, add the diced mangoes, stir gently, and set aside.

Use a fork to mix the chilled rice mixture until loosened and well combined, then divide among bowls or shallow plates. Sprinkle the meringue on top before spooning the mango and syrup over the pudding. Finish with the passion fruit pulp.

Also pictured on page 312

MERINGUE ROULADE WITH ROSE PETALS AND FRESH RASPBERRIES

SERVES EIGHT

Meringue
4 egg whites
1¼ cups/250 g superfine sugar
1 tsp vanilla extract
1 tsp white wine vinegar
1 tsp cornstarch

Cream
½ cup/100 g mascarpone
1 tbsp confectioners' sugar
1½ tbsp rose water
1⅔ cups/400 ml heavy cream

1¼ cups/150 g fresh raspberries
2 tbsp dried rose petals
confectioner's sugar, for dusting
1 tsp slivered pistachios (or regular, if unavailable, crushed)

Light, pretty, festive, and special, this can pull off the trick of being either the Christmas Yule log (without the chocolate or the sponge) or the perfect pudding for a midsummer lunch.

Preheat the oven to 325°F/160°C.

Line the base and sides of a 13 by 9-inch/33 by 23-cm jelly roll pan with parchment paper. Allow the paper to rise about ⅜-inch/1-cm above the sides of the pan.

To make the meringue, in a large bowl, beat the egg whites with an electric mixer until they begin to firm up. Add the superfine sugar to the whites in spoonfuls or tip into the bowl in a slow stream. Continue beating until a firm, glossy meringue forms. Using a large metal spoon, gently fold in the vanilla, vinegar, and cornstarch. Spread the mixture inside the prepared pan and level with an offset spatula.

Bake for 30 minutes, until a crust forms and the meringue is cooked through (it will still feel soft to the touch). Remove from the oven and allow to cool in the pan.

Unmold the cooled meringue onto a fresh piece of parchment paper. Carefully peel off the lining paper.

Meanwhile, make the cream. Place the mascarpone, confectioners' sugar, and rose water in a large bowl and whisk by hand until smooth. Add the cream and whisk for about 4 minutes, until the cream just holds its shape. (You can do this in an electric mixer but keep a close eye on it as it's easy to overmix.)

Spread most of the mascarpone cream over the original underside of the meringue, reserving a few tablespoons. Leave a small border around the edge of the meringue. Scatter most of the raspberries and 1½ tablespoons of rose petals evenly over the cream.

Using the paper to assist you and starting from a long edge, roll up the meringue into a perfect log shape. Carefully transfer the log onto a serving dish. Use the remaining cream to create a rough wavy strip along the top of the log (see picture). Chill for at least 30 minutes.

When ready to serve, dust the log with confectioners' sugar, dot with the remaining raspberries, and scatter the remaining rose petals and the pistachios evenly over the top.

INDEX

A

Almonds
  Apricot, Walnut, and Lavender Cake, 308
  Black Currant Friands, 286
  Crunchy Root Vegetables, 15
  Esme's Old-Fashioned Apple and Rhubarb Pudding, 310
  Fig and Goat Cheese Tart, 298–99
  Fregola and Artichoke Pilaf, 82
  Raw Beet and Herb Salad, 9
  Rice Salad with Nuts and Sour Cherries, 42
  Saffron, Date, and Almond Rice, 49
  Salbitxada Sauce, 203
  Tomato and Almond Tart, 272
Apples
  Esme's Old-Fashioned Apple and Rhubarb Pudding, 310
  Sort-of-Waldorf, 5
  Tart Apple and Celery Root Salad, 22
Apricots
  Apricot, Walnut, and Lavender Cake, 308
  Grilled Stone Fruit with Lemon Geranium Water, 302
Artichokes
  Baked Artichoke and Pearled Spelt Salad, 270
  Fregola and Artichoke Pilaf, 82
  Globe Artichoke and Mozzarella with Candied Lemon, 98
  Globe Artichoke Salad with Preserved Lemon Mayonnaise, 97
Arugula
  Caramelized Fig, Orange, and Feta Salad, 32
  Orange and Date Salad, 23
  Rice Salad with Nuts and Sour Cherries, 42
Asparagus
  Raw Vegetable Salad, 14
  Spring Salad, 28
Avocados
  Beet, Avocado, and Pea Salad, 65
  Polenta Chips with Avocado and Yogurt, 189
  Sprout Salad, Part Two, 25

B

Baigan Choka, 281
Banana Bread, Grilled, with Tahini and Honeycomb, 319
Barberries, 241
  Crispy Saffron Couscous Cakes, 205
  Eggplant Kuku, 241
  Iranian Vegetable Stew with Dried Lime, 134
Barley
  Baked Artichoke and Pearled Spelt Salad, 270
  Pot Barley and Lentils with Mushrooms and Sweet Spices, 211
  Pot Barley, Orange, and Sesame Pudding, 325
Basil Oil, 197
Batata Harra, 280
Beans
  Cannellini Bean Purée with Pickled Mushrooms and Pita Croutons, 229
  Carrot and Mung Bean Salad, 169
  Curry Laksa, 100
  Green Beans with Freekeh and Tahini, 110
  Hot-and-Sour Mushroom Soup, 83
  Indian Ratatouille, 128
  Legume (Noodle) Soup, 80
  Parsley, Lemon, and Cannellini Bean Salad, 22
  Spring Salad, 28
  Sprouting Broccoli and Edamame Salad with Curry Leaves and Coconut, 62
  Sprouting Broccoli with Sweet Tahini, 69
  See also Chickpeas; Edamame; Fava beans
Beets
  Beet and Rhubarb Salad, 178
  Beet, Avocado, and Pea Salad, 65
  Candy Beets with Lentils and Yuzu, 94
  Raw Beet and Herb Salad, 9
  Smoked Beets with Yogurt and Caramelized Macadamias, 173
Belgian endive
  Pink Grapefruit and Sumac Salad, 20
Berries
  Bitter Frozen Berries with White Chocolate Cream, 295
  See also individual berries
Blackberries, Stewed, with Bay Custard and Gin, 305
Bread
  Bread and Pumpkin "Fondue," 264
  Buttermilk-Crusted Okra with Tomato and Bread Sauce, 197
  Cannellini Bean Purée with Pickled Mushrooms and Pita Croutons, 229
  Grilled Banana Bread with Tahini and Honeycomb, 319
  Ricotta and Rosemary Bread Pudding, 275
  Slow-Cooked Chickpeas on Toast with Poached Egg, 106
  Super French Toast, 320
  Taleggio and Spinach Roulade, 278
Broccoli
  Sprouting Broccoli and Edamame Salad with Curry Leaves and Coconut, 62
  Sprouting Broccoli with Sweet Tahini, 69
Broccolini
  Miso Vegetables and Rice with Black Sesame Dressing, 50
Brussels sprouts
  Brussels Sprout Risotto, 76
  Brussels Sprouts with Caramelized Garlic and Lemon Peel, 201
  Roasted Brussels Sprouts with Pomelo and Star Anise, 170
Buckwheat Polenta, Butternut Squash with Tempura Lemon and, 124
Bulgur Soup, Spicy Chickpea and, 86

C

Cabbage
  Corn Slaw, 145
  Fancy Coleslaw, 8
  Sort-of-Waldorf, 5
Cakes
  Apricot, Walnut, and Lavender Cake, 308
  Walnut and Halvah Cake, 315
Carrots
  Carrot and Mung Bean Salad, 169
  Crunchy Root Vegetables, 15
  Crushed Carrots with Harissa and Pistachios, 230
  Curry-Roasted Root Vegetables with Lime Leaves and Juice, 177
  Honey-Roasted Carrots with Tahini Yogurt, 163
  Root Mash with Wine-Braised Shallots, 218
  Root Vegetable Pies, 282
  Seaweed, Ginger, and Carrot Salad, 58
Cashews, Spiced, 8
Cauliflower
  Alphonso Mango and Curried Chickpea Salad, 93
  Cauliflower Cake, 246
  Cauliflower, Grape, and Cheddar Salad, 166
  Fried Cauliflower with Mint and Tamarind Dipping Sauce, 200
  Raw Vegetable Salad, 14
Celery
  Celery Salad with Feta and Soft-Boiled Egg, 11
  Sort-of-Waldorf, 5
Celery root
  Root Mash with Wine-Braised Shallots, 218
  Tart Apple and Celery Root Salad, 22
Cheese
  Baked Orzo with Mozzarella and Oregano, 276
  Bread and Pumpkin "Fondue," 264
  Brussels Sprout Risotto, 76
  Caramelized Fig, Orange, and Feta Salad, 32
  Cauliflower Cake, 246
  Cauliflower, Grape, and Cheddar Salad, 166
  Celery Salad with Feta and Soft-Boiled Egg, 11
  Corsican Pie with Zucchini Flowers, 260
  Crespéou, 238
  Crispy Saffron Couscous Cakes, 205
  Dakos, 31
  Eggplant Cheesecake, 242
  Eggplant Kadaifi Nests, 261
  Fava Bean Spread with Roasted Garlic Ricotta, 222
  Fig and Goat Cheese Tart, 298–99

334

Globe Artichoke and Mozzarella with Candied Lemon, 98
Grilled Ziti with Feta, 144
Kale and Cheese Pikelets, 254
Lightly Stewed Fava Beans, Peas, and Gem Lettuce with Parmesan Rice, 119
Marrow with Tomato and Feta, 155
Membrillo and Stilton Quiche, 249
Meringue Roulade with Rose Petals and Fresh Raspberries, 332
Mushrooms, Garlic, and Shallots with Lemon Ricotta, 133
Quinoa Porridge with Grilled Tomatoes and Garlic, 101
Ricotta and Rosemary Bread Pudding, 275
Ricotta Fritters with Orange and Honey, 322
Ricotta Pancakes with Gooseberry Relish, 311
Set "Cheesecake" with Plum Compote, 306
Smoky Polenta Fries, 194
Spicy Chickpea and Bulgur Soup, 86
Stuffed Peppers with Fondant Rutabaga and Goat Cheese, 269
Tagliatelle with Walnuts and Lemon, 75
Taleggio and Spinach Roulade, 278
Watercress Salad with Quail Eggs, Ricotta, and Seeds, 12
Winter Saffron Gratin, 271

Cherries
  Rice Salad with Nuts and Sour Cherries, 42
  Sort-of-Waldorf, 5
Chickpeas
  Alphonso Mango and Curried Chickpea Salad, 93
  Eggplants with Crushed Chickpeas and Herb Yogurt, 167
  Legume (Noodle) Soup, 80
  Slow-Cooked Chickpeas on Toast with Poached Egg, 106
  Spicy Chickpea and Bulgur Soup, 86
Chiles
  Chile-Infused Oil, 89
  Green Chile Oil, 193
  Green Chile Sauce, 82
Chocolate Sauce, 316
Cobnuts
  Sort-of-Waldorf, 5
Coconut
  Sprouting Broccoli and Edamame Salad with Curry Leaves and Coconut, 62
  Urad Dal with Coconut and Cilantro, 113
Corn
  Corn and Green Onion Pancakes, 250
  Corn on the Cob with Miso Mayonnaise, 154
  Corn Slaw, 145
  Fritter Roulette, 245
Corsican Pie with Zucchini Flowers, 260
Couscous Cakes, Crispy Saffron, 205
Crackers, Fennel Seed, 296
Cranberries
  Sort-of-Waldorf, 5
Crespéou, 238
Currant Friands, Black, 286
Curry Laksa, 100

D
Dakos, 31
Dates
  Orange and Date Salad, 23
  Saffron, Date, and Almond Rice, 49

E
Edamame
  Rice Noodles with Green Onions and Edamame, 57
  Sprouting Broccoli and Edamame Salad with Curry Leaves and Coconut, 62
  Sprout Salad, Part Two, 25
Eggplant
  Baigan Choka, 281
  Baked Orzo with Mozzarella and Oregano, 276
  Eggplant Cheesecake, 242
  Eggplant Kadaifi Nests, 261
  Eggplant Kuku, 241
  Eggplant Pahi, 214
  Eggplant, Potato, Tomato, 207
  Eggplants with Crushed Chickpeas and Herb Yogurt, 167
  Eggplant with Black Garlic, 158
  Iranian-Style Pasta, 104
  Mixed Vegetables and Yogurt with Green Chile Oil, 193
  Steamed Eggplant with Sesame and Green Onion, 40
  Udon Noodles with Fried Eggplant, Walnut, and Miso, 204
Eggs
  Cauliflower Cake, 246
  Celery Salad with Feta and Soft-Boiled Egg, 11
  Corn and Green Onion Pancakes, 250
  Crespéou, 238
  Eggplant Cheesecake, 242
  Eggplant Kuku, 241
  Eggplant, Potato, Tomato, 207
  Fried Upma with Poached Egg, 198
  Fritter Roulette, 245
  Kale and Cheese Pikelets, 254
  Membrillo and Stilton Quiche, 249
  Meringue Roulade with Rose Petals and Fresh Raspberries, 332
  Slow-Cooked Chickpeas on Toast with Poached Egg, 106
  Spicy Scrambled Eggs, 253
  Watercress Salad with Quail Eggs, Ricotta, and Seeds, 12
Esme's Old-Fashioned Apple and Rhubarb Pudding, 310

F
Farro, Grilled Lettuce with Lemon and, 139
Fava, 221
Fava beans
  Fava Bean Spread with Roasted Garlic Ricotta, 222
  Fava Beans with Lemon and Cilantro, 120
  Lightly Stewed Fava Beans, Peas, and Gem Lettuce with Parmesan Rice, 119
  Quinoa and Fennel Salad, 109
  Spring Salad, 28
Fennel
  Fancy Coleslaw, 8
  Fennel with Capers and Olives, 131
  Quinoa and Fennel Salad, 109
  Zucchini and Fennel with Saffron Crumbs, 140
Figs
  Caramelized Fig, Orange, and Feta Salad, 32
  Fig and Goat Cheese Tart, 298–99
  Fig Salad, 16
  Grilled Stone Fruit with Lemon Geranium Water, 302
  Roasted Figs with Pomegranate Molasses and Orange Zest, 301
Freekeh, Green Beans with Tahini and, 110
Fregola and Artichoke Pilaf, 82
French Toast, Super, 320
Friands, Black Currant, 286
Fritters
  Fritter Roulette, 245
  Ricotta Fritters with Orange and Honey, 322

G
Garlic
  Brussels Sprouts with Caramelized Garlic and Lemon Peel, 201
  Eggplant with Black Garlic, 158
  Fava Bean Spread with Roasted Garlic Ricotta, 222
  Mushrooms, Garlic, and Shallots with Lemon Ricotta, 133
Gazpacho, Tomato and Watermelon, 90
Gooseberry Relish, Ricotta Pancakes with, 311
Grape, Cauliflower, and Cheddar Salad, 166
Grapefruit, Pink, and Sumac Salad, 20

H
Halvah
  Halvah Ice Cream with Chocolate Sauce and Roasted Peanuts, 316
  Walnut and Halvah Cake, 315
Hazelnuts
  Caramelized Brandy Pears with Fennel Seed Crackers, 296
  Cauliflower, Grape, and Cheddar Salad, 166
  Fig Salad, 16
  Set "Cheesecake" with Plum Compote, 306
  Sort-of-Waldorf, 5

I
Ice cream
  Halvah Ice Cream with Chocolate Sauce and Roasted Peanuts, 316
  Stewed Blackberries with Bay Custard and Gin, 305
Indian Ratatouille, 128

INDEX **335**

Iranian-Style Pasta, 104
Iranian Vegetable Stew with Dried Lime, 134

J

Jerusalem artichokes
    Winter Saffron Gratin, 271

K

Kadaifi Nests, Eggplant, 261
Kale
    Braised Kale with Crispy Shallots, 121
    Kale and Cheese Pikelets, 254
Kashk, 87
    Green Onion Soup, 87
    Iranian-Style Pasta, 104
Kohlrabi
    Crunchy Root Vegetables, 15
    Sprout Salad, 24
    Sprout Salad, Part Two, 25
    Winter Saffron Gratin, 271
Kuku, Eggplant, 241

L

Labneh, 291
    Baked Rhubarb with Sweet Labneh, 291
    Squash with Labneh and Pickled Walnut Salsa, 142
Leeks, Sweet-and-Sour, with Goat's Curd and Currants, 123
Legume (Noodle) Soup, 80
Lemons
    Butternut Squash with Buckwheat Polenta and Tempura Lemon, 124
    Globe Artichoke and Mozzarella with Candied Lemon, 98
    Grilled Lettuce with Farro and Lemon, 139
    Lemon and Curry Leaf Rice, 45
    Lemon Glaze, 286
    Lentils with Mushroom and Preserved Lemon Ragout, 116
    Parsley, Lemon, and Cannellini Bean Salad, 22
    Preserved Lemon Mayonnaise, 97
    Tagliatelle with Walnuts and Lemon, 75
    Tomato and Roasted Lemon Salad, 54
Lentils
    Candy Beets with Lentils and Yuzu, 94
    Crushed Puy Lentils with Tahini and Cumin, 226
    Lentils, Radicchio, and Walnuts with Manuka Honey, 126
    Lentils with Mushroom and Preserved Lemon Ragout, 116
    Pot Barley and Lentils with Mushrooms and Sweet Spices, 211
    Root Mash with Wine-Braised Shallots, 218
    Thai Red Lentil Soup with Aromatic Chile Oil, 89
    Urad Dal with Coconut and Cilantro, 113
Lettuce
    Globe Artichoke and Mozzarella with Candied Lemon, 98
    Grilled Lettuce with Farro and Lemon, 139

Lightly Stewed Fava Beans, Peas, and Gem Lettuce with Parmesan Rice, 119
Orange and Date Salad, 23
Limes
    Cold Rice and Pandan Pudding with Alphonso Mango and Lime Syrup, 331
    Curry-Roasted Root Vegetables with Lime Leaves and Juice, 177
    Iranian Vegetable Stew with Dried Lime, 134

M

Macadamias, Caramelized, Smoked Beets with Yogurt and, 173
Mangoes
    Alphonso Mango and Curried Chickpea Salad, 93
    Cold Rice and Pandan Pudding with Alphonso Mango and Lime Syrup, 331
    Pomelo Salad, 19
    Seaweed, Ginger, and Carrot Salad, 58
Membrillo and Stilton Quiche, 249
Meringue Roulade with Rose Petals and Fresh Raspberries, 332
Miso
    Corn on the Cob with Miso Mayonnaise, 154
    Miso Vegetables and Rice with Black Sesame Dressing, 50
    Udon Noodles with Fried Eggplant, Walnut, and Miso, 204
Mushrooms
    Cannellini Bean Purée with Pickled Mushrooms and Pita Croutons, 229
    Hot-and-Sour Mushroom Soup, 83
    Lentils with Mushroom and Preserved Lemon Ragout, 116
    Miso Vegetables and Rice with Black Sesame Dressing, 50
    Mushroom and Tarragon Pithivier, 266–67
    Mushrooms, Garlic, and Shallots with Lemon Ricotta, 133
    Pot Barley and Lentils with Mushrooms and Sweet Spices, 211
    Seared Chanterelles with Black Glutinous Rice, 190
    Soba Noodles with Quick-Pickled Mushrooms, 61

N

Nectarines
    Grilled Stone Fruit with Lemon Geranium Water, 302
Noodles. *See* Pasta and noodles

O

Okra
    Buttermilk-Crusted Okra with Tomato and Bread Sauce, 197
    Indian Ratatouille, 128
Olives
    Coated Olives with Spicy Yogurt, 208
    Dakos, 31
    Fennel with Capers and Olives, 131
    Fregola and Artichoke Pilaf, 82

Raw Vegetable Salad, 14
Tomato and Almond Tart, 272
Onions
    Corn and Green Onion Pancakes, 250
    Crespéou, 238
    Green Onion Soup, 87
    Red Onions with Walnut Salsa, 164
    Rice Noodles with Green Onions and Edamame, 57
Oranges
    Caramelized Fig, Orange, and Feta Salad, 32
    Orange and Date Salad, 23
    Pot Barley, Orange, and Sesame Pudding, 325
    Ricotta Fritters with Orange and Honey, 322
    Sweet Potatoes with Orange Bitters, 174

P

Pahi, Eggplant, 214
Pancakes
    Corn and Green Onion Pancakes, 250
    Kale and Cheese Pikelets, 254
    Ricotta Pancakes with Gooseberry Relish, 311
Pandan leaves, 326, 331
Parsley, Lemon, and Cannellini Bean Salad, 22
Parsnips
    Curry-Roasted Root Vegetables with Lime Leaves and Juice, 177
    Root Vegetable Pies, 282
    Winter Saffron Gratin, 271
Pasta and noodles
    Baked Orzo with Mozzarella and Oregano, 276
    Butternut Tataki and Udon Noodle Salad, 148
    Curry Laksa, 100
    Fregola and Artichoke Pilaf, 82
    Grilled Ziti with Feta, 144
    Iranian-Style Pasta, 104
    Legume (Noodle) Soup, 80
    Rice Noodles with Green Onions and Edamame, 57
    Soba Noodles with Quick-Pickled Mushrooms, 61
    Tagliatelle with Walnuts and Lemon, 75
    Udon Noodles with Fried Eggplant, Walnut, and Miso, 204
Peaches
    Grilled Stone Fruit with Lemon Geranium Water, 302
Peanuts
    Black Sesame Dressing, 50
    Halvah Ice Cream with Chocolate Sauce and Roasted Peanuts, 316
    Pomelo Salad, 19
    Seaweed, Ginger, and Carrot Salad, 58
Pears, Caramelized Brandy, with Fennel Seed Crackers, 296
Peas
    Baked Artichoke and Pearled Spelt Salad, 270
    Beet, Avocado, and Pea Salad, 65

Fava, 221
Green Onion Soup, 87
Legume (Noodle) Soup, 80
Lightly Stewed Fava Beans, Peas, and Gem Lettuce with Parmesan Rice, 119
Miso Vegetables and Rice with Black Sesame Dressing, 50
Pea and Mint Croquettes, 186
Peas with Sorrel and Mustard, 70
Raw Vegetable Salad, 14
Soba Noodles with Quick-Pickled Mushrooms, 61
Thai Red Lentil Soup with Aromatic Chile Oil, 89

Pecans
Grilled Banana Bread with Tahini and Honeycomb, 319

Peppers
Fritter Roulette, 245
Indian Ratatouille, 128
Mixed Vegetables and Yogurt with Green Chile Oil, 193
Red Pepper and Tomato Salsa, 261
Stuffed Peppers with Fondant Rutabaga and Goat Cheese, 269
See also Chiles

Pies
Corsican Pie with Zucchini Flowers, 260
Mushroom and Tarragon Pithivier, 266–67
Root Vegetable Pies, 282

Pikelets, Kale and Cheese, 254
Pilaf, Fregola and Artichoke, 82

Pineapple
Tau Fu Fa, 326

Pistachios
Black Currant Friands, 286
Crushed Carrots with Harissa and Pistachios, 230

Pithivier, Mushroom and Tarragon, 266–67
Plum Compote, Set "Cheesecake" with, 306

Polenta
Butternut Squash with Buckwheat Polenta and Tempura Lemon, 124
Polenta Chips with Avocado and Yogurt, 189
Smoky Polenta Fries, 194

Pomegranates
Crunchy Root Vegetables, 15
Quince Poached in Pomegranate Juice, 292
Roasted Figs with Pomegranate Molasses and Orange Zest, 301
Tomato and Pomegranate Salad, 3
Tomato and Roasted Lemon Salad, 54

Pomelo
Pomelo Salad, 19
Roasted Brussels Sprouts with Pomelo and Star Anise, 170

Potatoes
Batata Harra, 280
Eggplant, Potato, Tomato, 207
Globe Artichoke Salad with Preserved Lemon Mayonnaise, 97
Indian Ratatouille, 128
Iranian Vegetable Stew with Dried Lime, 134
Root Vegetable Pies, 282
Spice-Stuffed Potato Cakes, 232

Prunes
Hot-and-Sour Mushroom Soup, 83

Puddings
Cold Rice and Pandan Pudding with Alphonso Mango and Lime Syrup, 331
Esme's Old-Fashioned Apple and Rhubarb Pudding, 310
Pot Barley, Orange, and Sesame Pudding, 325
Ricotta and Rosemary Bread Pudding, 275
Pumpkin "Fondue," Bread and, 264

Q

Quiche, Membrillo and Stilton, 249

Quince
Membrillo and Stilton Quiche, 249
Quince Poached in Pomegranate Juice, 292

Quinoa
Parsley, Lemon, and Cannellini Bean Salad, 22
Quinoa and Fennel Salad, 109
Quinoa and Wild Garlic Cakes with Salbitxada Sauce, 203
Quinoa Porridge with Grilled Tomatoes and Garlic, 101
Rice Salad with Nuts and Sour Cherries, 42
Tart Apple and Celery Root Salad, 22

R

Radicchio
Fancy Coleslaw, 8
Fig Salad, 16
Lentils, Radicchio, and Walnuts with Manuka Honey, 126
Soba Noodles with Quick-Pickled Mushrooms, 61
Sprout Salad, Part Two, 25

Radishes
Orange and Date Salad, 23
Raw Vegetable Salad, 14
Sprout Salad, 24

Raspberries, Fresh, Meringue Roulade with Rose Petals and, 332
Ratatouille, Indian, 128

Rhubarb
Baked Rhubarb with Sweet Labneh, 291
Beet and Rhubarb Salad, 178
Esme's Old-Fashioned Apple and Rhubarb Pudding, 310

Rice
Brussels Sprout Risotto, 76
Cold Rice and Pandan Pudding with Alphonso Mango and Lime Syrup, 331
Lemon and Curry Leaf Rice, 45
Lightly Stewed Fava Beans, Peas, and Gem Lettuce with Parmesan Rice, 119
Miso Vegetables and Rice with Black Sesame Dressing, 50
Rice Salad with Nuts and Sour Cherries, 42
Saffron, Date, and Almond Rice, 49
Seared Chanterelles with Black Glutinous Rice, 190
Stuffed Zucchini, 105
Risotto, Brussels Sprout, 76

Rutabaga
Crunchy Root Vegetables, 15
Curry-Roasted Root Vegetables with Lime Leaves and Juice, 177
Stuffed Peppers with Fondant Rutabaga and Goat Cheese, 269
Winter Saffron Gratin, 271

S

Saffron
Crispy Saffron Couscous Cakes, 205
Saffron, Date, and Almond Rice, 49
Winter Saffron Gratin, 271
Zucchini and Fennel with Saffron Crumbs, 140

Salads
Alphonso Mango and Curried Chickpea Salad, 93
Baked Artichoke and Pearled Spelt Salad, 270
Beet and Rhubarb Salad, 178
Beet, Avocado, and Pea Salad, 65
Butternut Tataki and Udon Noodle Salad, 148
Caramelized Fig, Orange, and Feta Salad, 32
Carrot and Mung Bean Salad, 169
Cauliflower, Grape, and Cheddar Salad, 166
Celery Salad with Feta and Soft-Boiled Egg, 11
Corn Slaw, 145
Dakos, 31
Fancy Coleslaw, 8
Fig Salad, 16
Globe Artichoke Salad with Preserved Lemon Mayonnaise, 97
Orange and Date Salad, 23
Parsley, Lemon, and Cannellini Bean Salad, 22
Pink Grapefruit and Sumac Salad, 20
Pomelo Salad, 19
Quinoa and Fennel Salad, 109
Raw Beet and Herb Salad, 9
Raw Vegetable Salad, 14
Rice Salad with Nuts and Sour Cherries, 42
Seaweed, Ginger, and Carrot Salad, 58
Sort-of-Waldorf, 5
Spring Salad, 28
Sprouting Broccoli and Edamame Salad with Curry Leaves and Coconut, 62
Sprout Salad, 24
Sprout Salad, Part Two, 25
Tart Apple and Celery Root Salad, 22
Tomato and Pomegranate Salad, 3
Tomato and Roasted Lemon Salad, 54
Watercress Salad with Quail Eggs, Ricotta, and Seeds, 12

Salbitxada Sauce, 203
Seaweed
    Seaweed, Ginger, and Carrot Salad, 58
    Soba Noodles with Quick-Pickled Mushrooms, 61
Sesame Dressing, Black, 50
Set "Cheesecake" with Plum Compote, 306
Shallots, Wine-Braised, Root Mash with, 218
Slaws
    Corn Slaw, 145
    Fancy Coleslaw, 8
    Sort-of-Waldorf, 5
Soups
    Curry Laksa, 100
    Green Onion Soup, 87
    Hot-and-Sour Mushroom Soup, 83
    Legume (Noodle) Soup, 80
    Spicy Chickpea and Bulgur Soup, 86
    Thai Red Lentil Soup with Aromatic Chile Oil, 89
    Tomato and Watermelon Gazpacho, 90
    Spelt Salad, Pearled, Baked Artichoke and, 270
Spinach
    Iranian Vegetable Stew with Dried Lime, 134
    Legume (Noodle) Soup, 80
    Spring Salad, 28
    Sprout Salad, 24
    Taleggio and Spinach Roulade, 278
    Spring Salad, 28
Sprouts
    Curry Laksa, 100
    Hot-and-Sour Mushroom Soup, 83
    Sprout Salad, 24
    Sprout Salad, Part Two, 25
Squash
    Butternut Squash with Buckwheat Polenta and Tempura Lemon, 124
    Butternut Tataki and Udon Noodle Salad, 148
    Fritter Roulette, 245
    Iranian Vegetable Stew with Dried Lime, 134
    Marrow with Tomato and Feta, 155
    Membrillo and Stilton Quiche, 249
    Root Mash with Wine-Braised Shallots, 218
    Root Vegetable Pies, 282
    Squash with Cardamom and Nigella Seeds, 160
    Squash with Chile Yogurt and Cilantro Sauce, 181
    Squash with Labneh and Pickled Walnut Salsa, 142
    See also Zucchini
Sweet potatoes
    Root Mash with Wine-Braised Shallots, 218
    Sweet Potatoes with Orange Bitters, 174
Swiss chard
    Corsican Pie with Zucchini Flowers, 260

T
Tarts
    Corsican Pie with Zucchini Flowers, 260
    Fig and Goat Cheese Tart, 298–99
    Tomato and Almond Tart, 272
Tau Fu Fa, 326
Thai Red Lentil Soup with Aromatic Chile Oil, 89
Tofu puffs
    Curry Laksa, 100
Tomatoes
    Baked Orzo with Mozzarella and Oregano, 276
    Buttermilk-Crusted Okra with Tomato and Bread Sauce, 197
    Crushed Puy Lentils with Tahini and Cumin, 226
    Dakos, 31
    Eggplant Cheesecake, 242
    Eggplant, Potato, Tomato, 207
    Grilled Ziti with Feta, 144
    Indian Ratatouille, 128
    Iranian Vegetable Stew with Dried Lime, 134
    Marrow with Tomato and Feta, 155
    Mixed Vegetables and Yogurt with Green Chile Oil, 193
    Quinoa Porridge with Grilled Tomatoes and Garlic, 101
    Red Pepper and Tomato Salsa, 261
    Salbitxada Sauce, 203
    Spicy Scrambled Eggs, 253
    Sprout Salad, 24
    Taleggio and Spinach Roulade, 278
    Tomato and Almond Tart, 272
    Tomato and Pomegranate Salad, 3
    Tomato and Roasted Lemon Salad, 54
    Tomato and Watermelon Gazpacho, 90
    Urad Dal with Coconut and Cilantro, 113
Turnips
    Bread and Pumpkin "Fondue," 264
    Crunchy Root Vegetables, 15
    Ricotta and Rosemary Bread Pudding, 275
    Spicy Turnip, 60

U
Upma, Fried, with Poached Egg, 198
Urad Dal with Coconut and Cilantro, 113

V
Vegetables, mixed
    Crunchy Root Vegetables, 15
    Curry-Roasted Root Vegetables with Lime Leaves and Juice, 177
    Iranian Vegetable Stew with Dried Lime, 134
    Miso Vegetables and Rice with Black Sesame Dressing, 50
    Mixed Vegetables and Yogurt with Green Chile Oil, 193
    Raw Vegetable Salad, 14
    Root Mash with Wine-Braised Shallots, 218
    Root Vegetable Pies, 282
    Winter Saffron Gratin, 271
    See also individual vegetables

W
Waldorf, Sort-of-, 5
Walnuts
    Apricot, Walnut, and Lavender Cake, 308
    Lentils, Radicchio, and Walnuts with Manuka Honey, 126
    Red Onions with Walnut Salsa, 164
    Squash with Labneh and Pickled Walnut Salsa, 142
    Tagliatelle with Walnuts and Lemon, 75
    Udon Noodles with Fried Eggplant, Walnut, and Miso, 204
    Walnut and Halvah Cake, 315
Watercress
    Fig Salad, 16
    Pink Grapefruit and Sumac Salad, 20
    Pomelo Salad, 19
    Raw Vegetable Salad, 14
    Watercress Salad with Quail Eggs, Ricotta, and Seeds, 12
Watermelon Gazpacho, Tomato and, 90
White Chocolate Cream, Bitter Frozen Berries with, 295
Wild rice
Rice Salad with Nuts and Sour Cherries, 42
Winter Saffron Gratin, 271

Y
Yogurt
Coated Olives with Spicy Yogurt, 208
Eggplants with Crushed Chickpeas and Herb Yogurt, 167
Honey-Roasted Carrots with Tahini Yogurt, 163
Mixed Vegetables and Yogurt with Green Chile Oil, 193
Polenta Chips with Avocado and Yogurt, 189
Smoked Beets with Yogurt and Caramelized Macadamias, 173
Squash with Chile Yogurt and Cilantro Sauce, 181
Yogurt and Kaffir Lime Leaf Spread, 234
See also Labneh

Z
Zucchini
Corsican Pie with Zucchini Flowers, 260
Green Onion Soup, 87
Mixed Vegetables and Yogurt with Green Chile Oil, 193
Stuffed Zucchini, 105
Yogurt and Kaffir Lime Leaf Spread, 234
Zucchini and Fennel with Saffron Crumbs, 140
Zucchini "Baba Ghanoush," 151

ACKNOWLEDGMENTS

All the dishes in this book have been created under the watchful eyes of Sarah Joseph, Tara Wigley, Esme Robinson, and Claudine Boulstridge. Their input is priceless. Tara deserves extra recognition for her enormous contribution in both research and imaginative writing. Noam Bar, as always, was involved throughout, constantly giving his fresh outlook.

Jonathan Lovekin and Caz Hildebrand, my close creative partners, made another book, which, in my mind, is unusually beautiful; Felicity Rubinstein and Sarah Lavelle are credited with allowing us to take this thrilling ride and for making it so smooth.

I would also like to thank my family, close friends and colleagues for their ongoing support: Karl Allen, Michael and Ruth Ottolenghi, Tirza, Danny and the Florentin family, Pete and Greta Allen, Cornelia Staeubli, Peter Lowe, Sami Tamimi, Jeremy Kelly, Helen Goh, David Kausman, Alex Meitlis, Tamara Meitlis, Garry Chang, Ramael Scully, Lucy Henry, Shachar Argov, Alison Quinn, Maria Mok, Basia Murphy, Heidi Knudsen, Luana Knudsen, Paulina Bembel, Charissa Fraser, Faiscal Barakat, Toni Birbara, Laura Clifford, Angelita Pereira, Francis Pereira, Sarit Packer, Itamar Srulovich, Lingchee Ang, Gemma Bell, Bob Granleese, Merope Mills, Fiona MacIntyre, Sarah Bennie, Mark Hutchinson, Imogen Fortes, Sanjana Lovekin, Keren Margalit, Yoram Ever-Hadani, Itzik Lederfeind, Ilana Lederfeind, and Amos, Ariela, and David Oppenheim.

Finally, I sincerely thank all the team members at Ottolenghi and NOPI for their endless commitment and hard work.

YOTAM OTTOLENGHI

Copyright © 2014 by Yotam Ottolenghi, LLP
Photographs copyright © 2014 by Jonathan Lovekin

All rights reserved.
Published in the United States by Ten Speed Press, an imprint of
Random House, a division of Penguin Random House LLC, New York.
www.tenspeed.com

Originally published in the United States in hardcover by Ten Speed
Press, an imprint of Random House, a division of Penguin Random
House LLC and in slightly different form in Great Britain by Ebury
Press, an imprint of Ebury Publishing, a Penguin Random House
Company, London, in 2014.

Ten Speed Press and the Ten Speed Press colophon are registered
trademarks of Random House LLC.

Design by Caz Hildebrand and Sakiko Kobayashi, Here Design

10 9 8 7 6

2019 Trade Paperback Box Edition